Joanna van Oppen

MUSEUM OF SCOTLAND

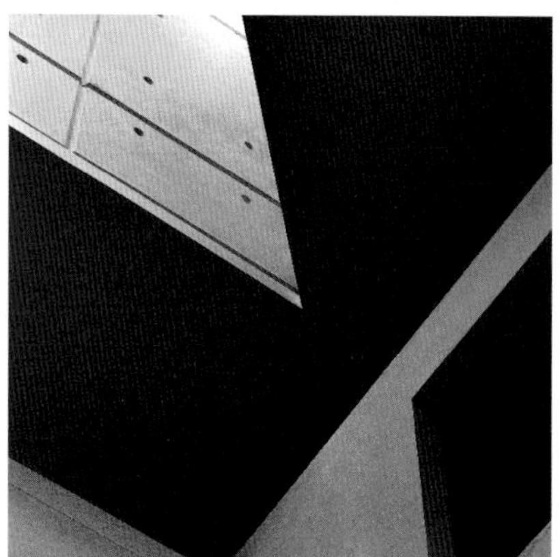

Foreword

Sir Colin St John Wilson

The Museum of Scotland has entered the scene at a colourful moment both politically at a time of historic change and architecturally at a time when, all over the world, the building of public monuments has gathered a new energy and significance. I believe that it has matched both the hour and the need with authority and abundant relish.

The ancient Greeks held that the mother of the arts was Mnemosyne, the goddess of memory and not, as so frequently suggested, the art of architecture. The categories are quite different from each other so that the confusion is quite arbitrary; and yet today we have to recognise that due to a certain convergence of cultural interests and political priorities architecture has after all become ordained to be the very embodiment and celebration of not only the goddess herself but also to be the champion for cities across the world in competition to be crowned as the city of culture. What began forty years ago with that distant precursor of "the landmark building" in Sydney has slowly gathered momentum to a rivalry of city states like that of Renaissance Italy, so that the building of a museum or gallery or cultural centre becomes not just a celebration of possessions but also a symbol of local identity just at the time when the tourist industry has amassed its hordes of pilgrims in search of new holy lands. As the millennium draws nigh the competition becomes feverish: after all, whoever went to Bilbao before the satellite Guggenheim landed there?

But this new ebullience has not all been benign, for here and there it has led to the eruption of a deviant species of construction which is neither quite architecture nor sculpture, but is perceived to be a new art form offering sensational spatial experiences of a novel kind or a metaphysical object of contemplation in its own right, empty of content other than its own symbolic play of forms in light – in short what the 18th century architects called "a folly", and these, assuredly, are not dedicated to the service of the muse.

Mercifully the Museum of Scotland explores with conviction the traditional responsibilities of the hall of memory and enjoys to the full the multiplicity of evocative objects thrown up by the tides of history. Mercifully too we are spared the directives of "politically correct" programmes. The essential magic of a museum is disclosed when a twelve-year-old or a sixty-year-old makes a discovery for himself or herself which glows like a personal secret.

Of course the celebration of memory has broader implications than the stimulation of personal chemistry in this way, but it is the task of the architecture to create the aura in which the mysteries of such chemistry are invited to take place. I once heard Le Corbusier commend the "atmosphere" of a building as he walked around it, and Aalto use the word "mood". These were not fashionable terms but they went straight to the heart of the issue of engaging visitors to a building in a participatory and possessive way.

The broader obligations to which I referred lie in the way that a museum may embody the relation between past, present and future as a living and changing continuum. In his celebrated essay "Tradition and the Individual Talent" TS Eliot unveiled a dynamic two-way relationship between the terms as follows:

"What happens when a new work of art is created is something that happens simultaneously to all the works of art, which precede it. The existing monuments form an ideal order among themselves, which is modified by the introduction of the new (the really new) work of art among them. The existing order is complete before the new work arrives; for order to persist after the supervention of novelty the whole existing order must be, if ever so slightly, altered; and so the relations, proportions, values of each work of art toward the whole are readjusted. Whoever has approved this idea of order… will not find it preposterous that the past is altered by the present as much as the present is directed by the past."

I believe that the Museum of Scotland does create the aura in which this play on time, back and forth as on a keyboard, can be enjoyed by all. The character of every one of the tactical inventions deployed by the architects (and there are many) has been evolved out of the study and understanding of the particular object, group or episode to be celebrated. The same vein of relevance drives the broader strategies. Although it is big, this building does not "put you down". Whether it is the framing of a relic or a view of the city without, the placing and the sense of proportion are unfailingly just. By the same token the visitors to the building are drawn into a narrative that offers both focal points to study at close quarters and enticements to further destinations. What is technically admirable in these situations is that, in a large volume of space, both natural light and artificial light meld together as one – even the areas limited to levels of 50 lux somehow manage to convey the impression of no constraint. That is no mean feat!

An equally positive air declares the public presence of the building in its urban context, both to its neighbours and its historic location in the city. It bulges with energy, all of a piece, and the last two stations of its climbing narrative within emerge again under the sky to enjoy magnificent vistas across the city which are also, in their range of targets from the Castle to the Firth of Forth, crowded with the echoes of history.

In the serious business of making this monumental building the architects Benson + Forsyth have clearly enjoyed themselves and that enjoyment is catching. I believe this building will be blessed with affection by citizens and visitors alike.

6

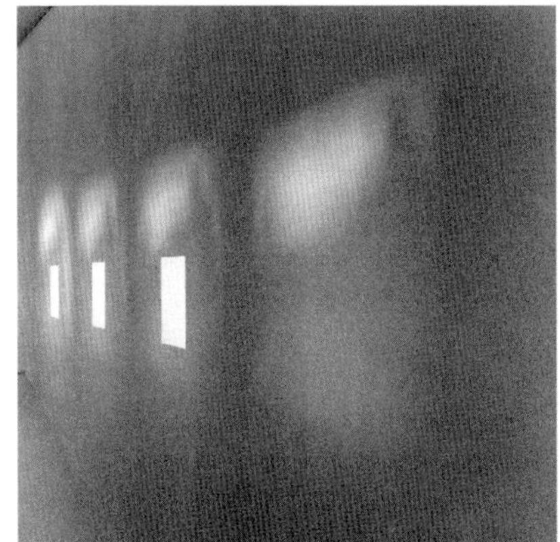

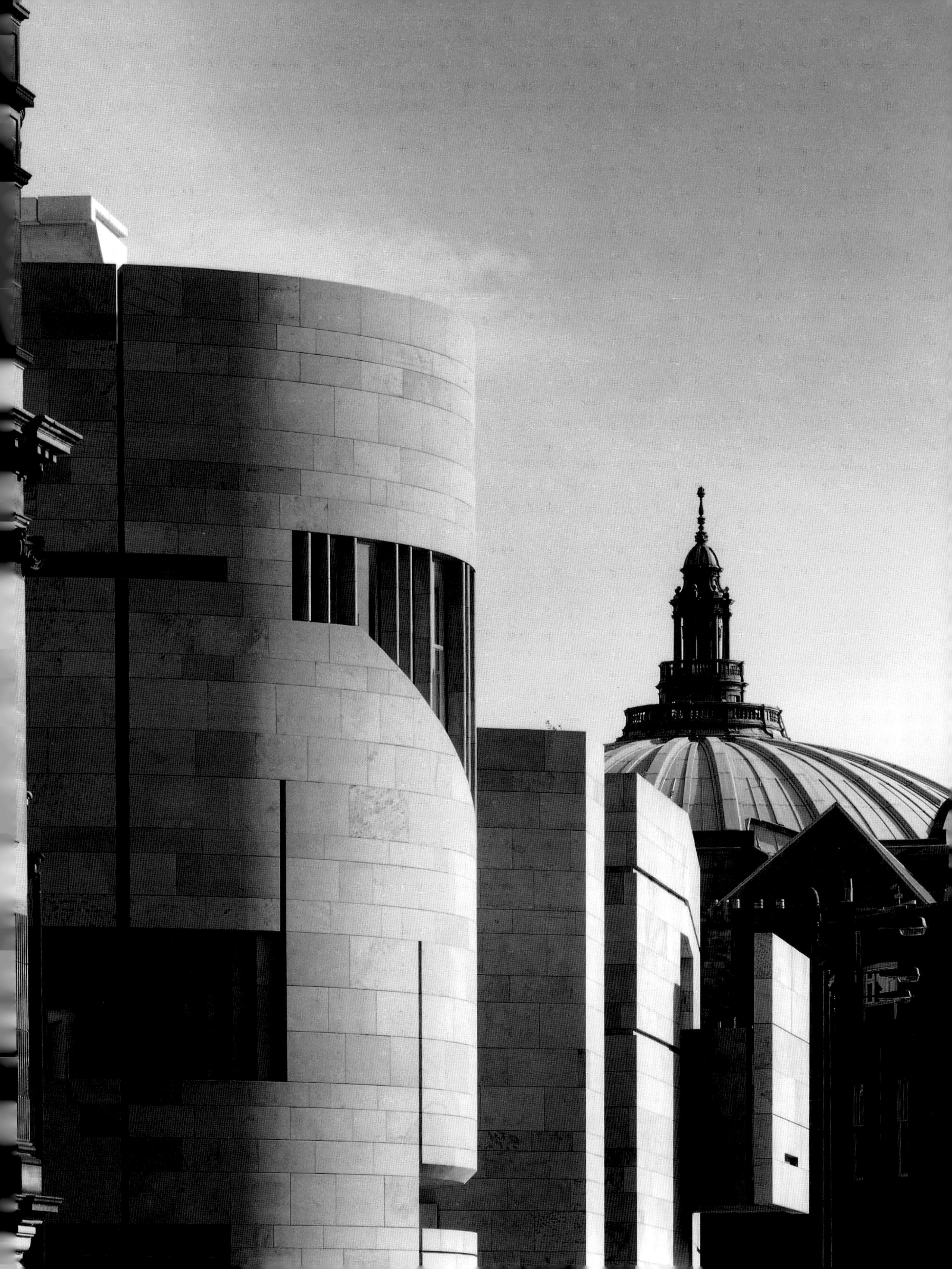

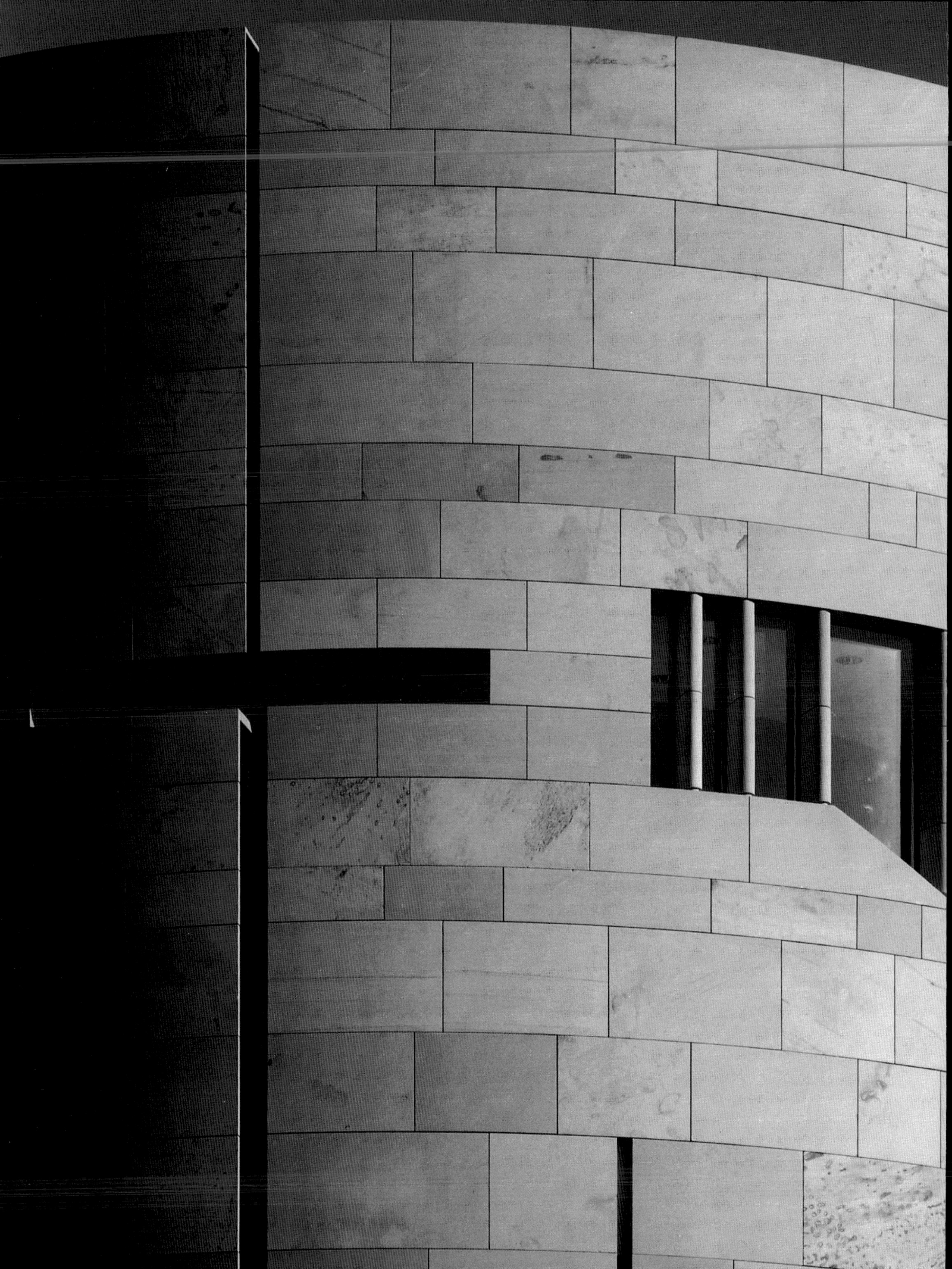

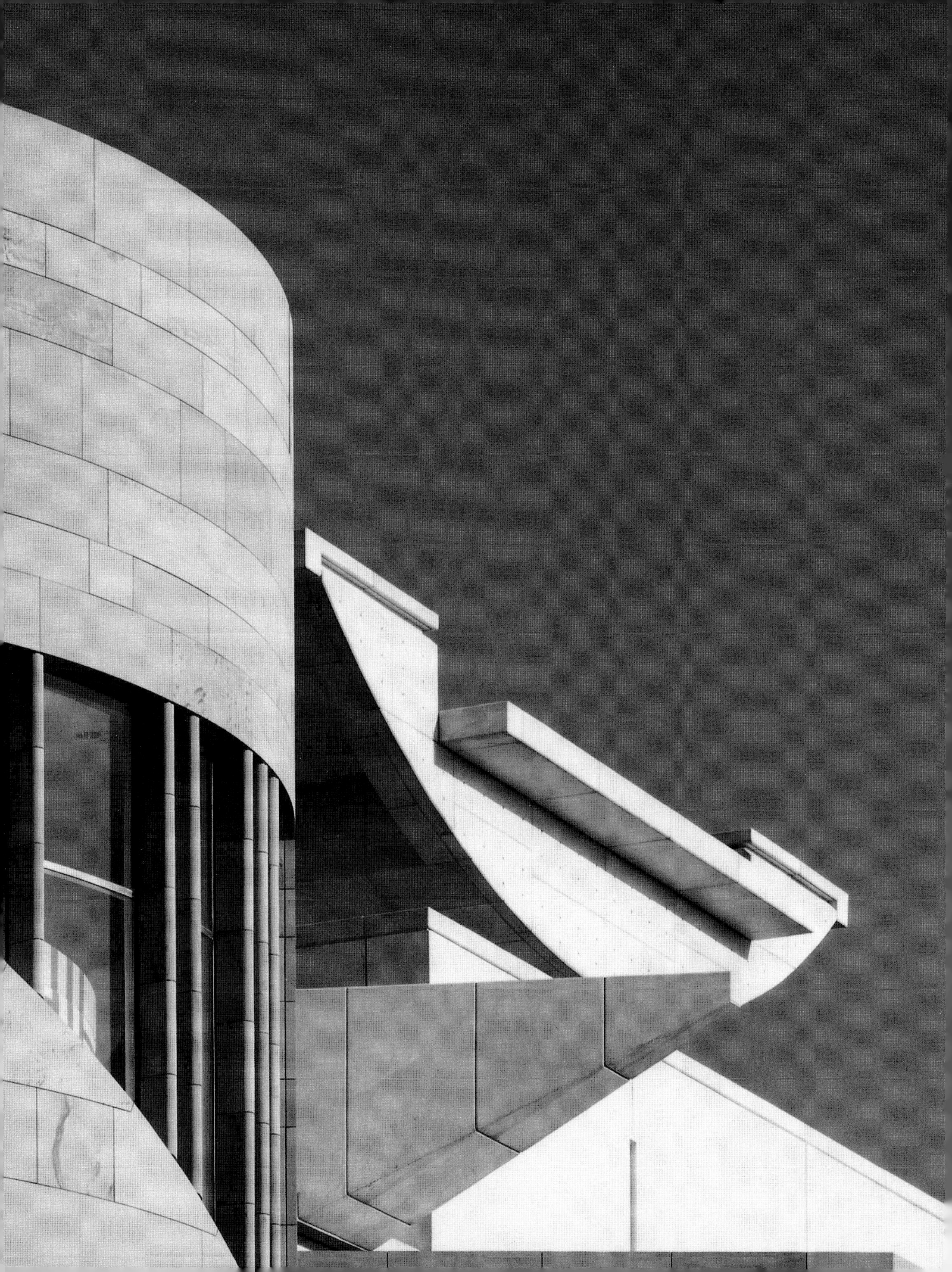

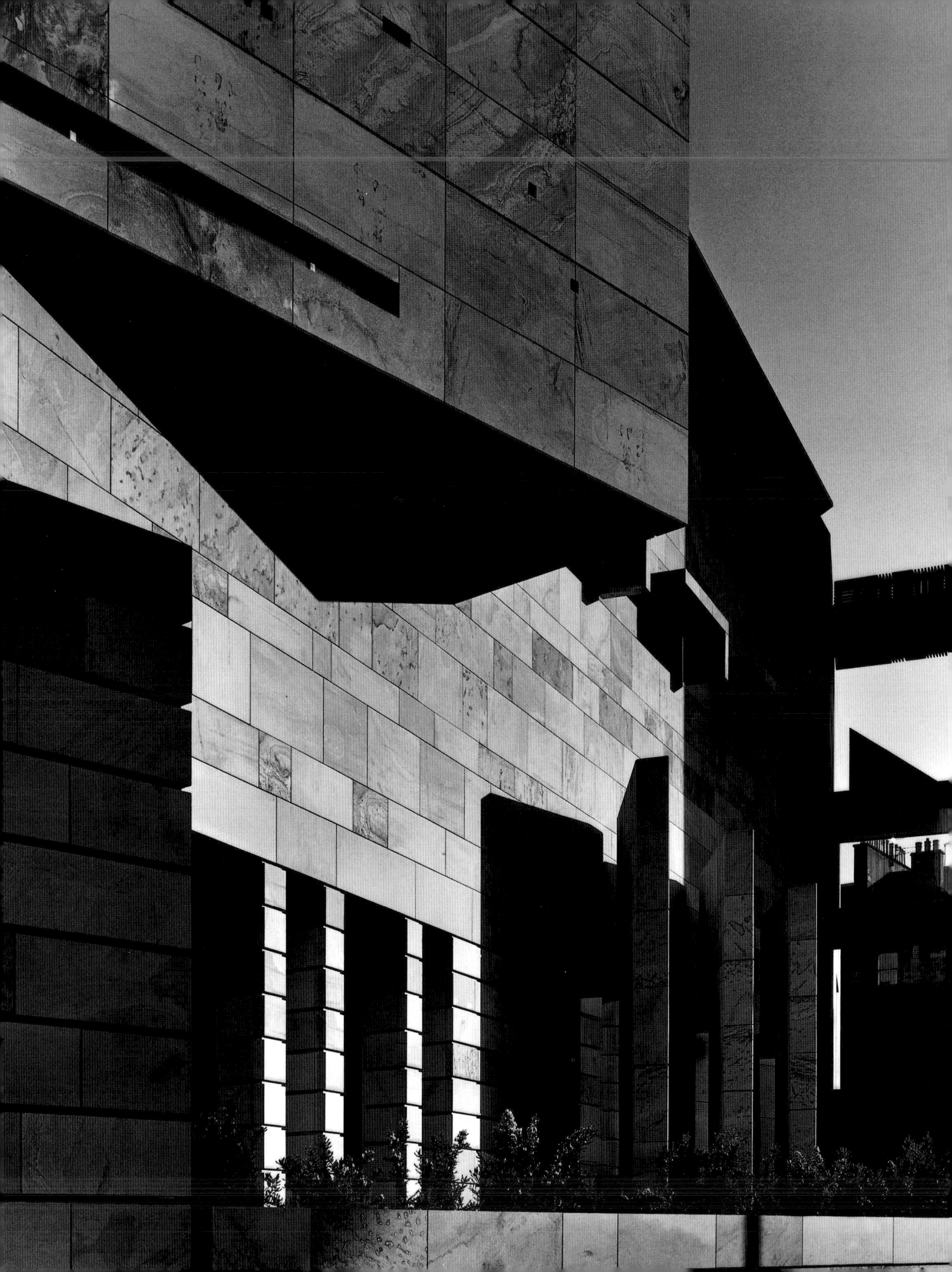

12

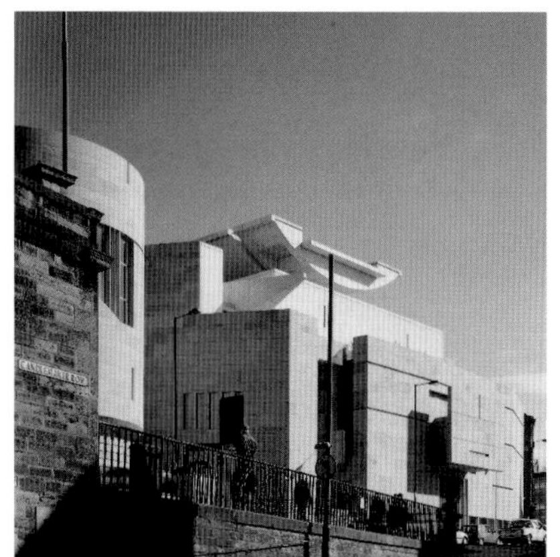

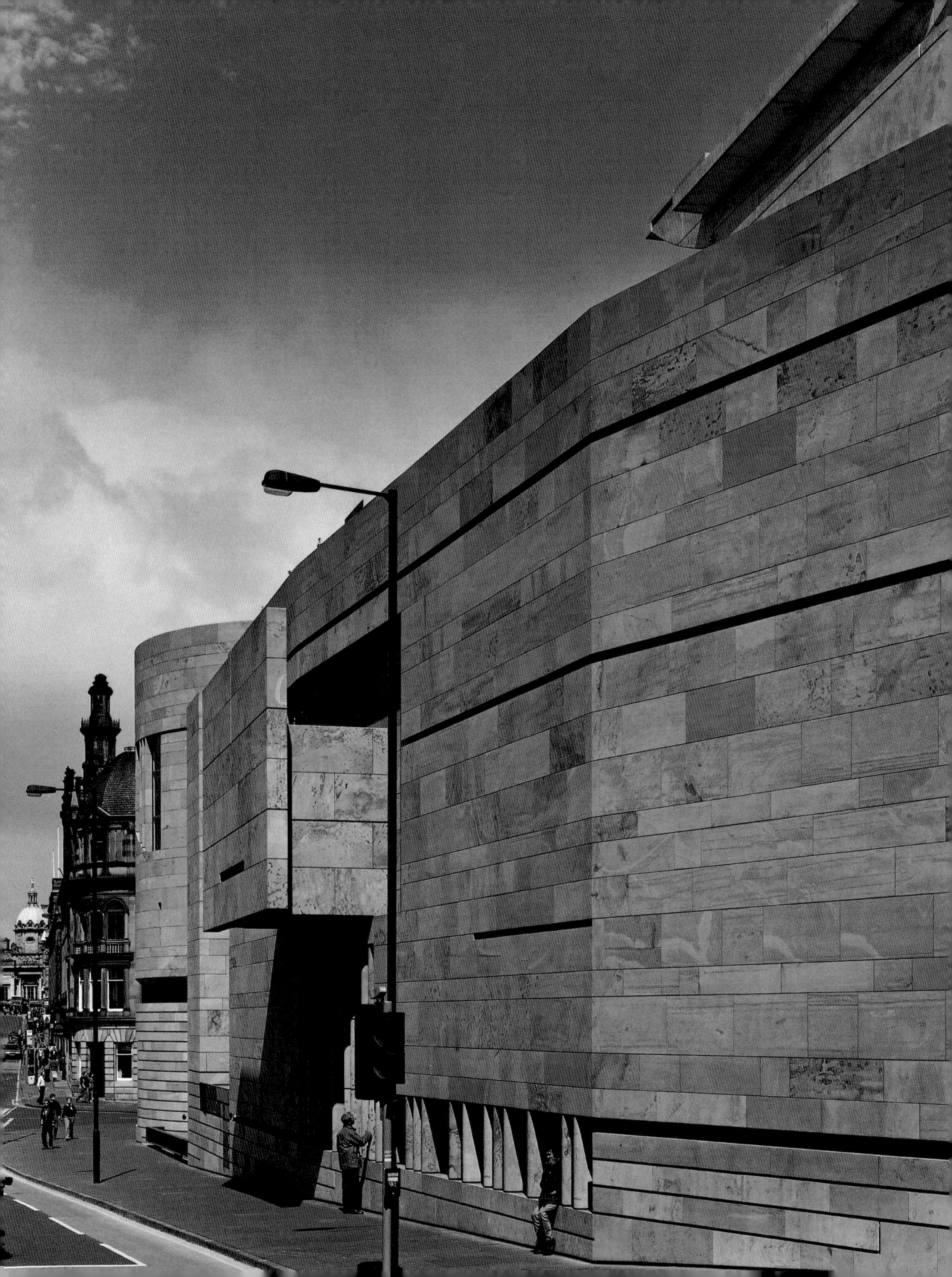

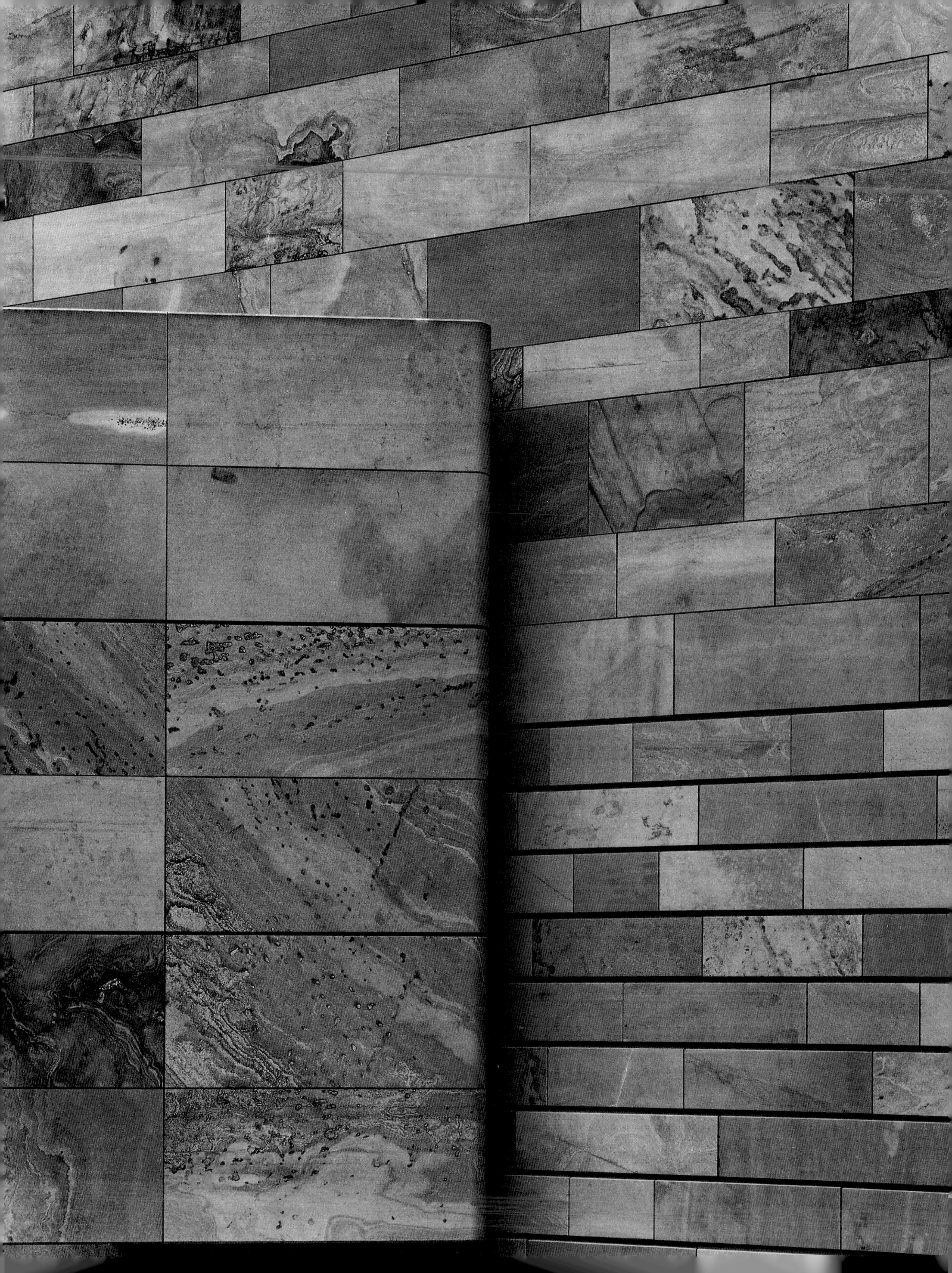

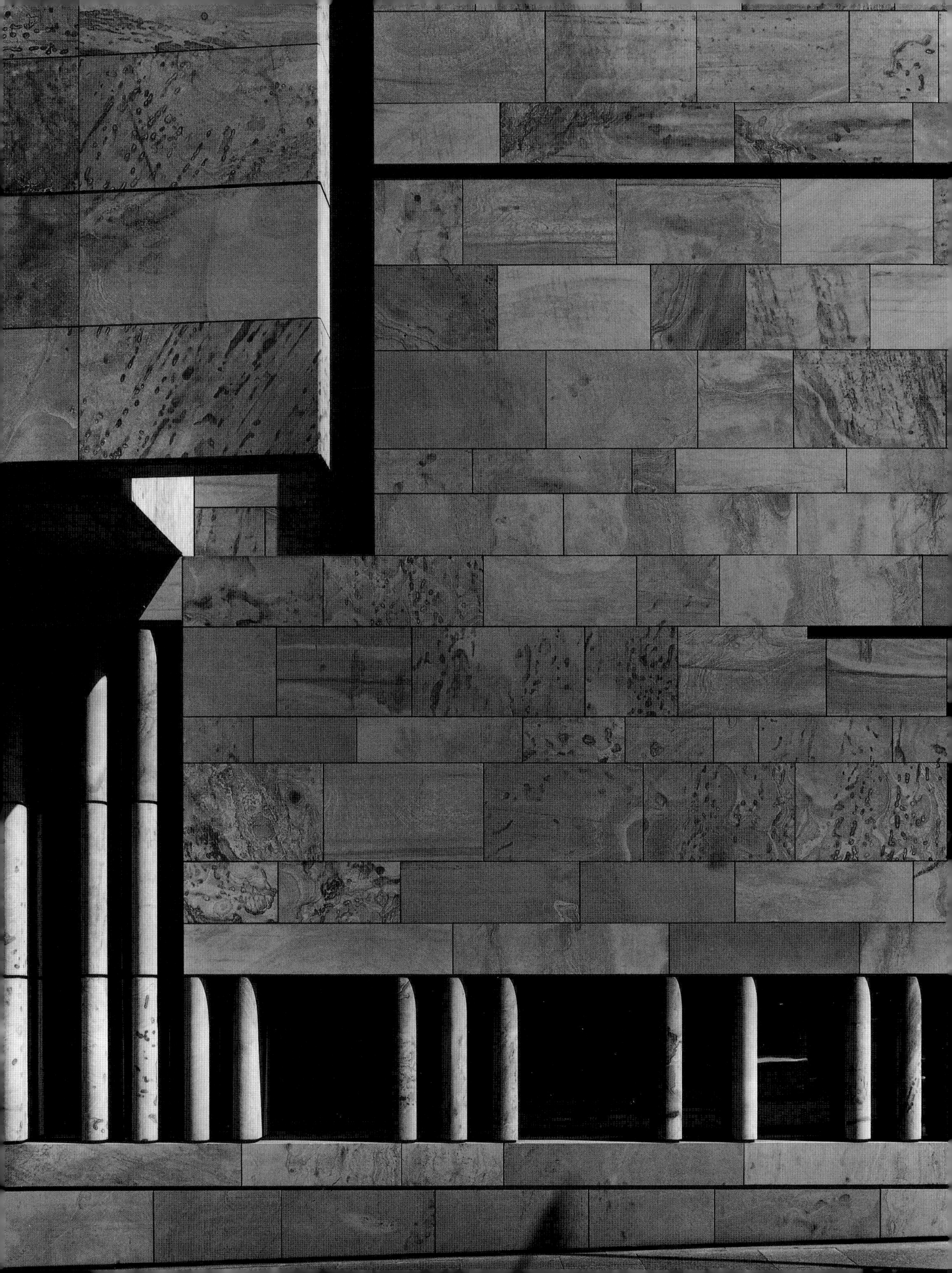

16

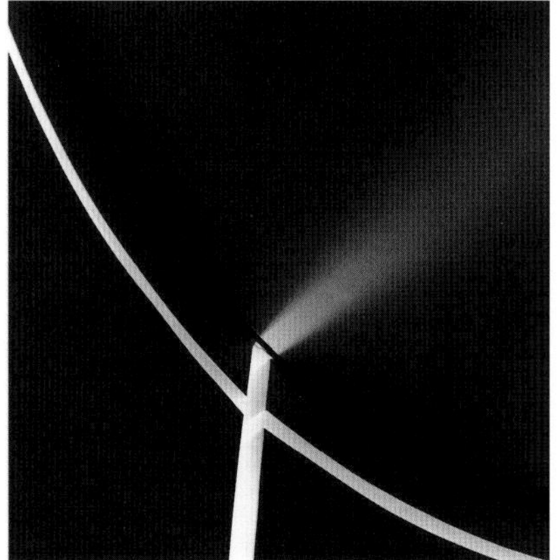

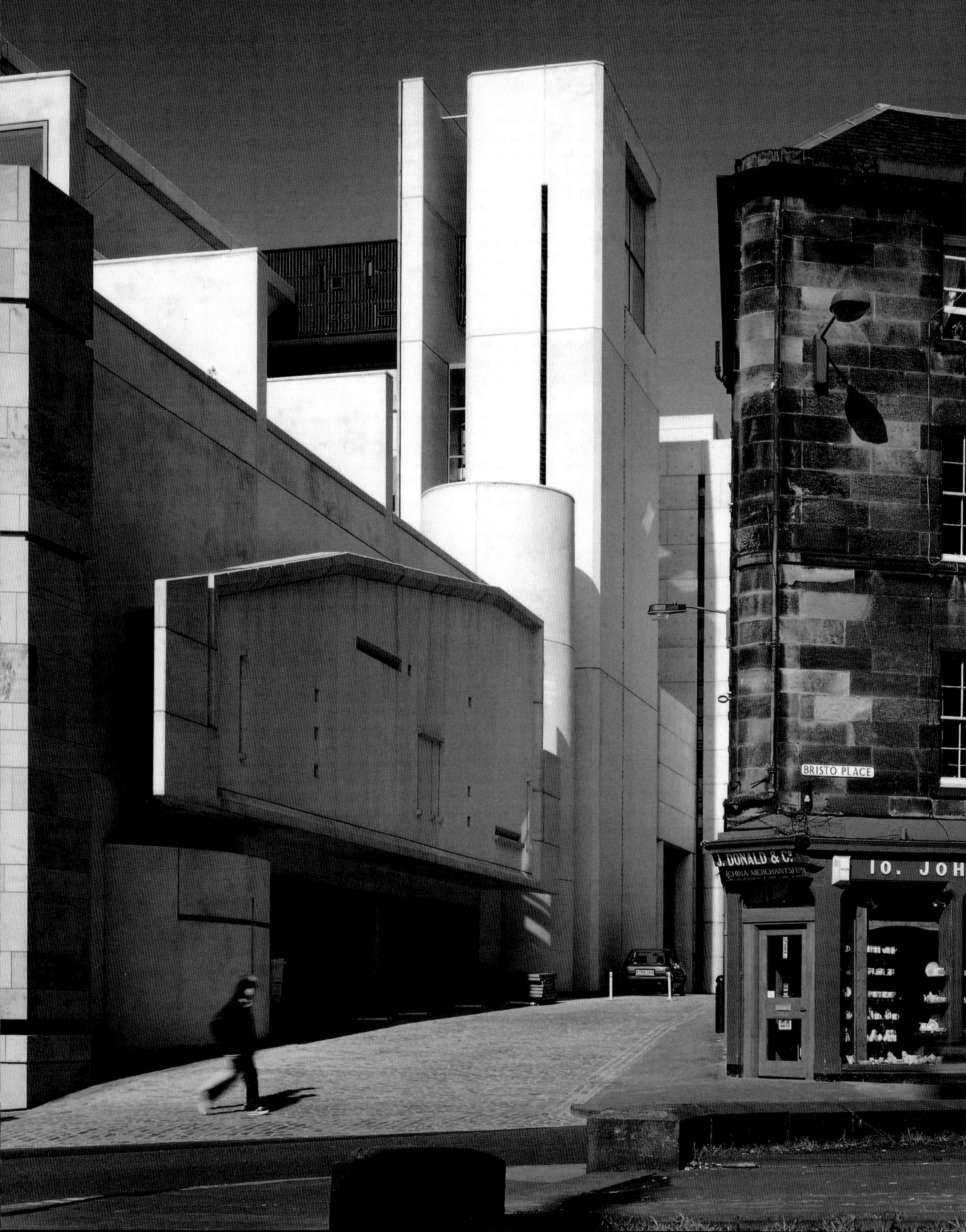
BRISTO PLACE
J. DONALD & Co
(CHINA MERCHANTS) Ltd
10. JOH

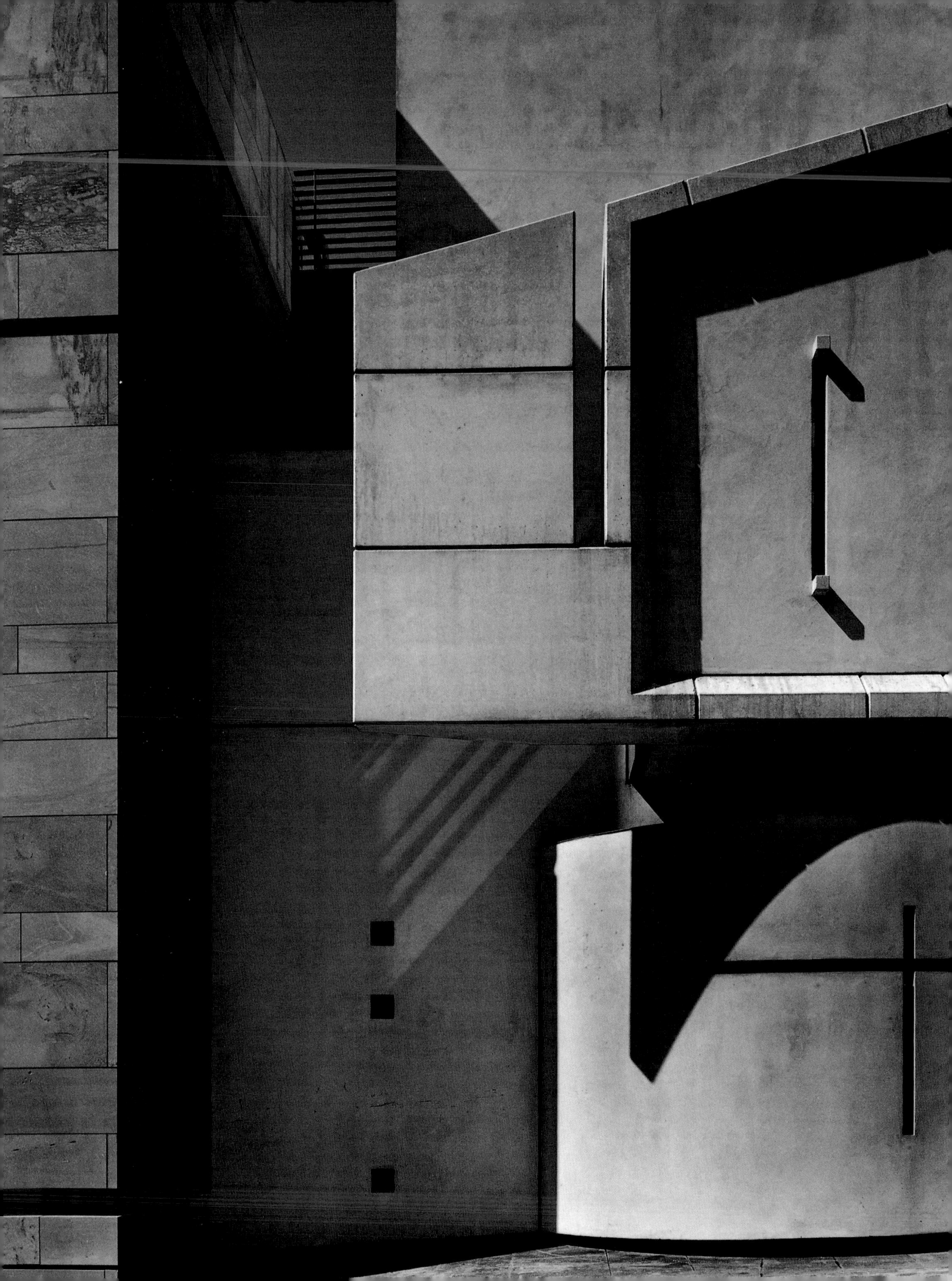

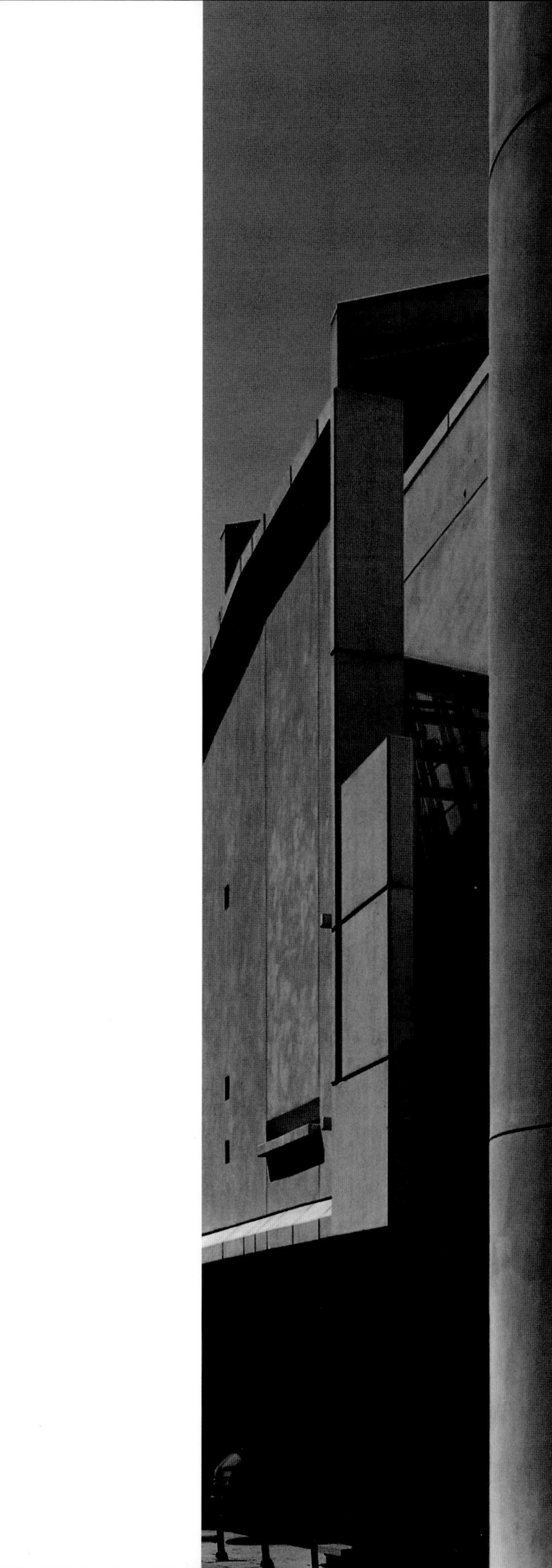

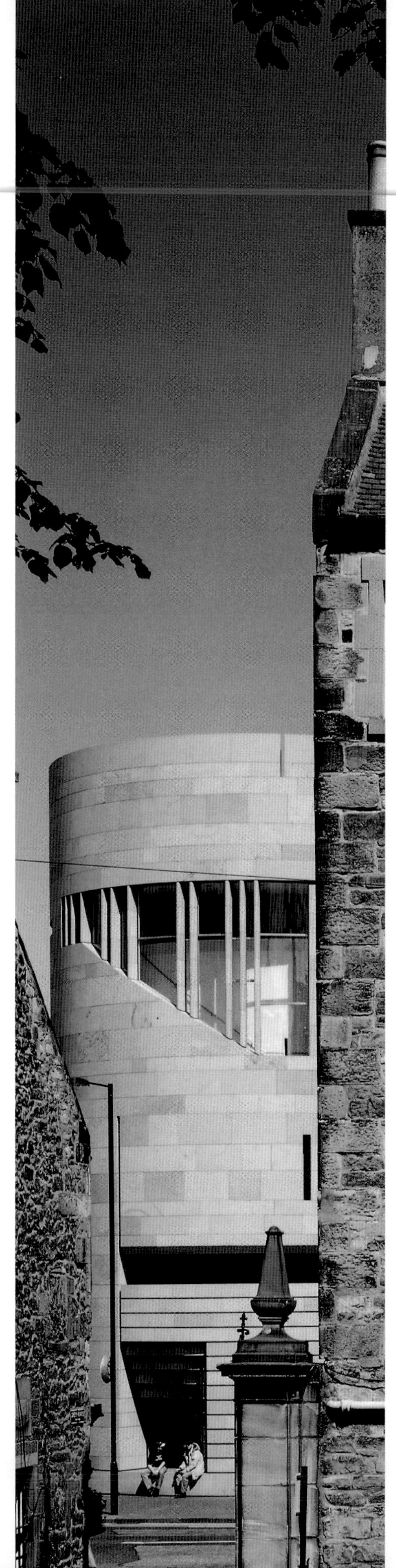

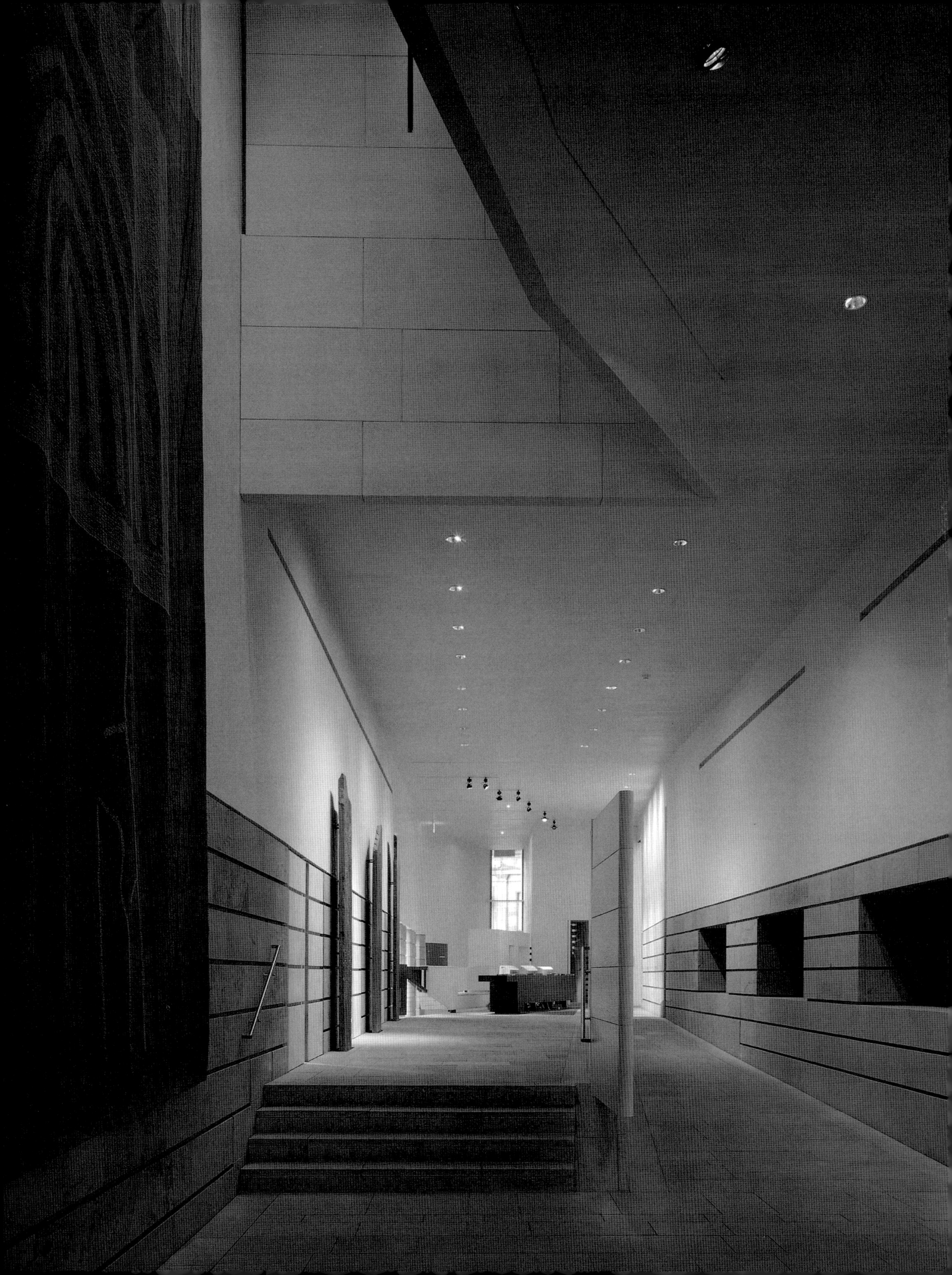

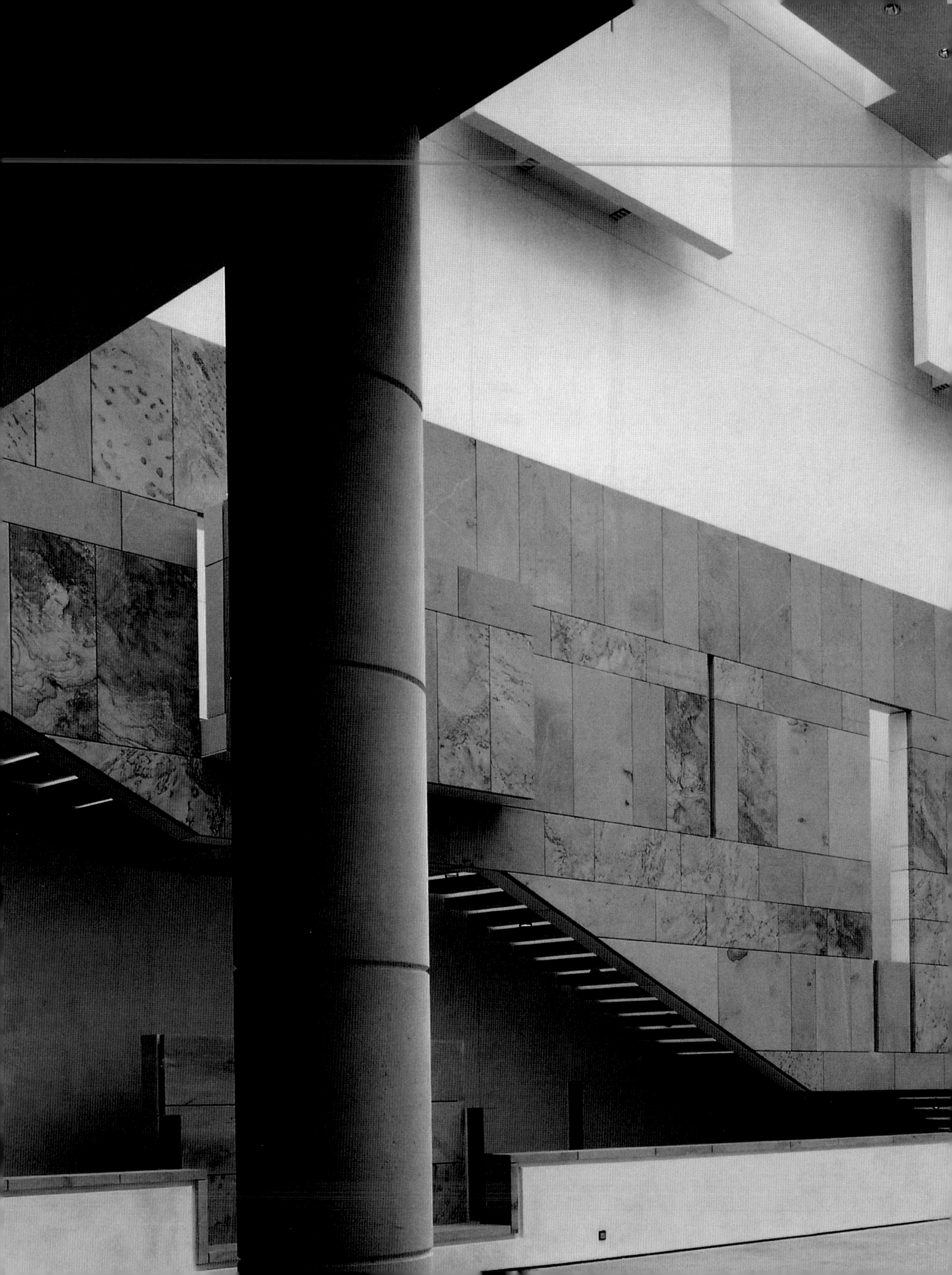

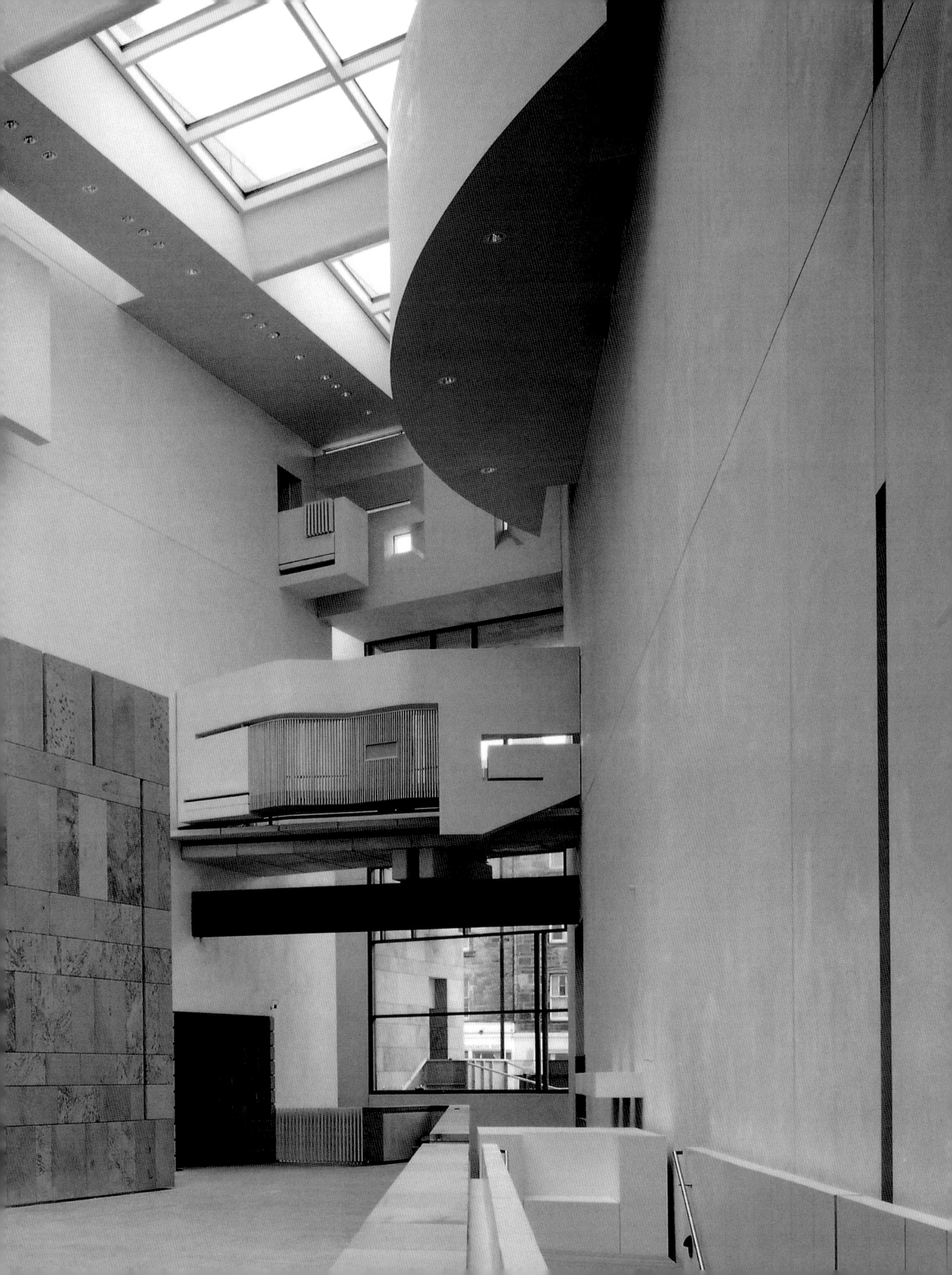

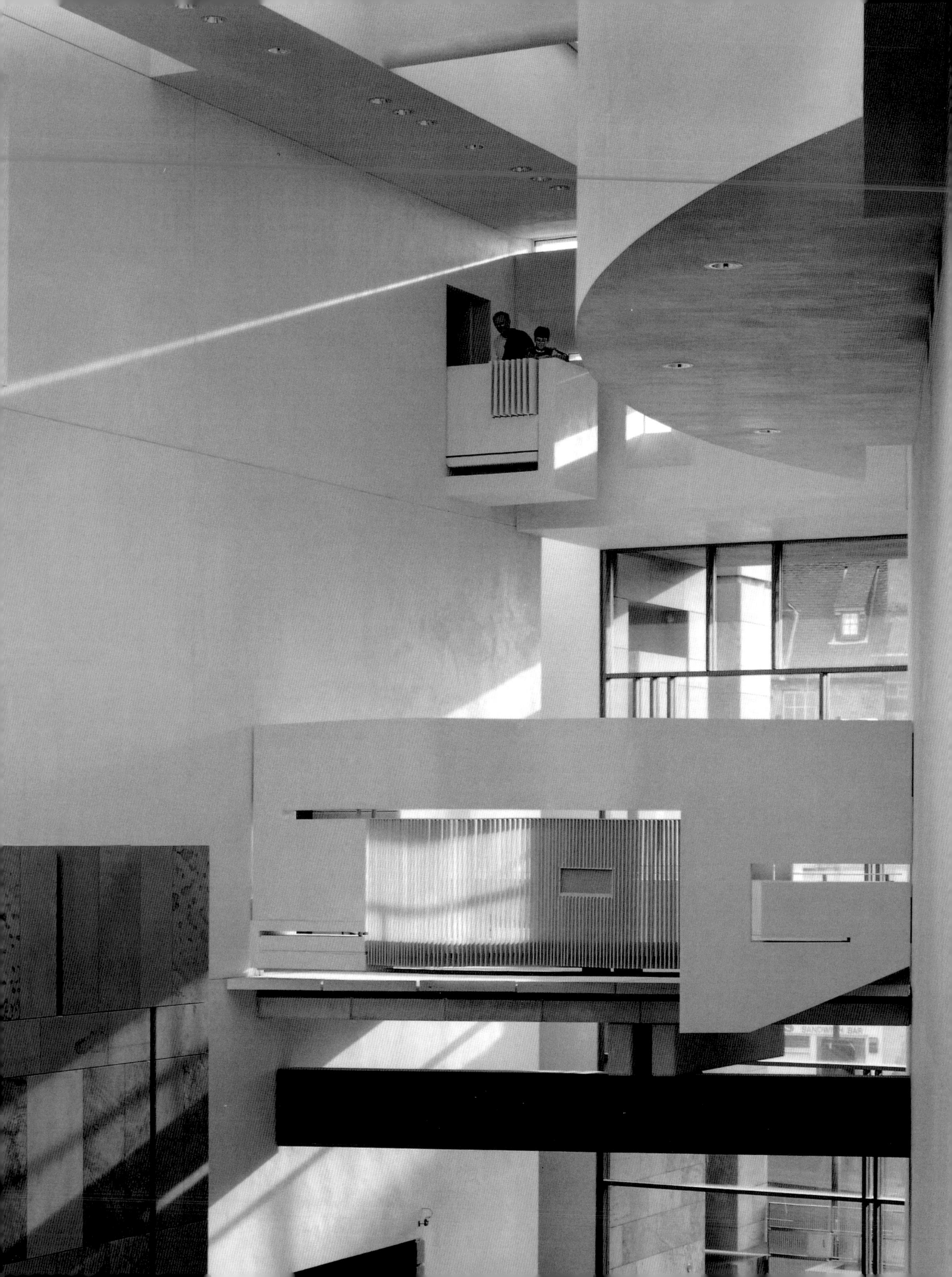

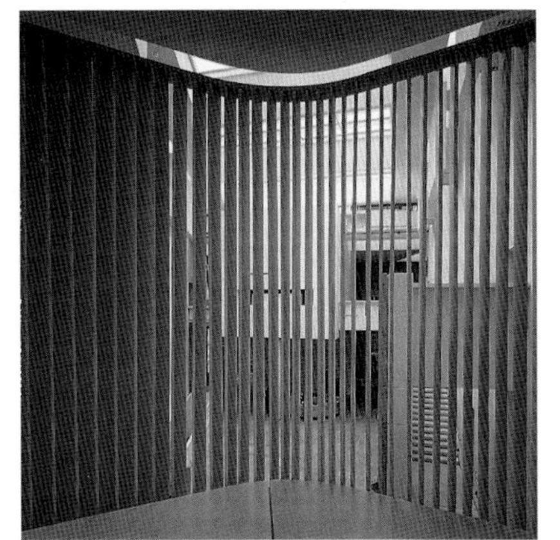

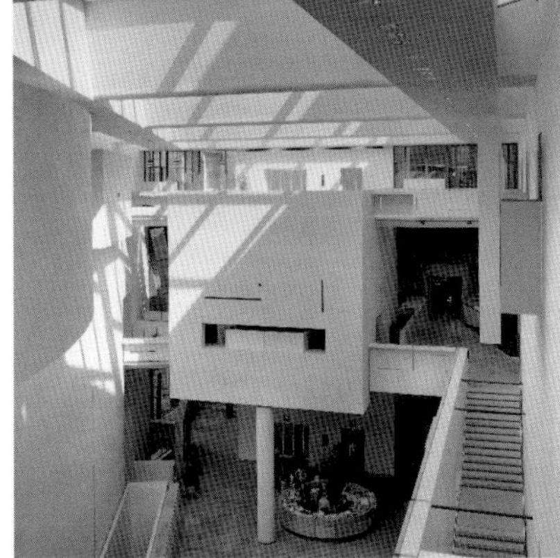

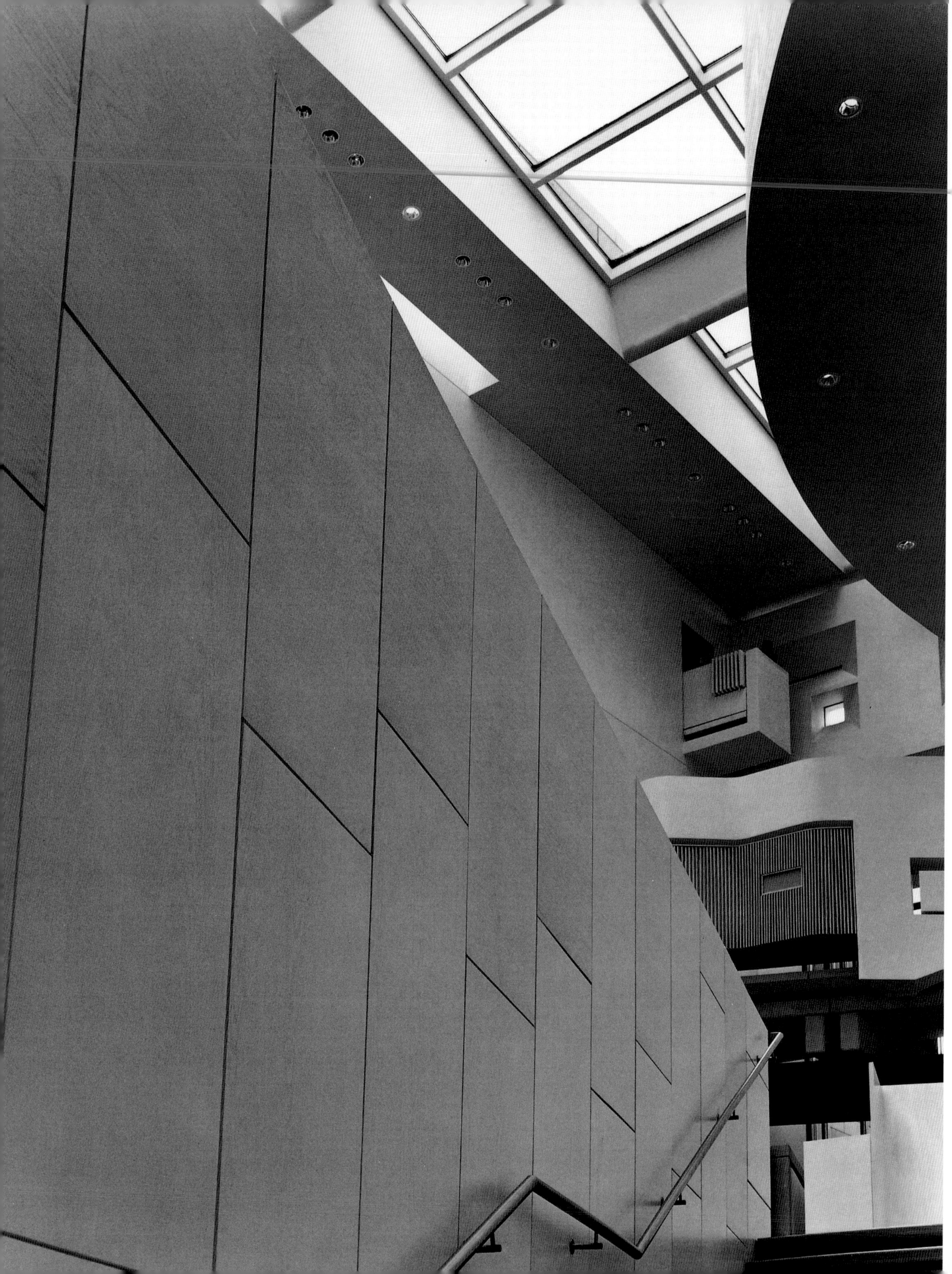

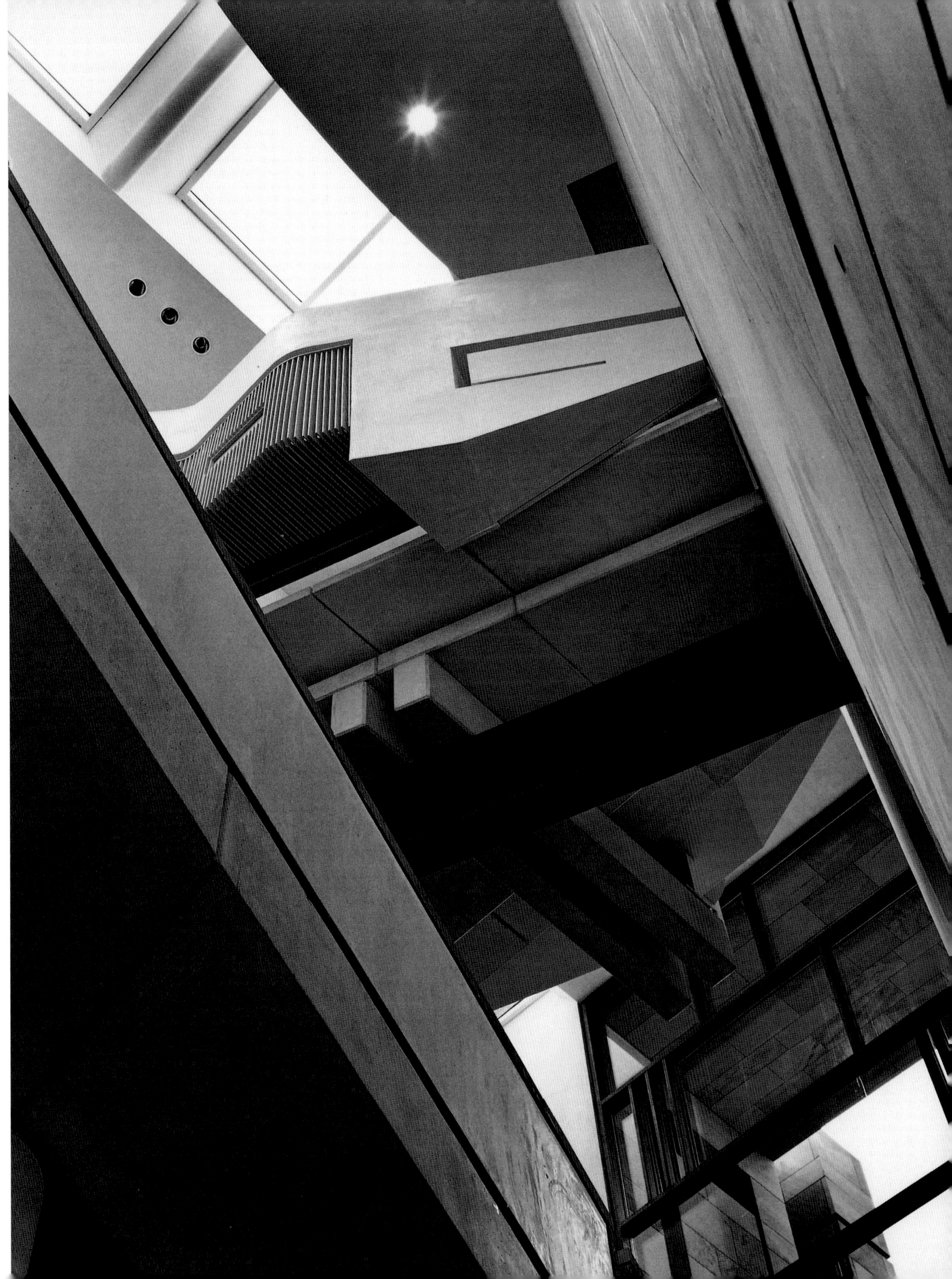

28

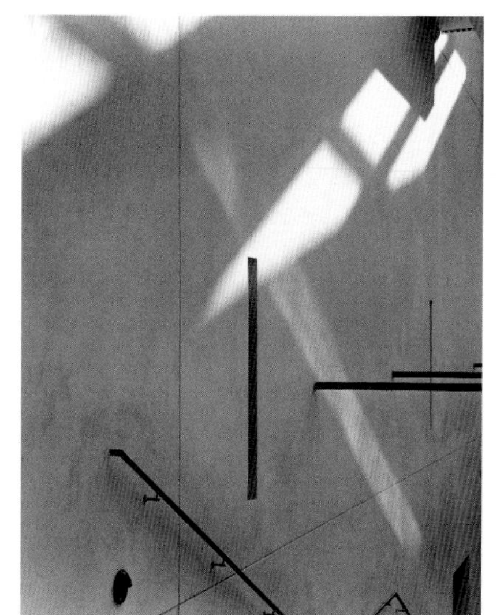

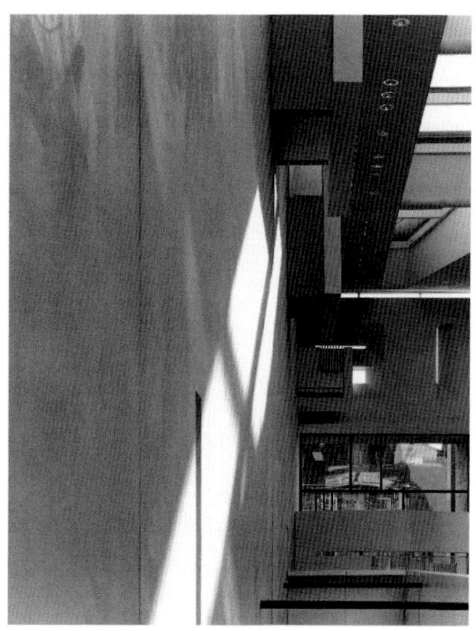

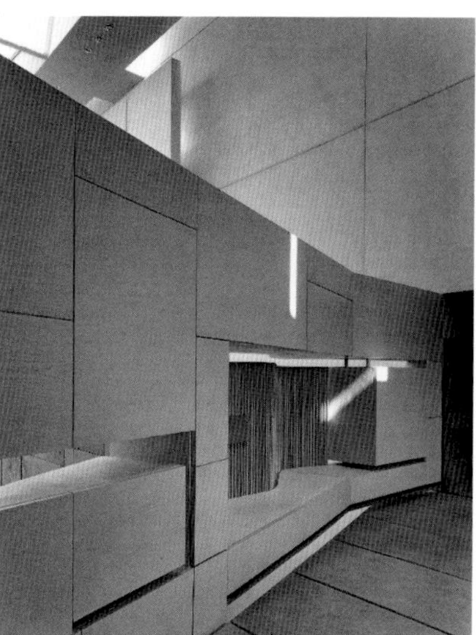

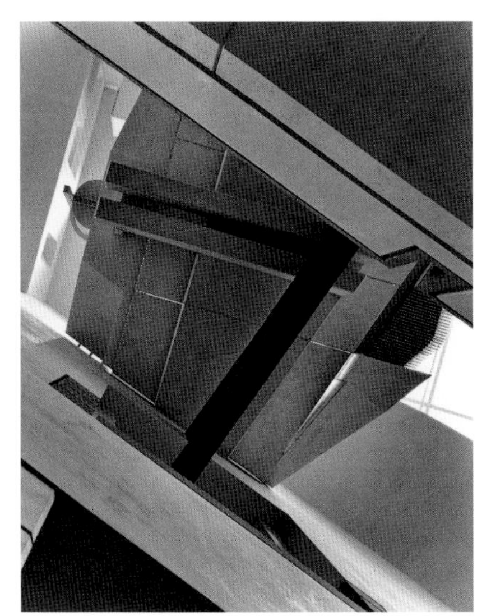

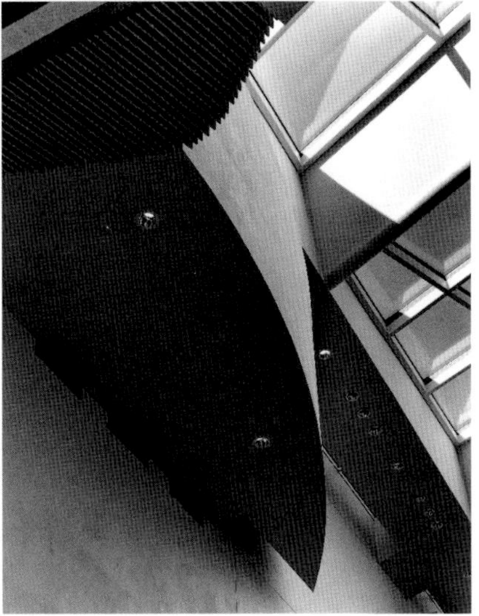

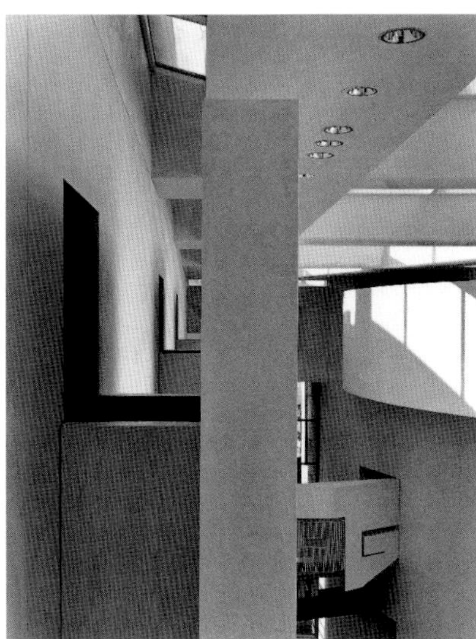

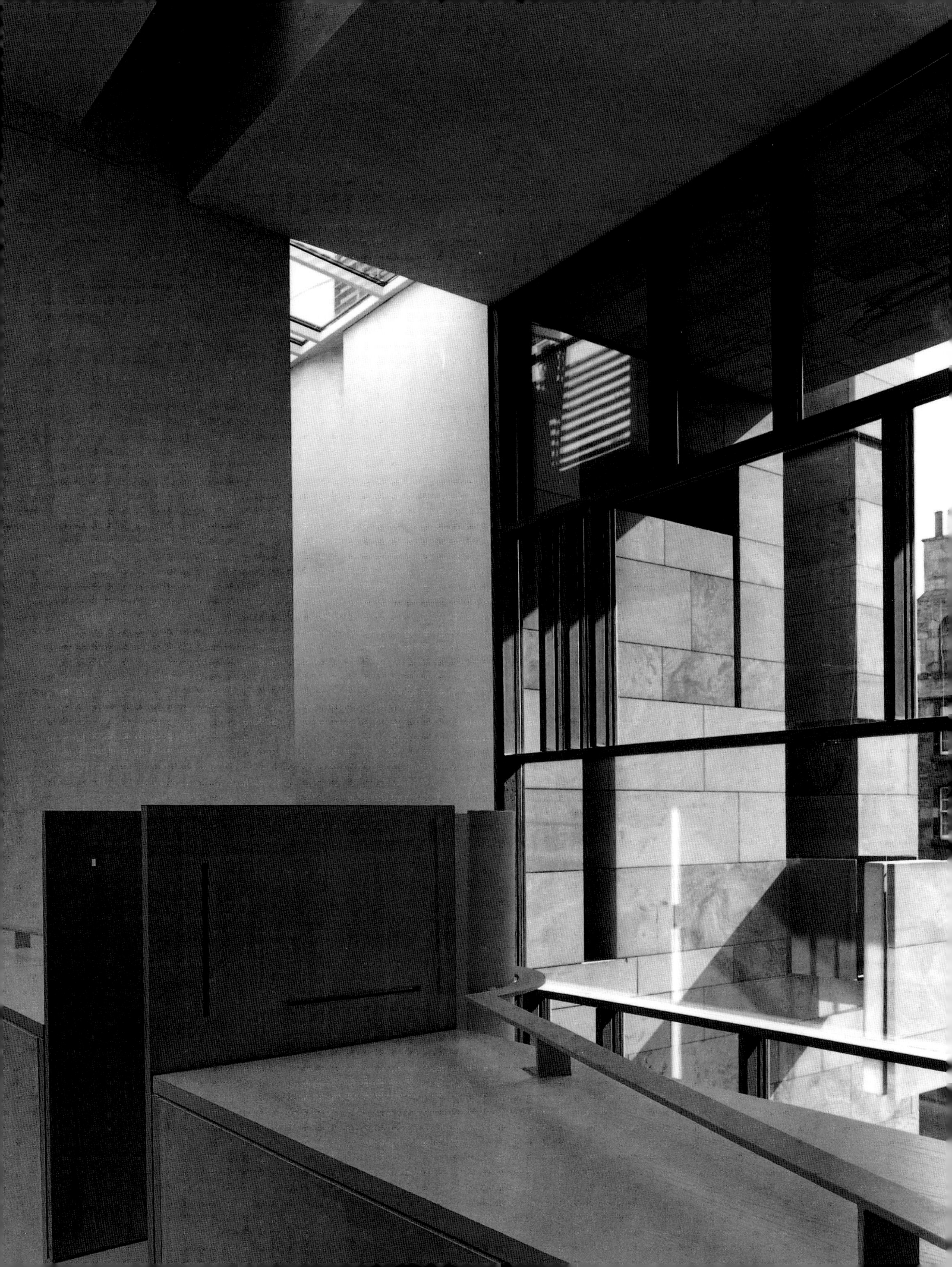

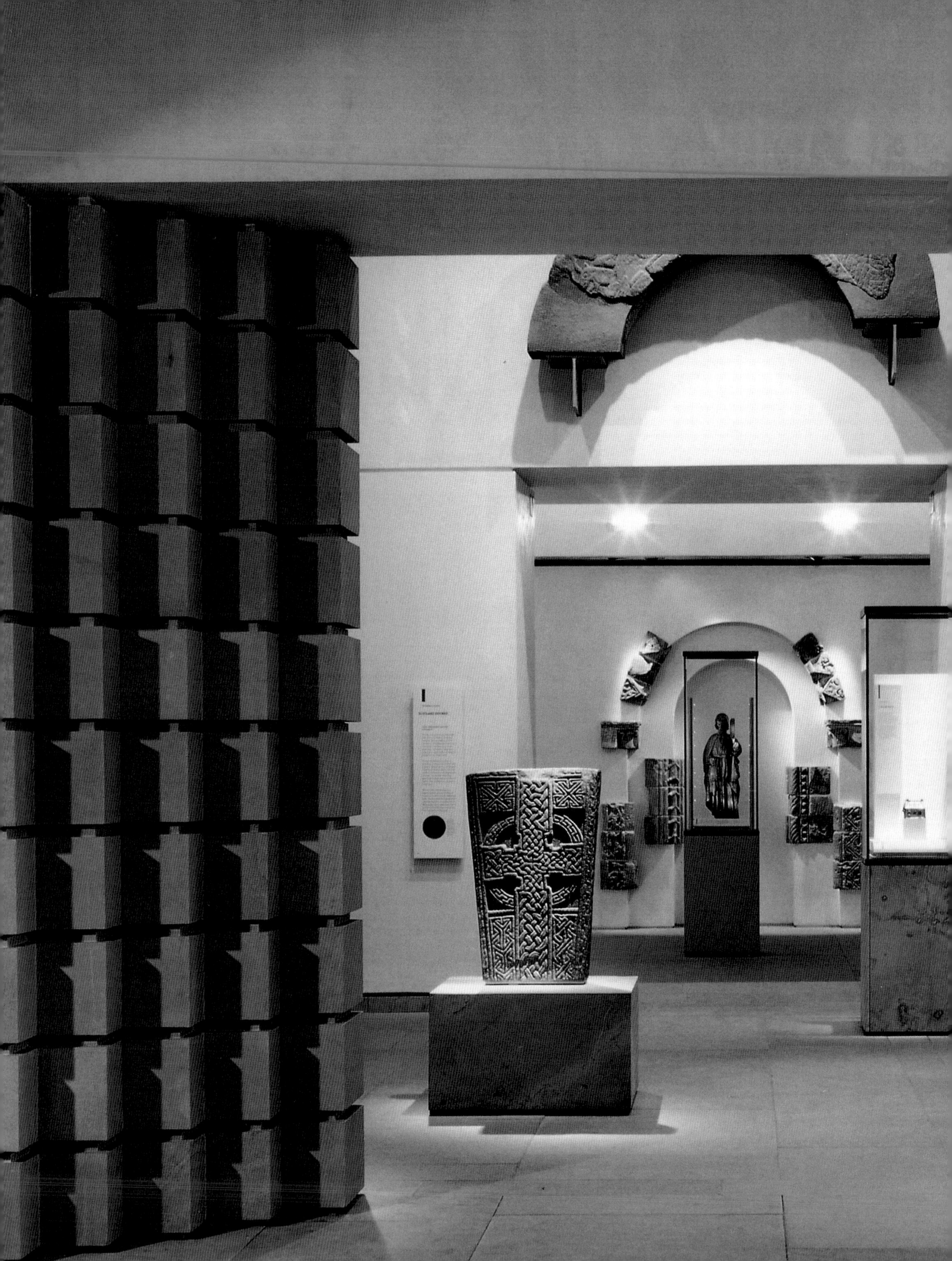

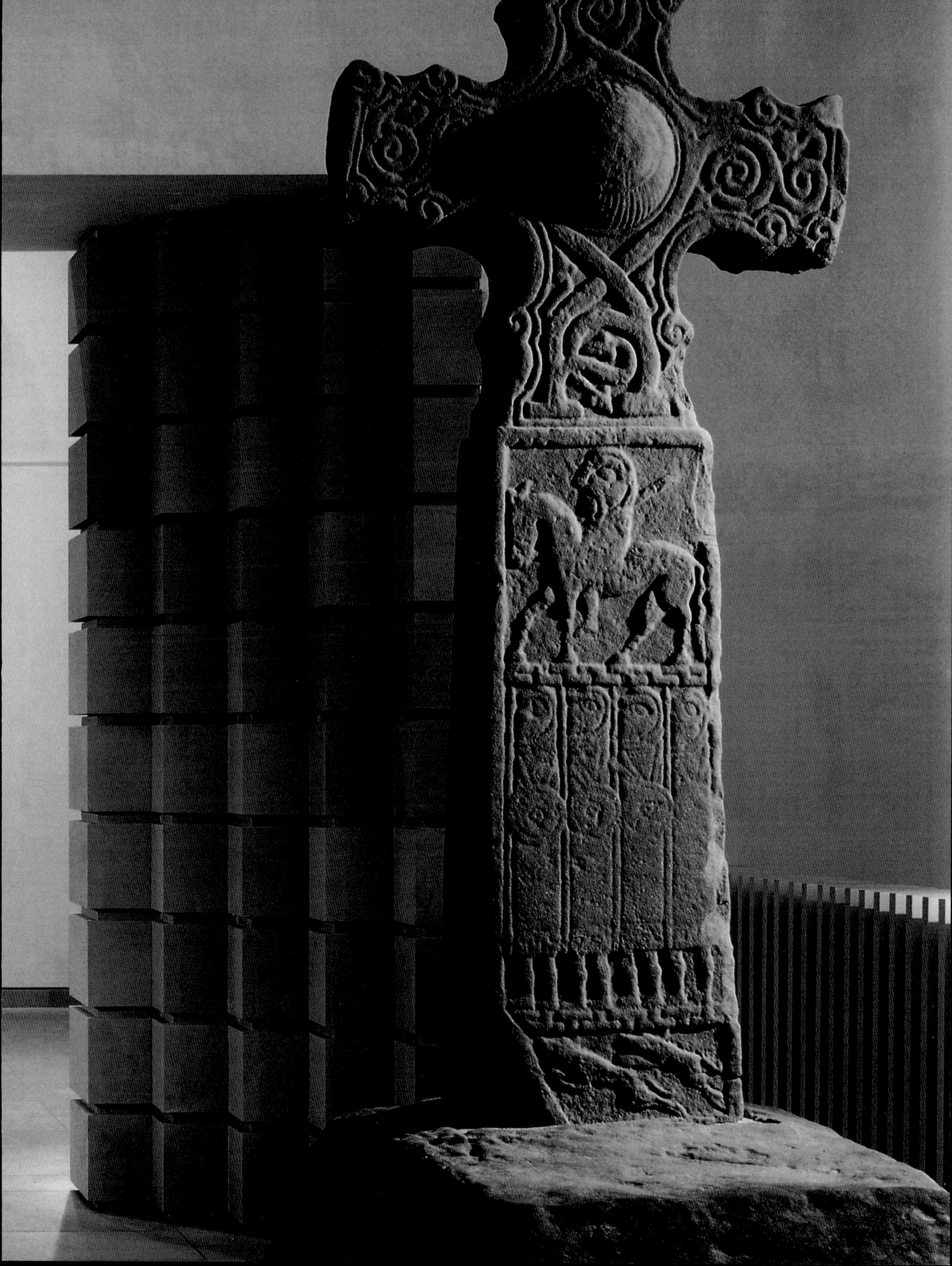

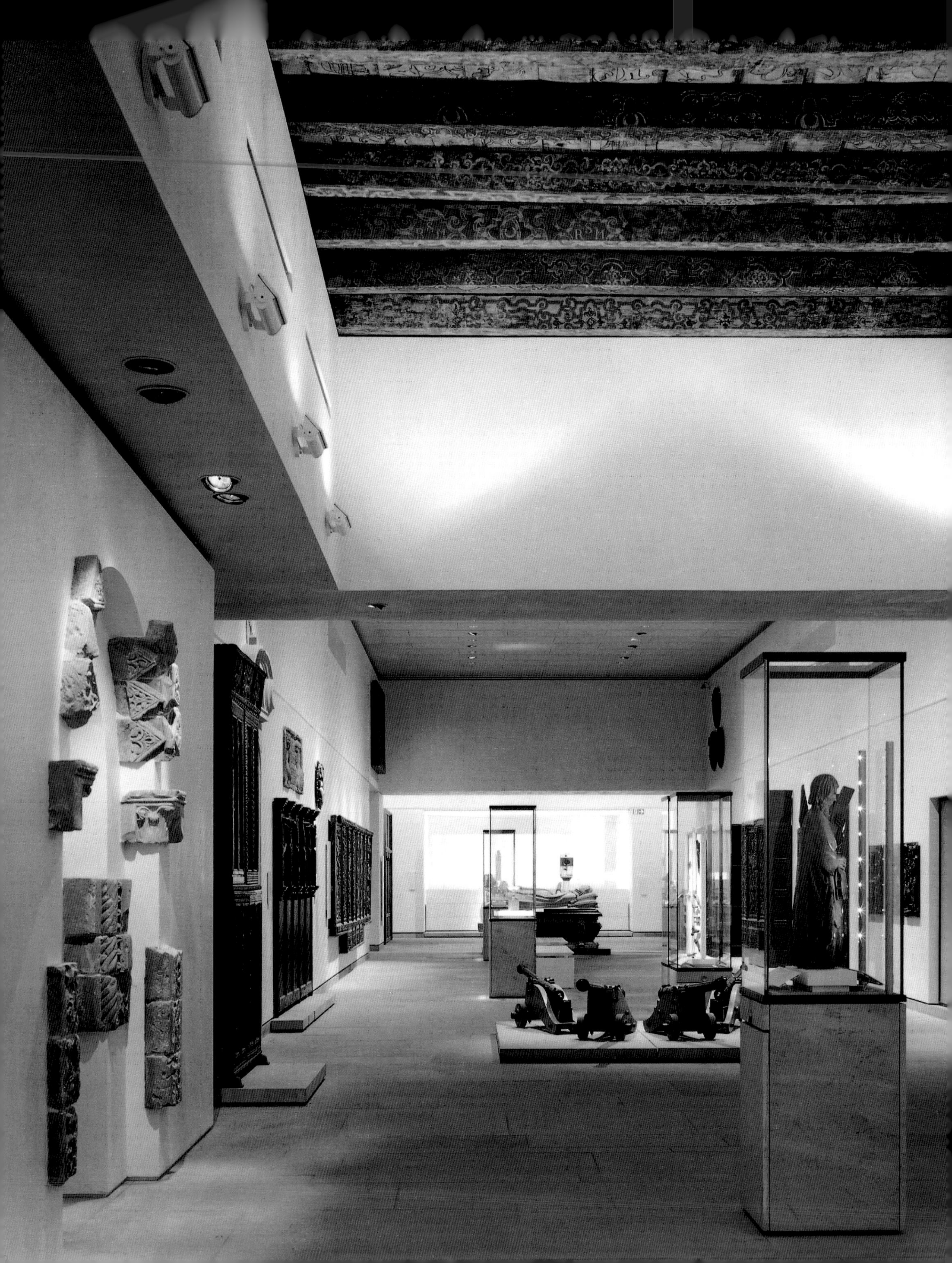

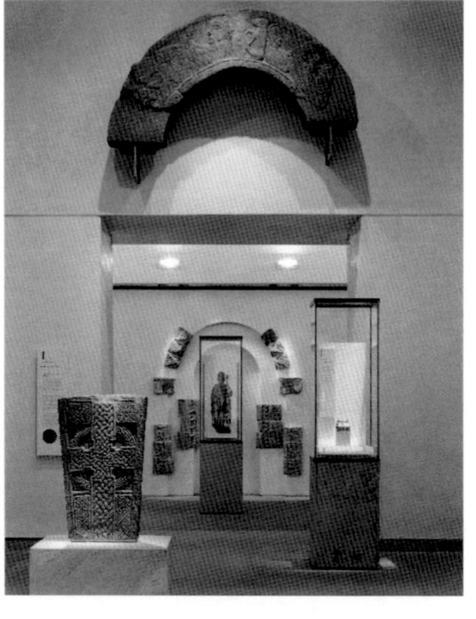

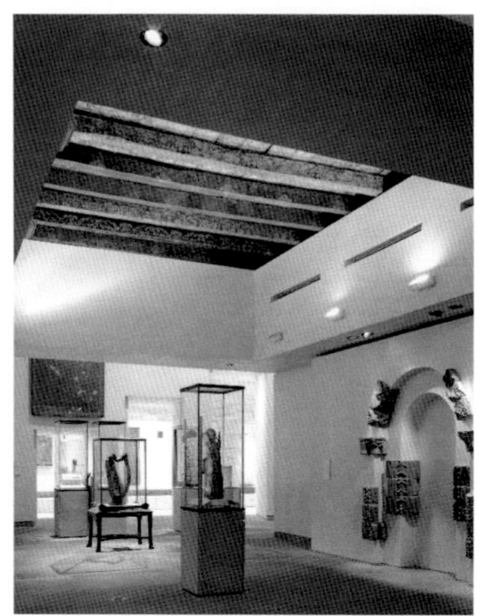

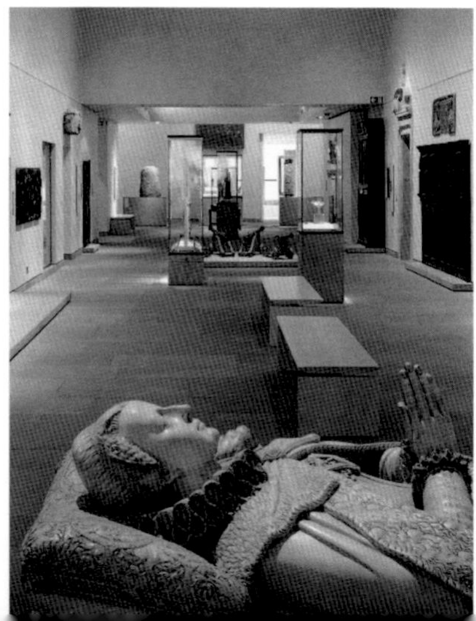

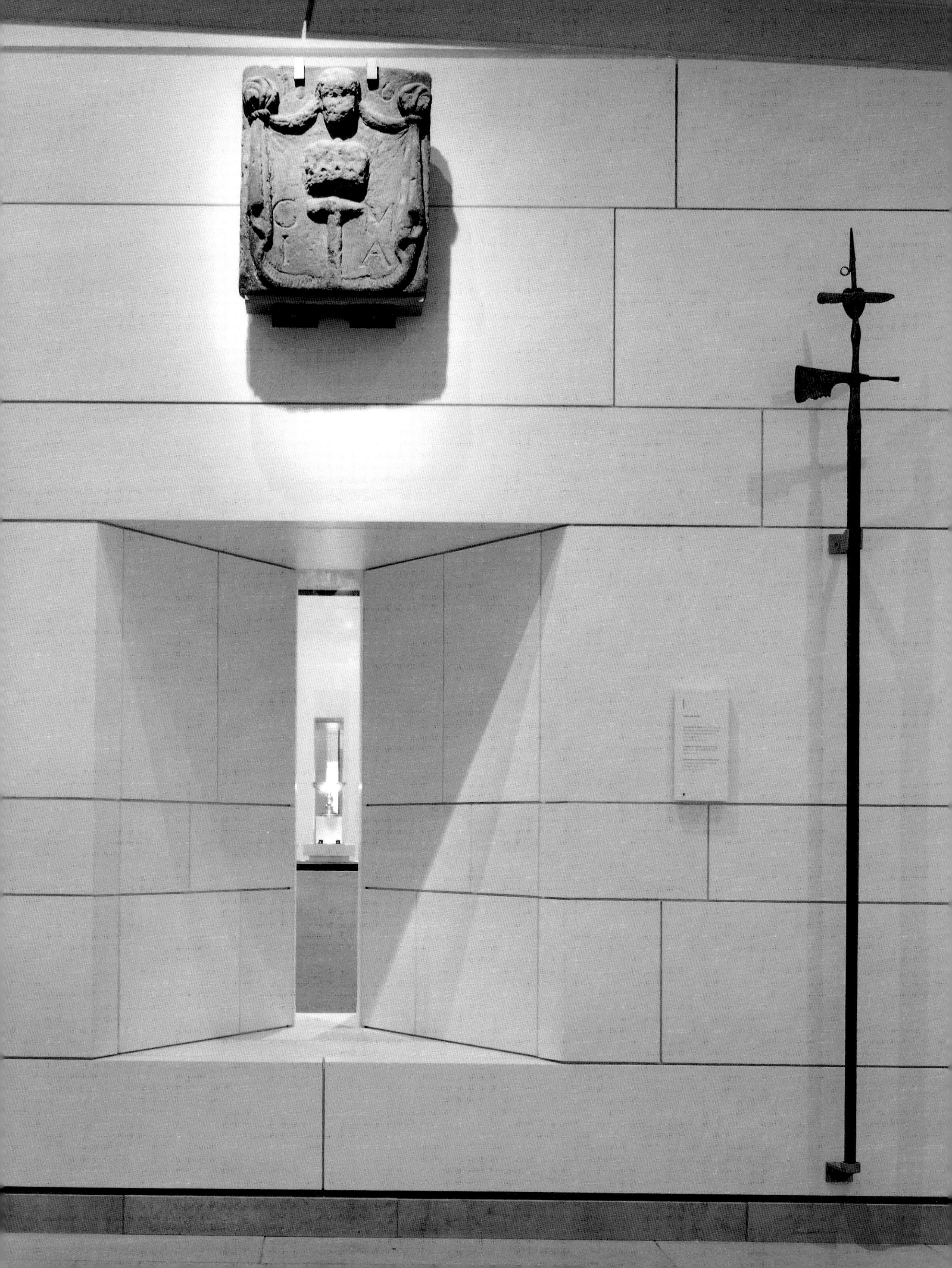

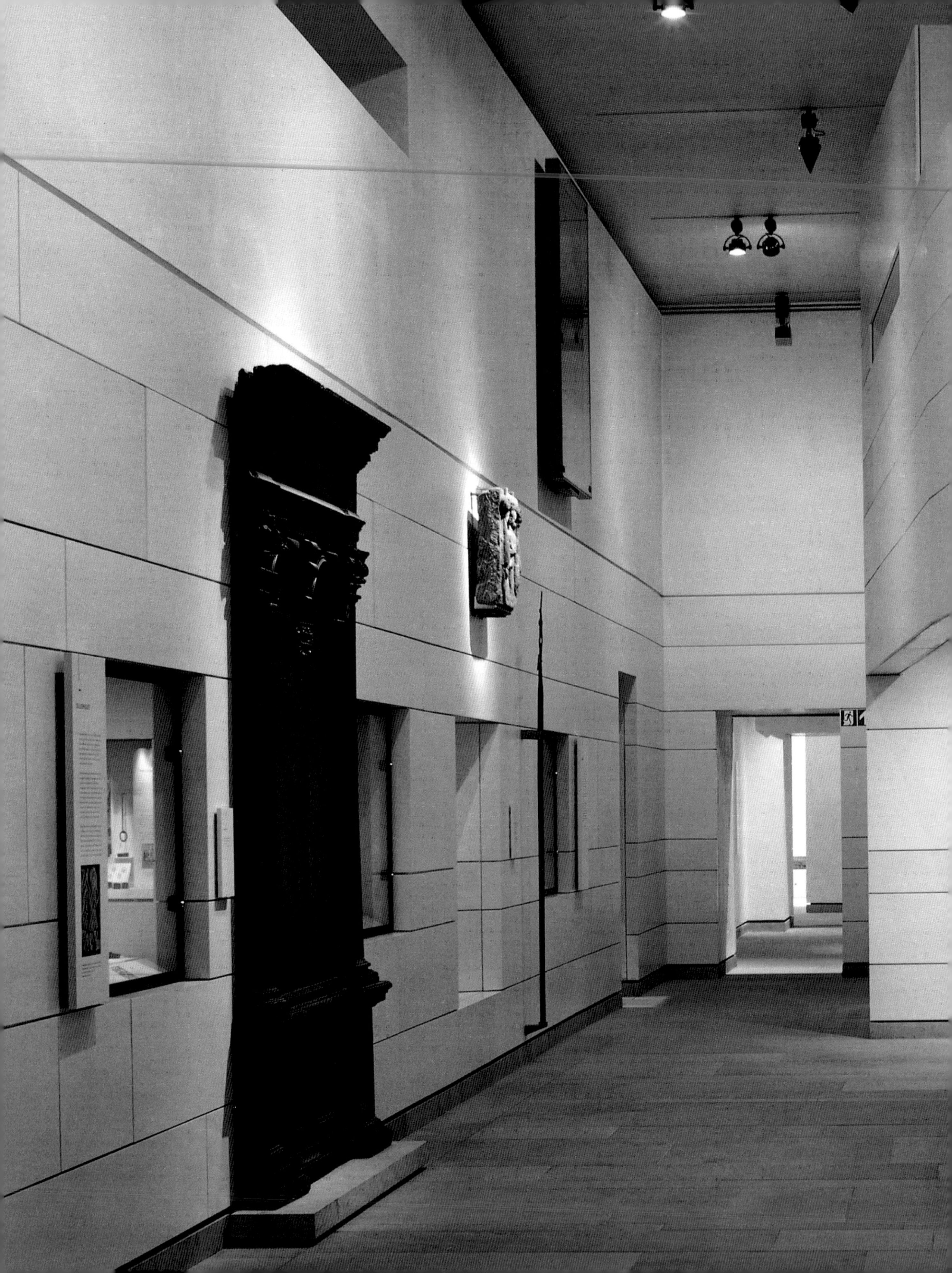

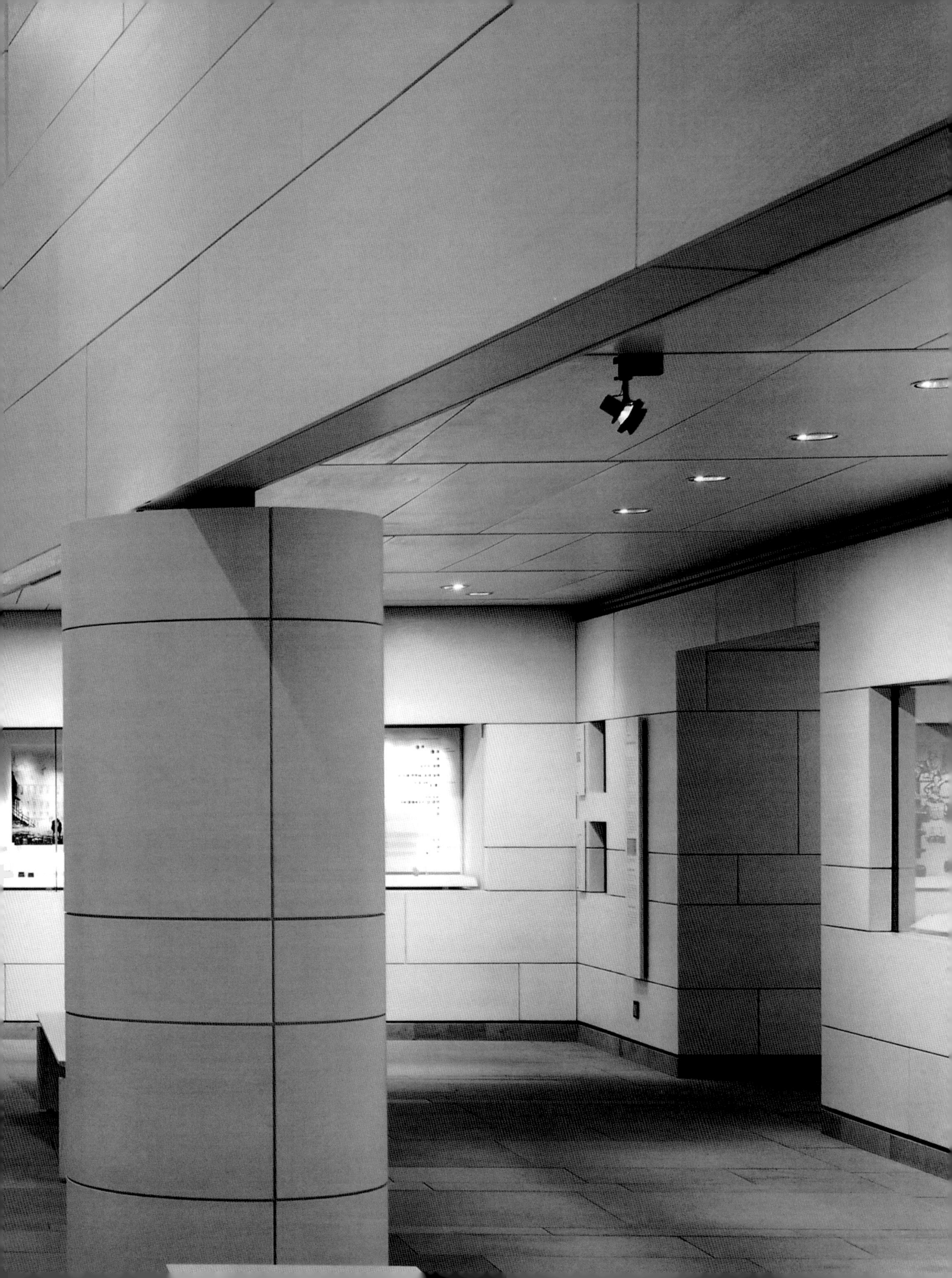

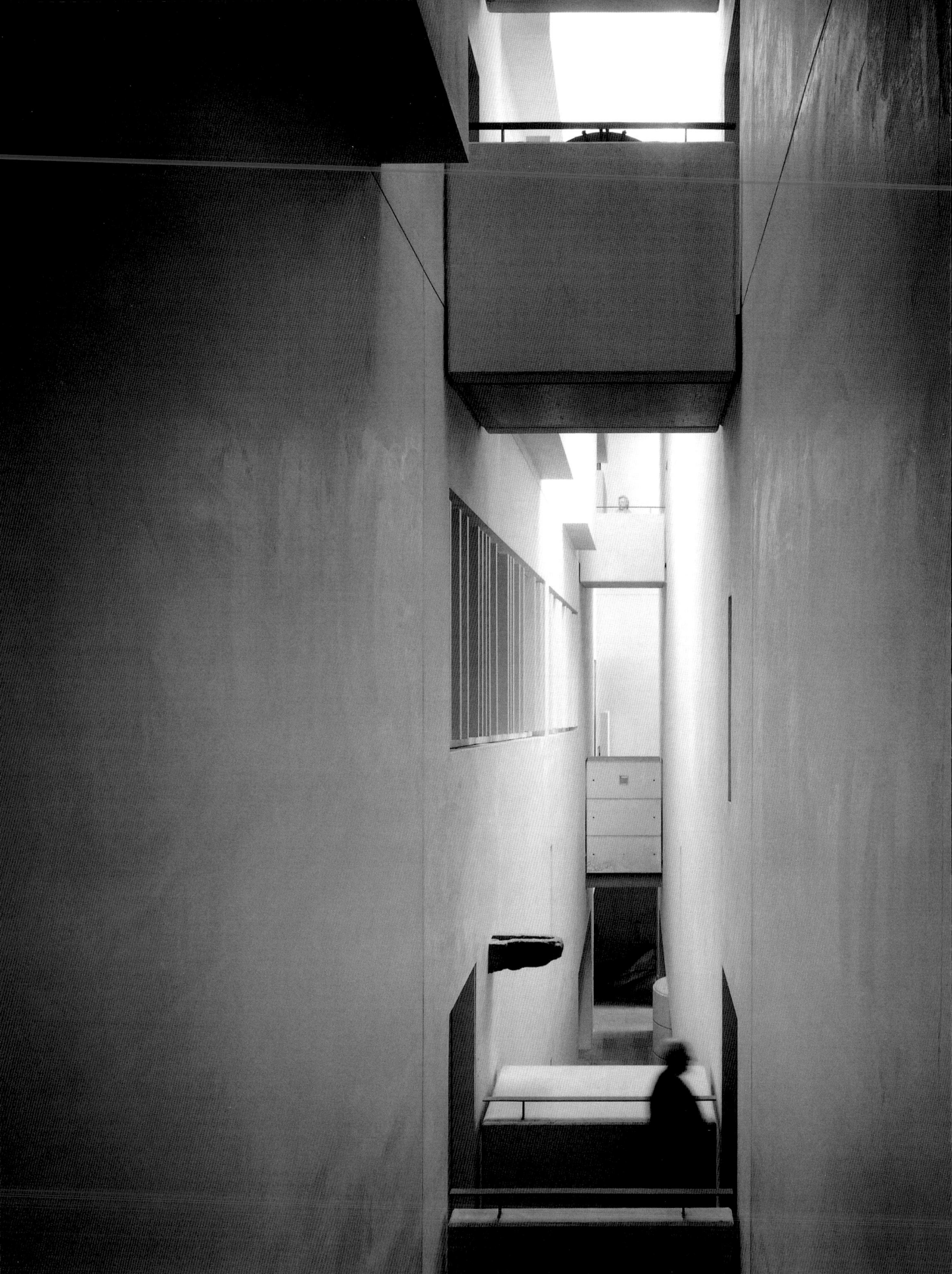

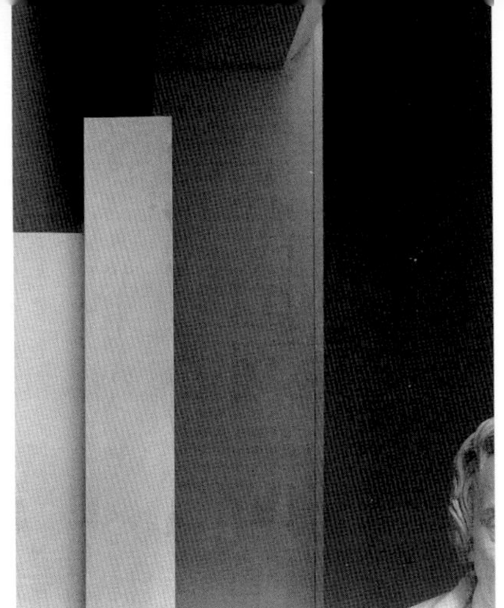

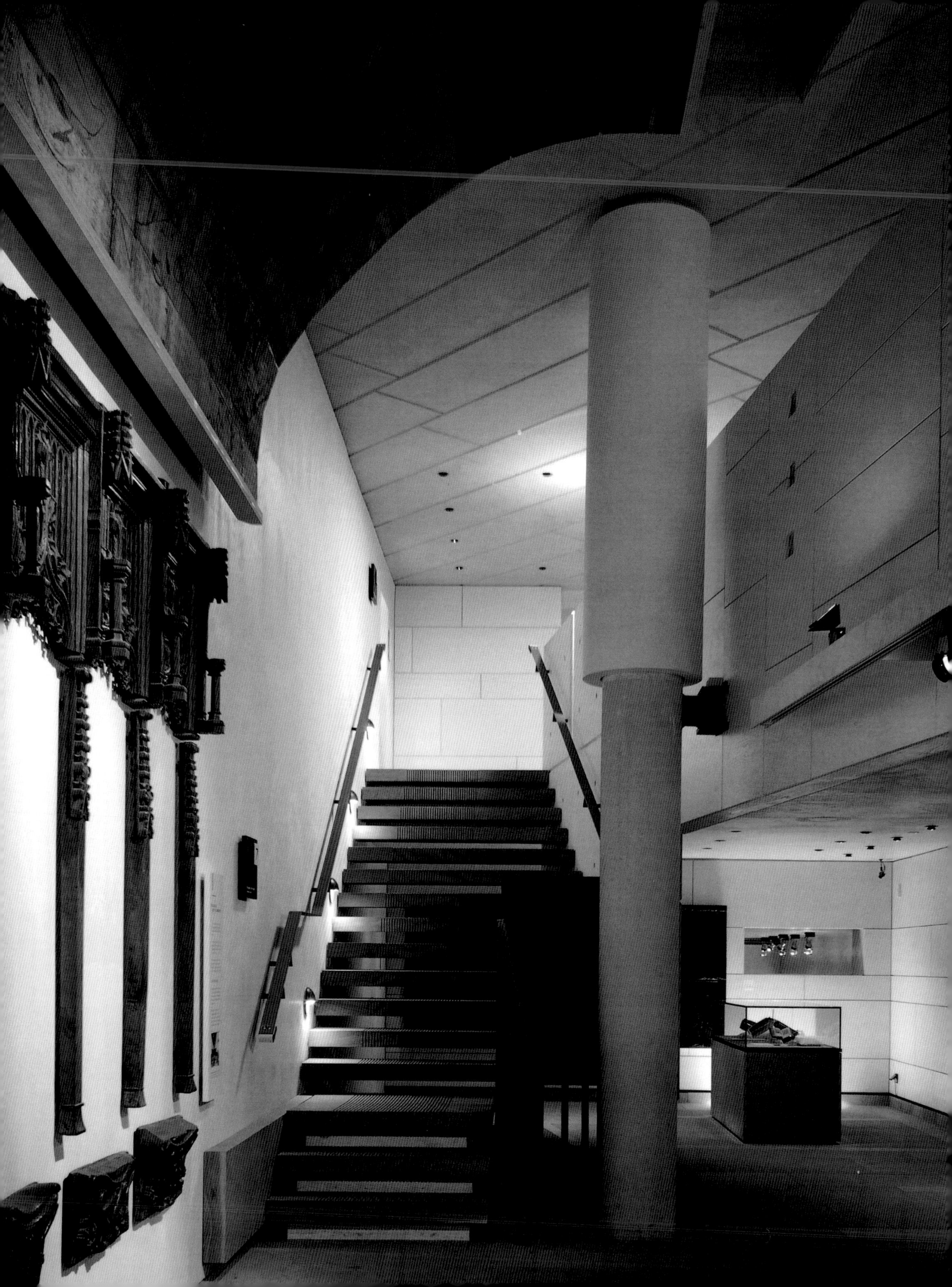

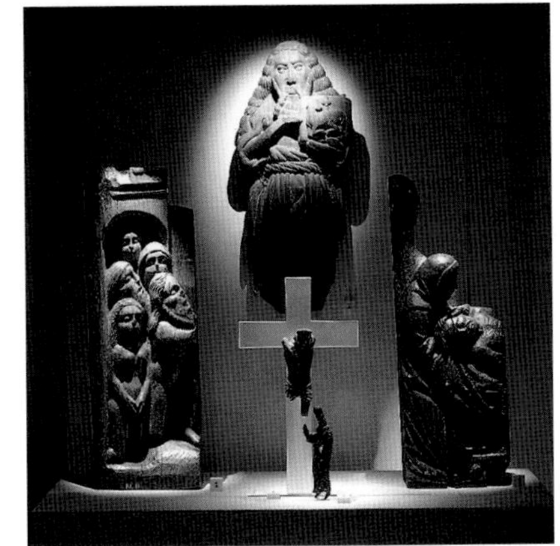

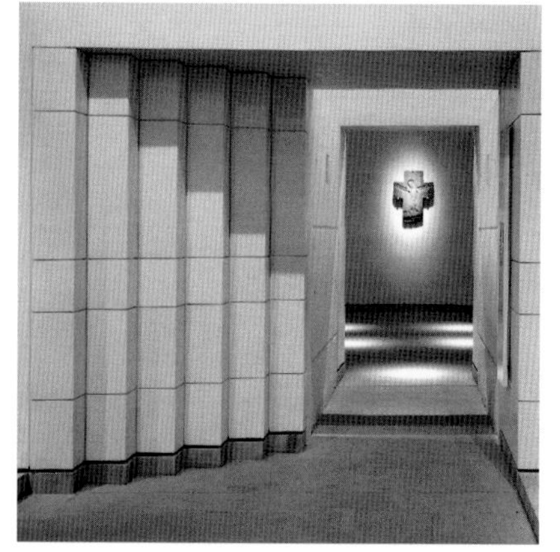

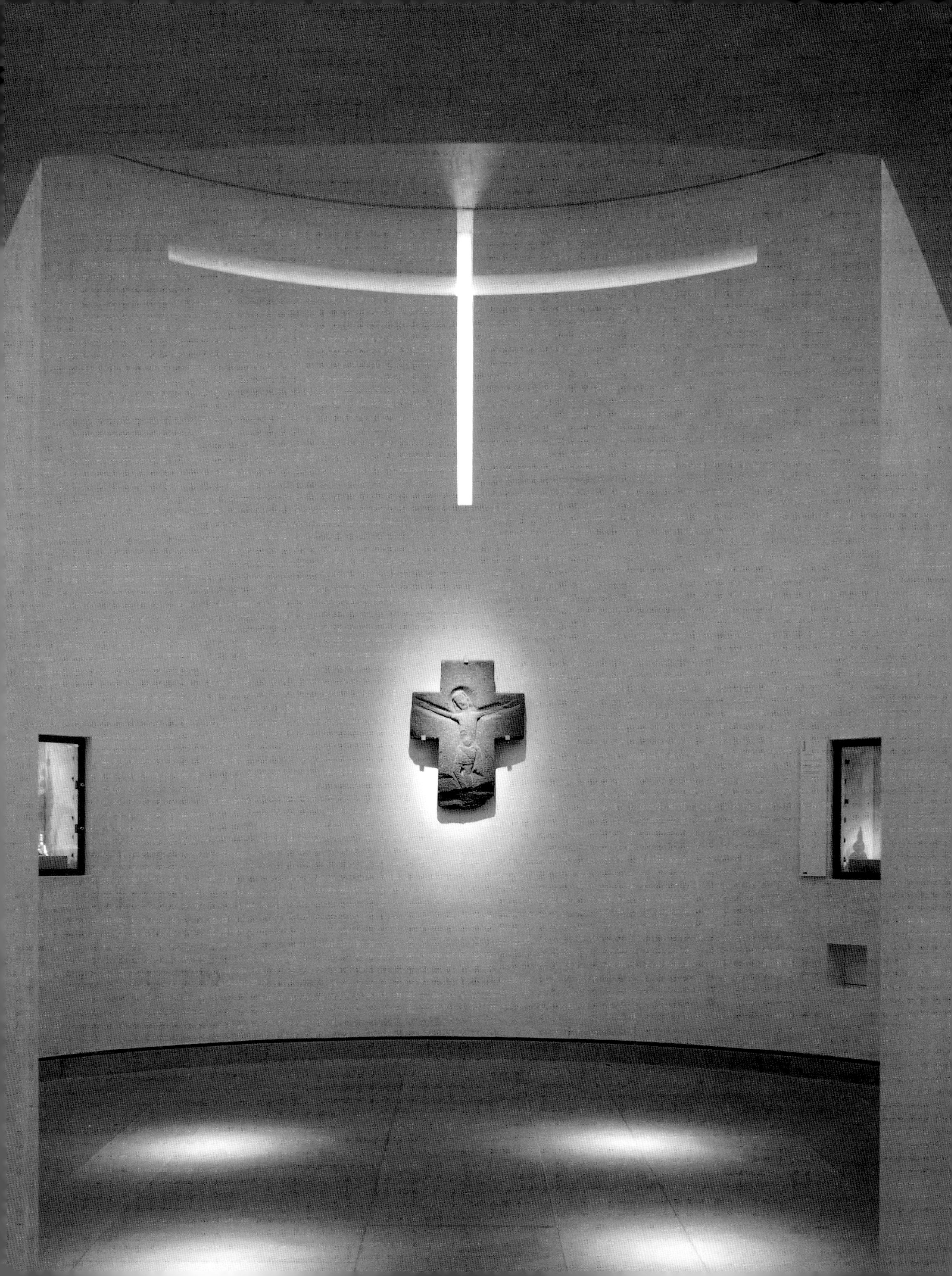

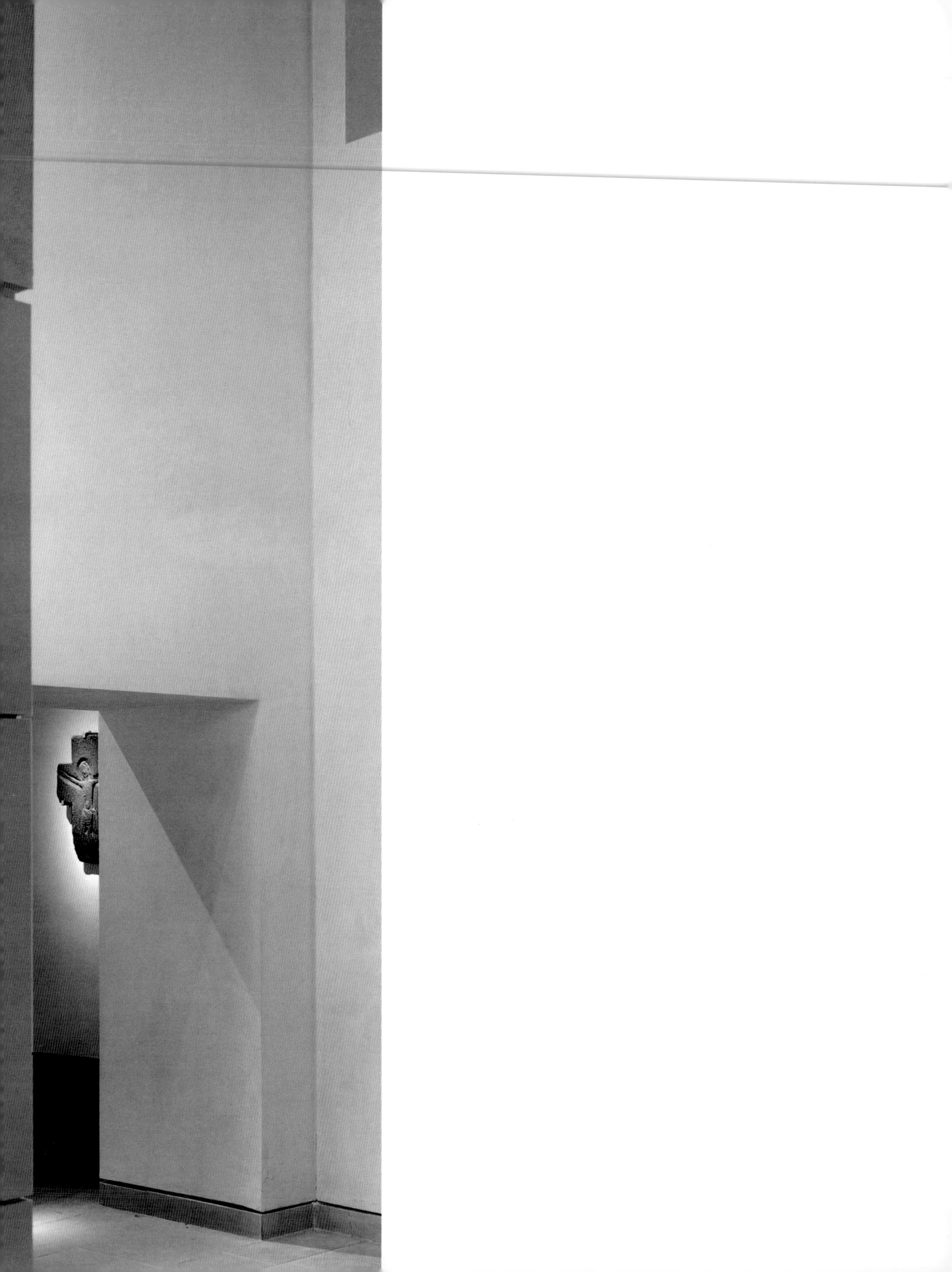

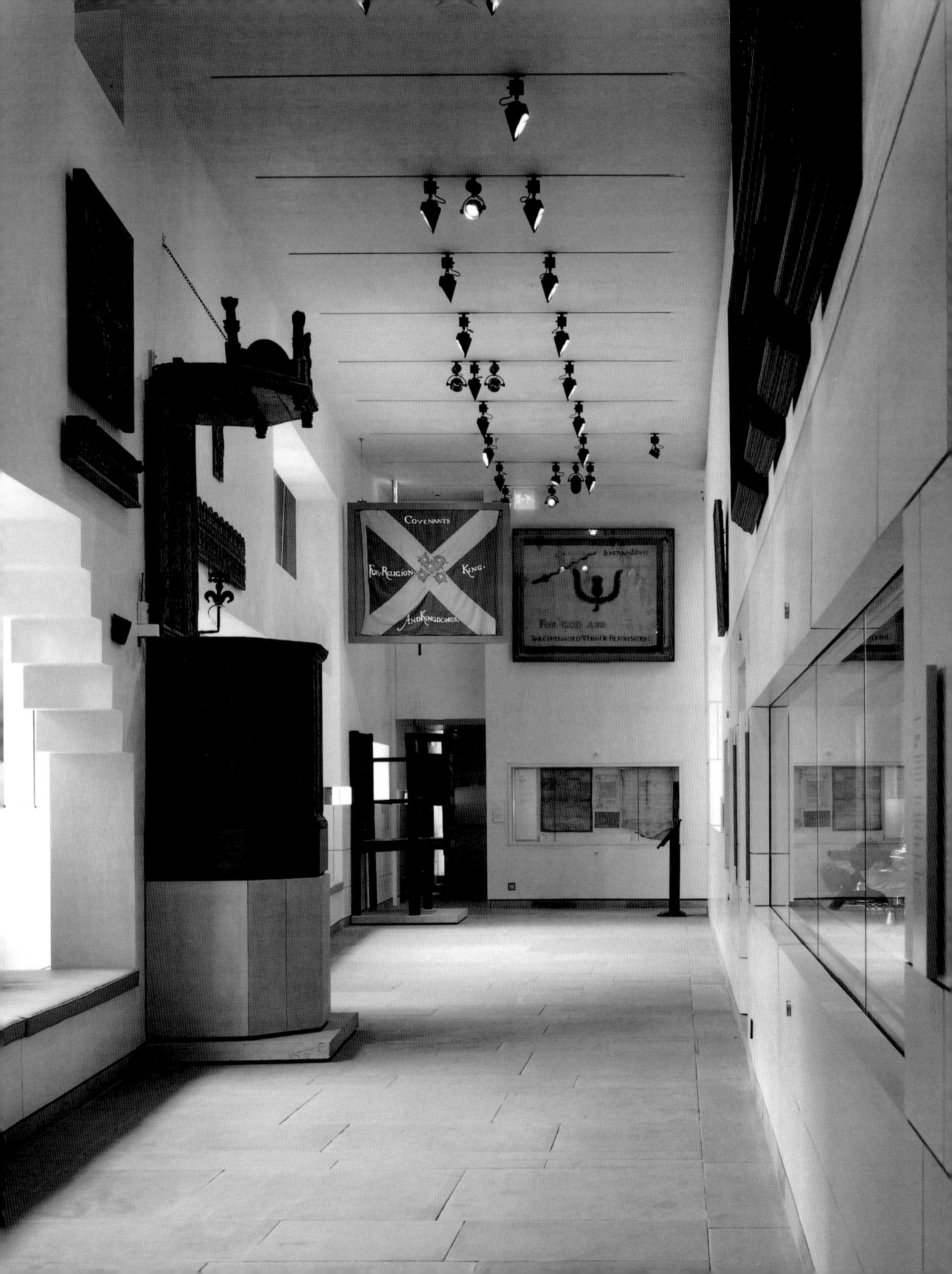
COVENANTS
FOR RELIGION
KING
AND KINGDOMES

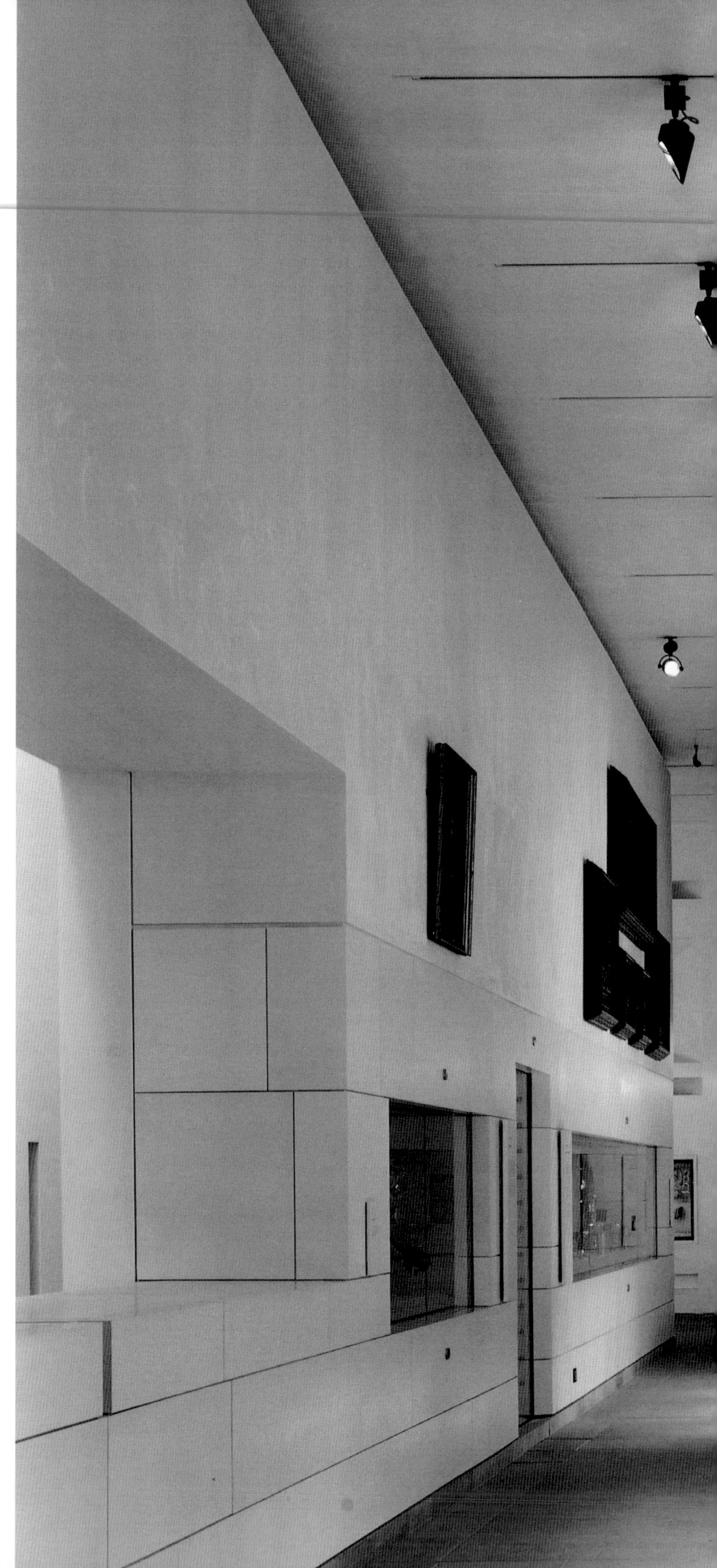

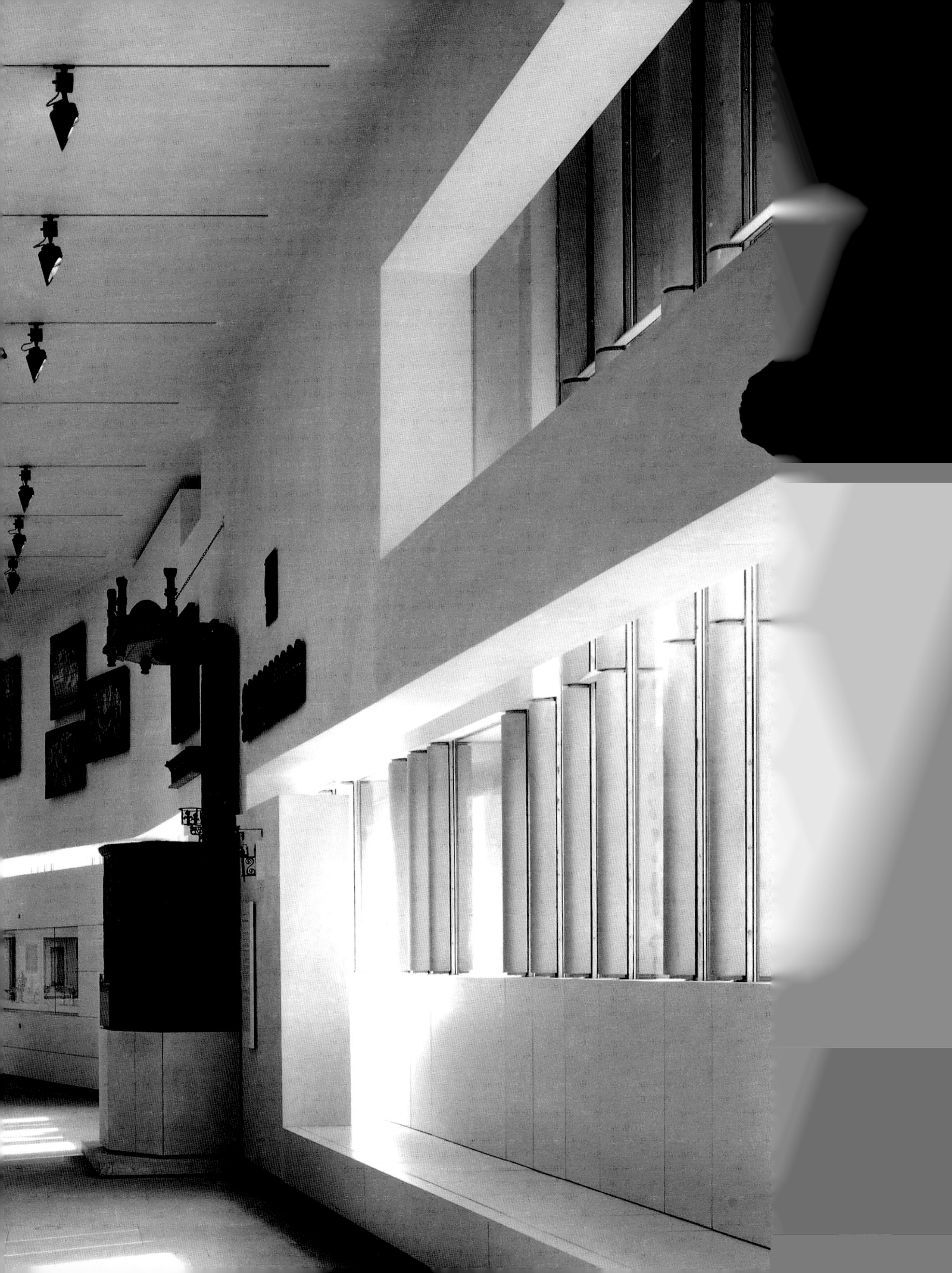

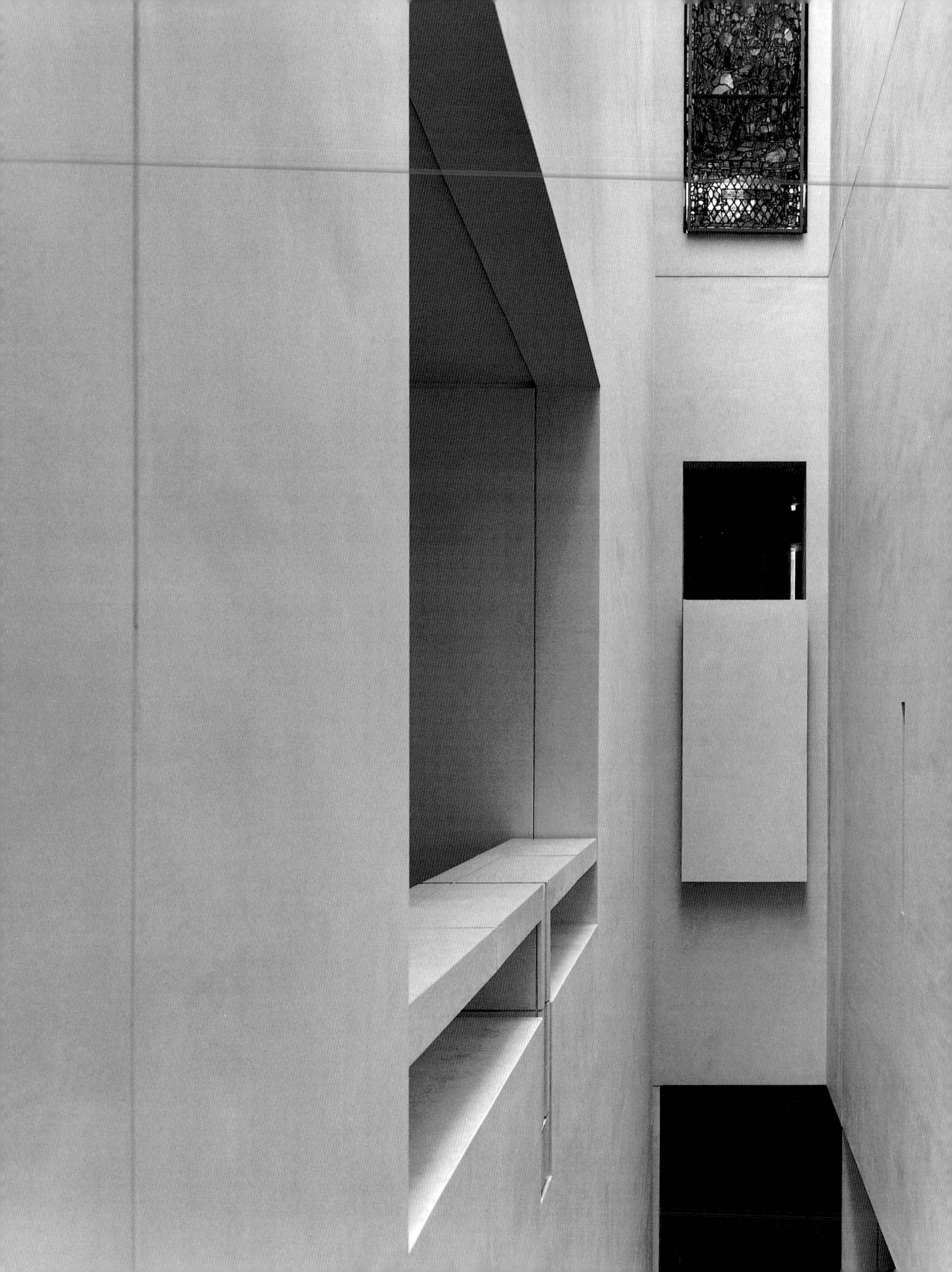

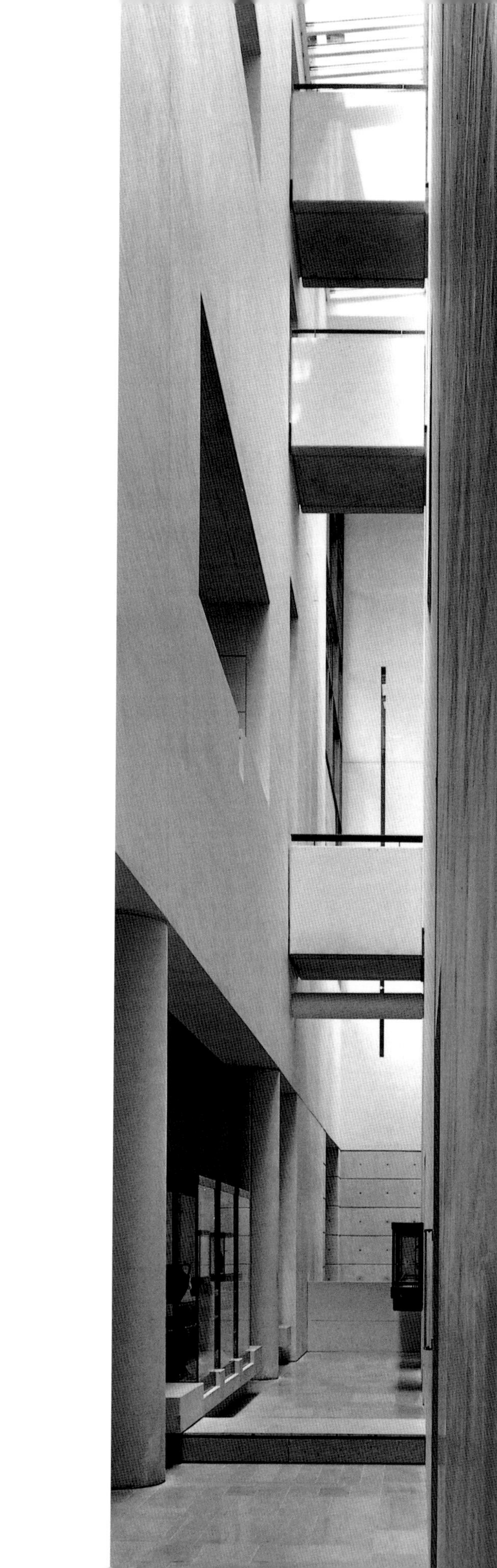

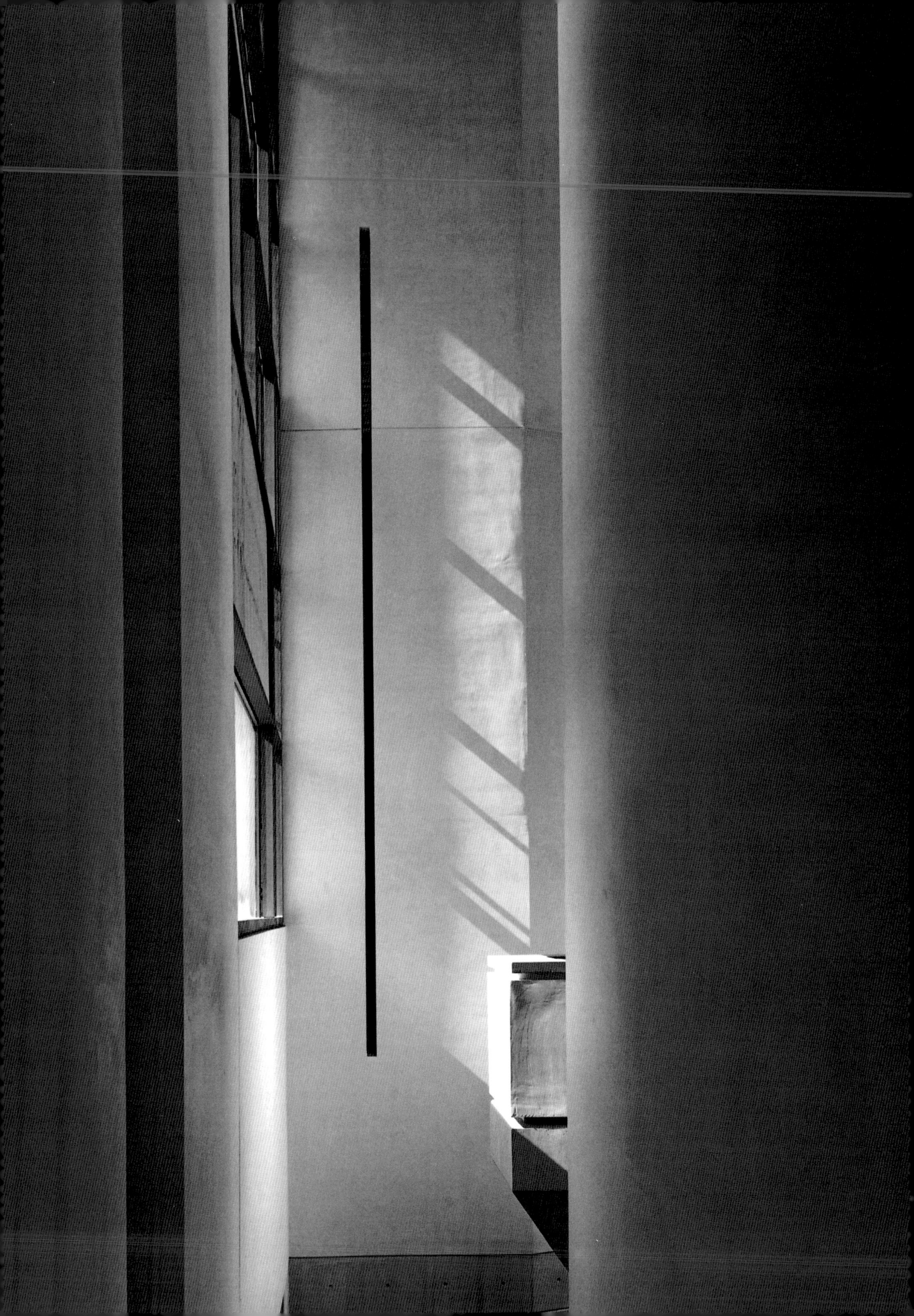

First floor

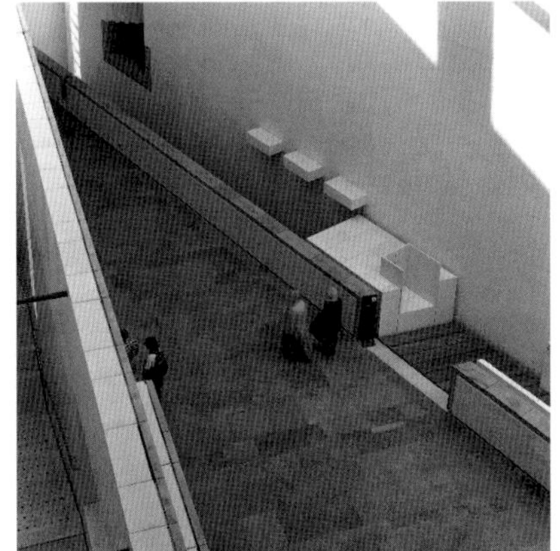

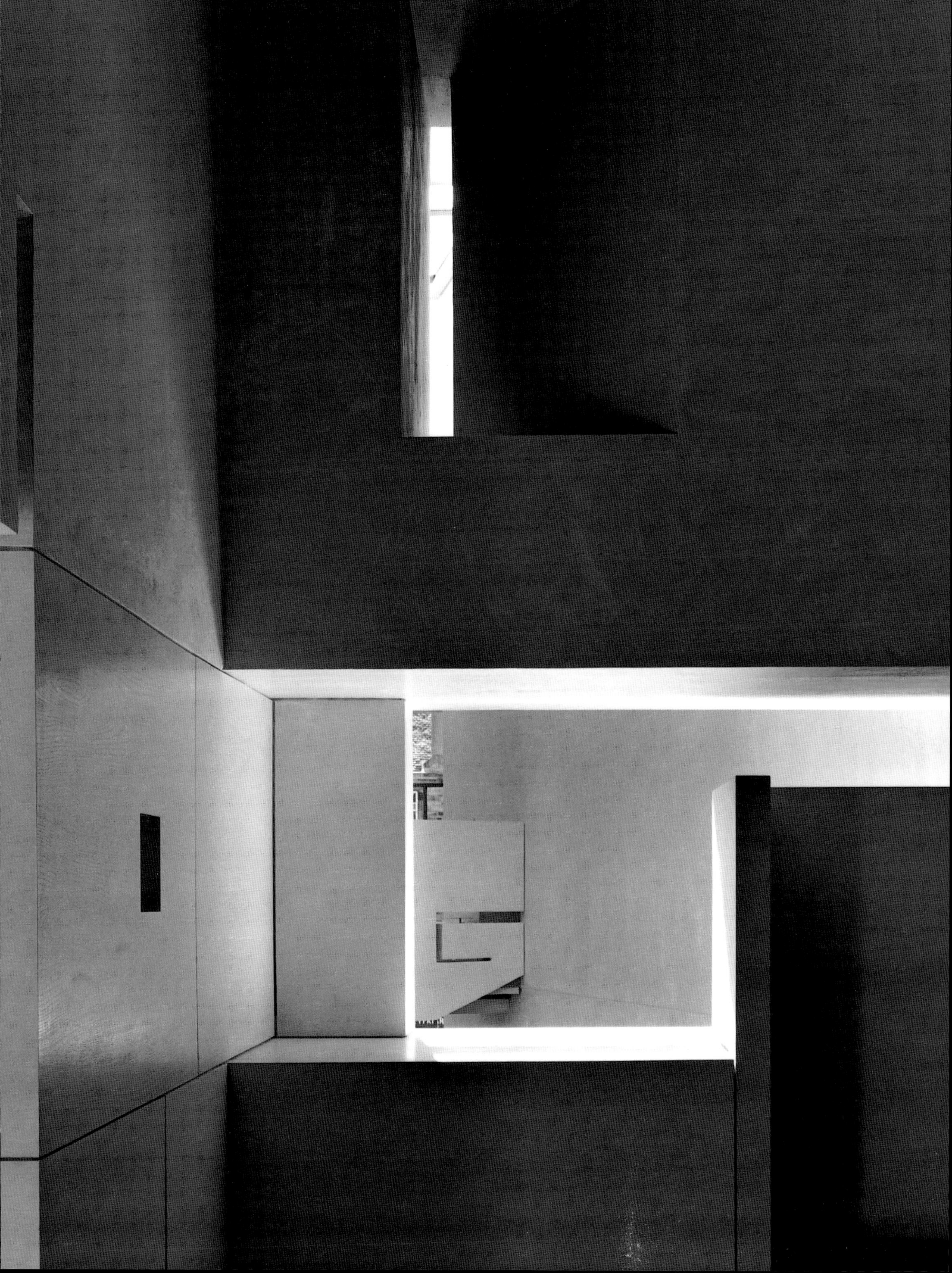

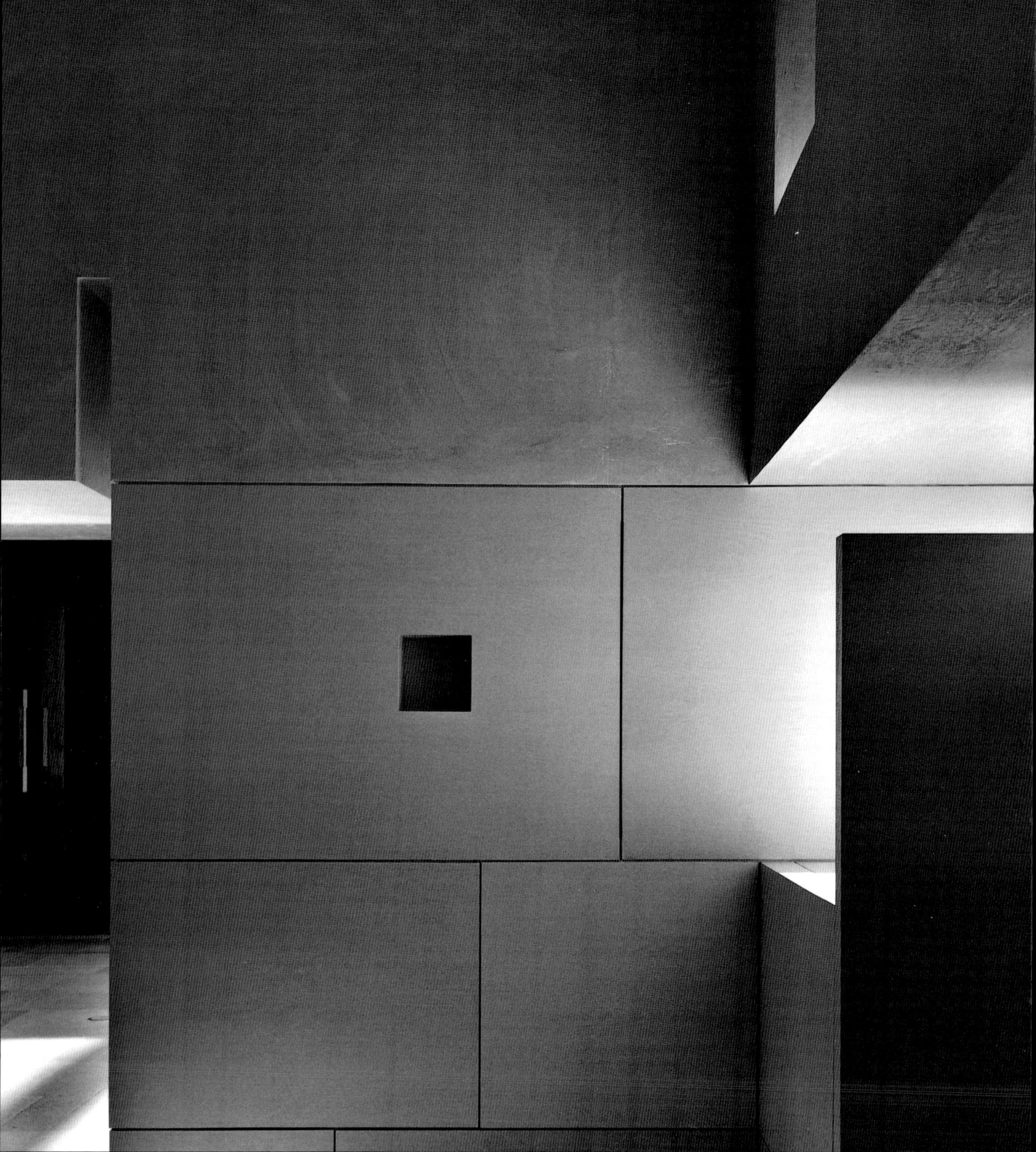

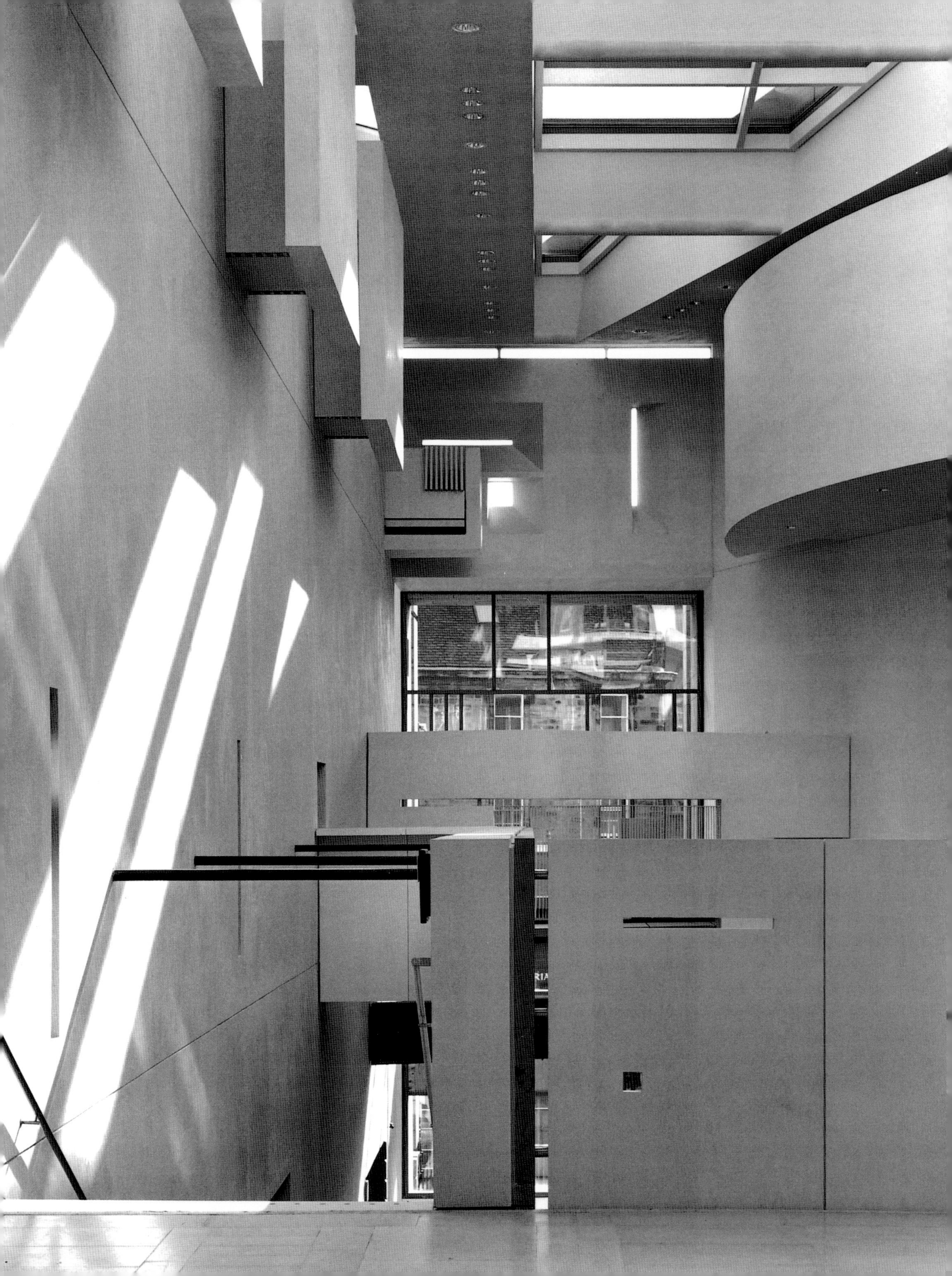

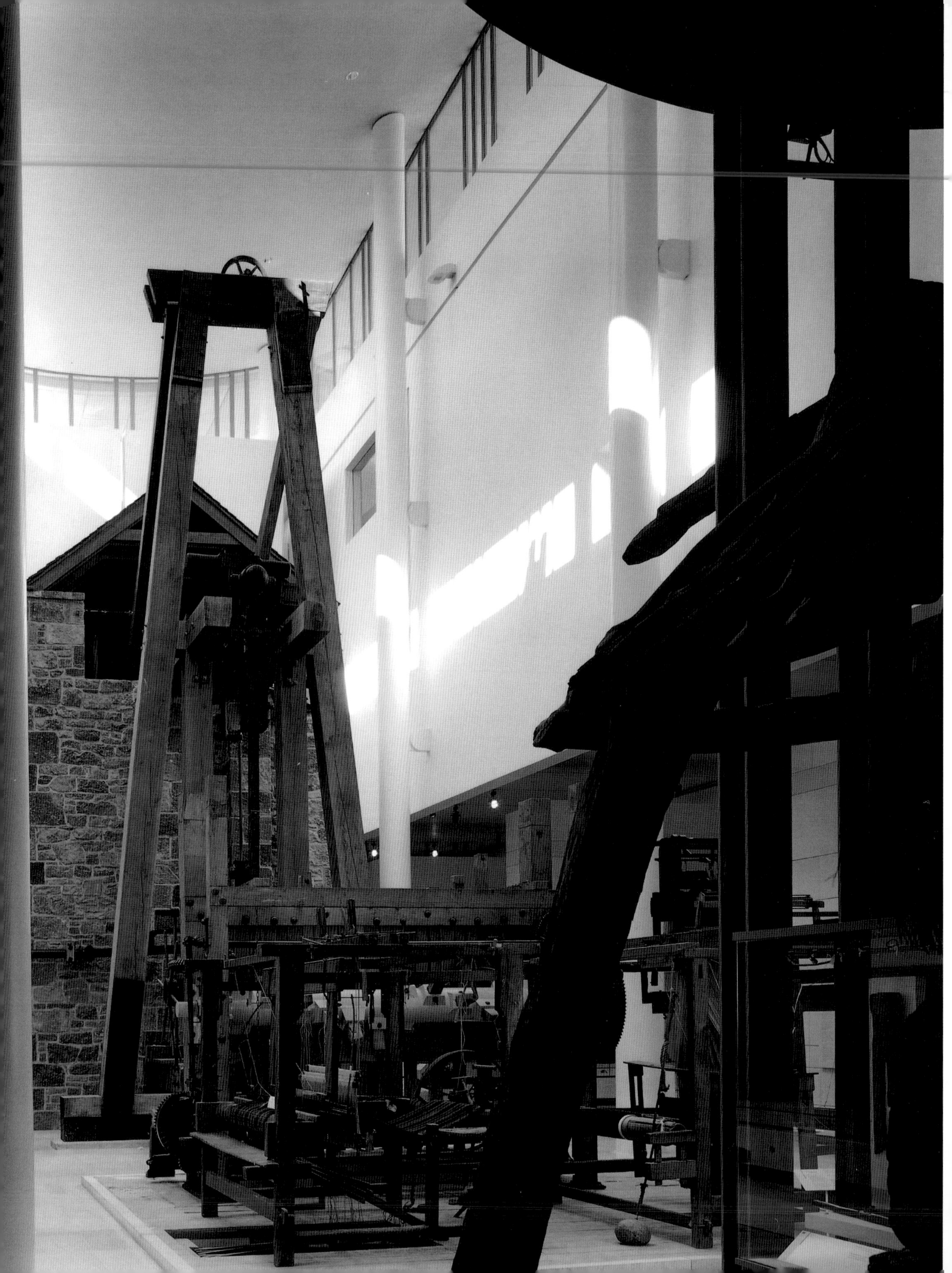

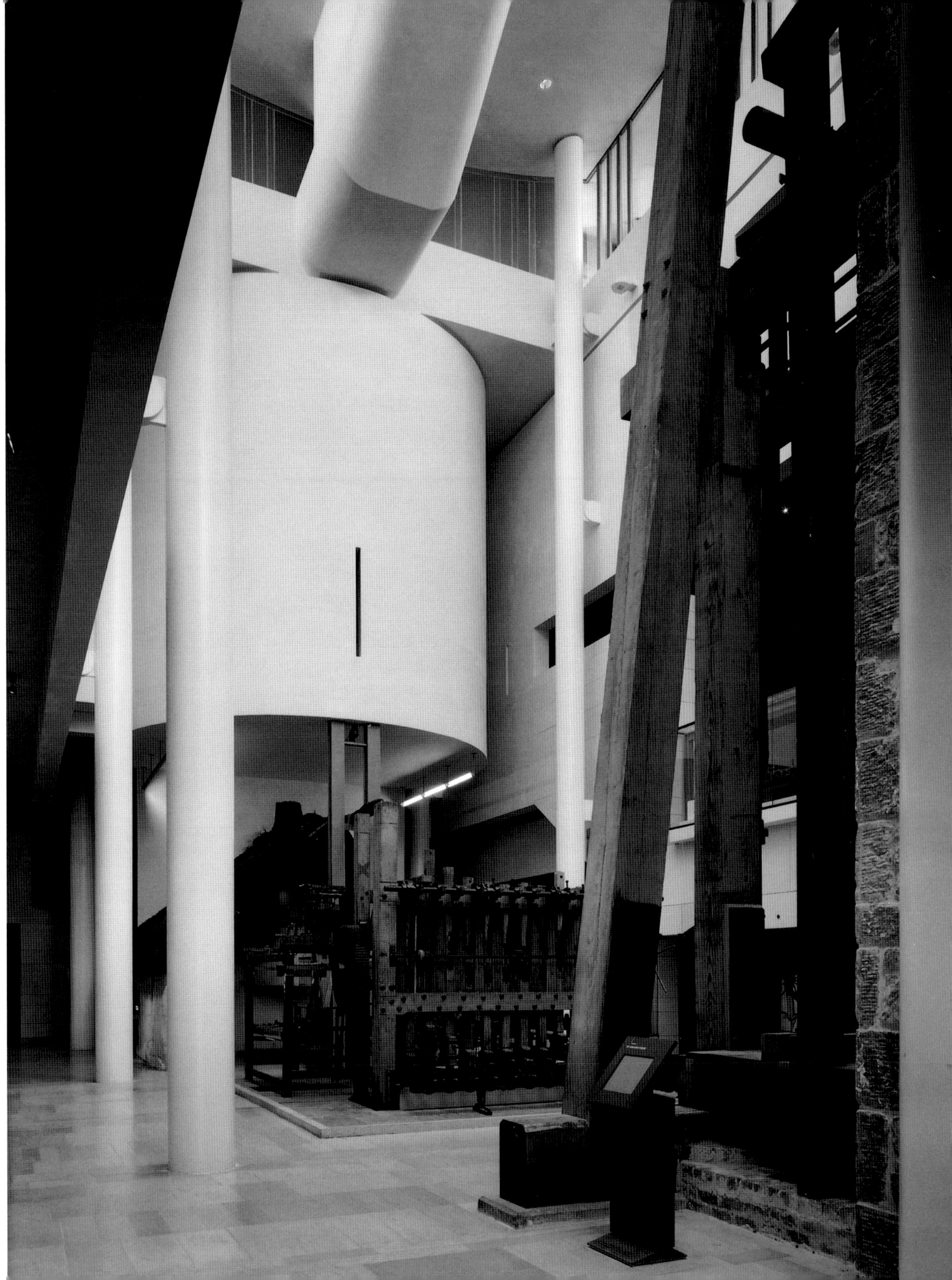

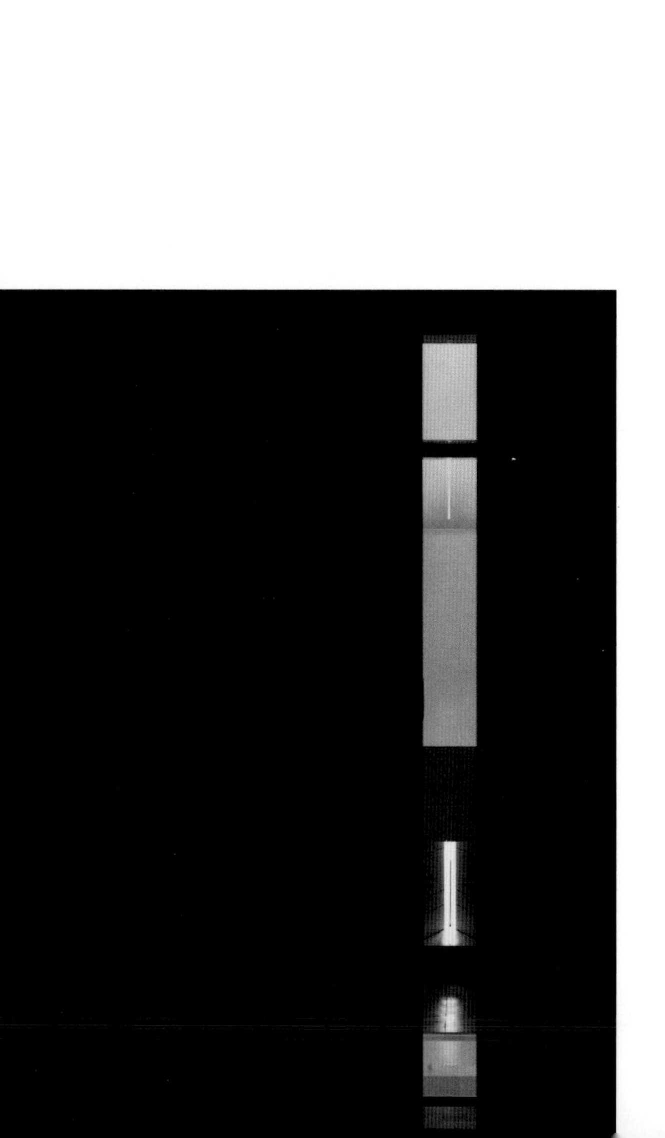

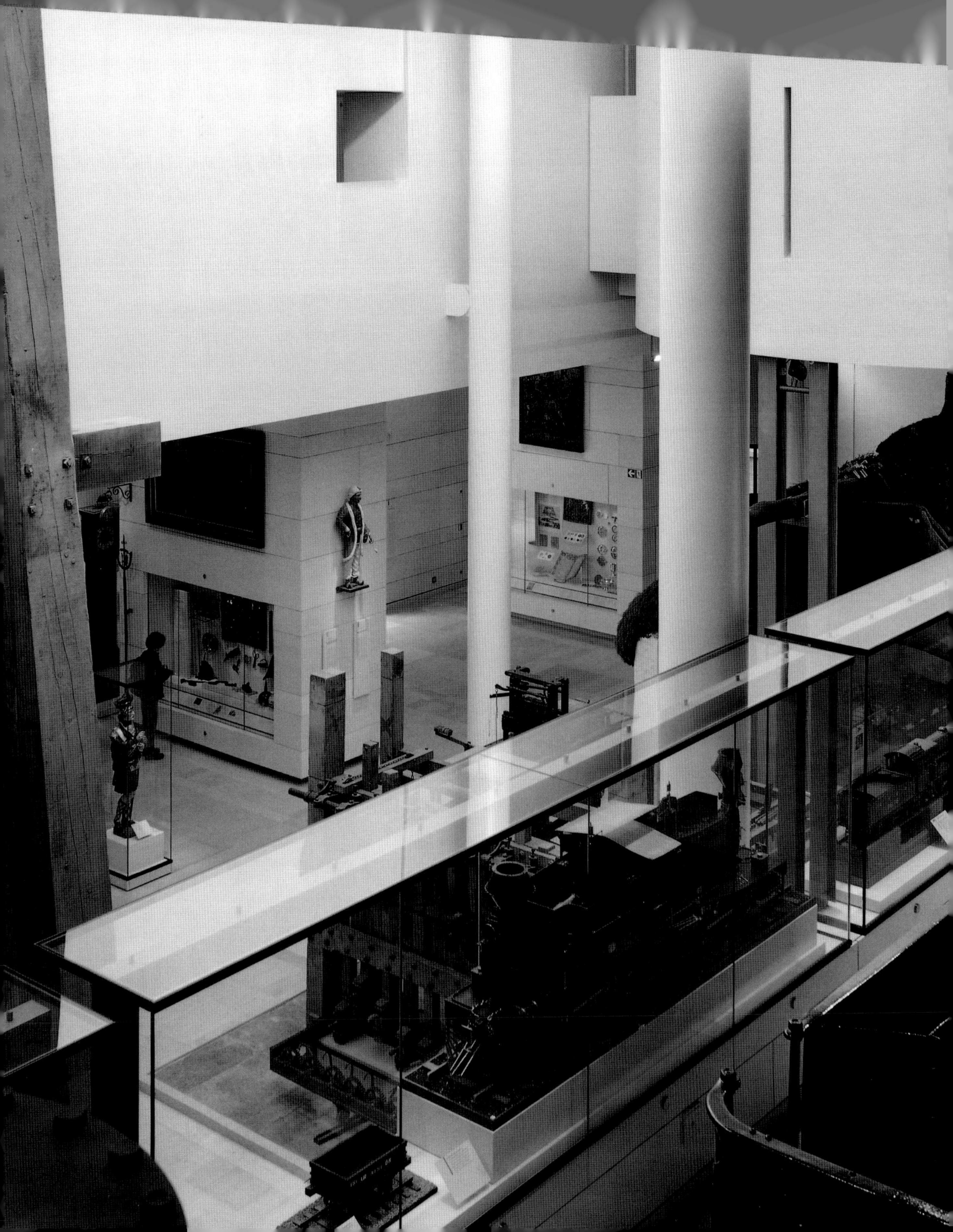

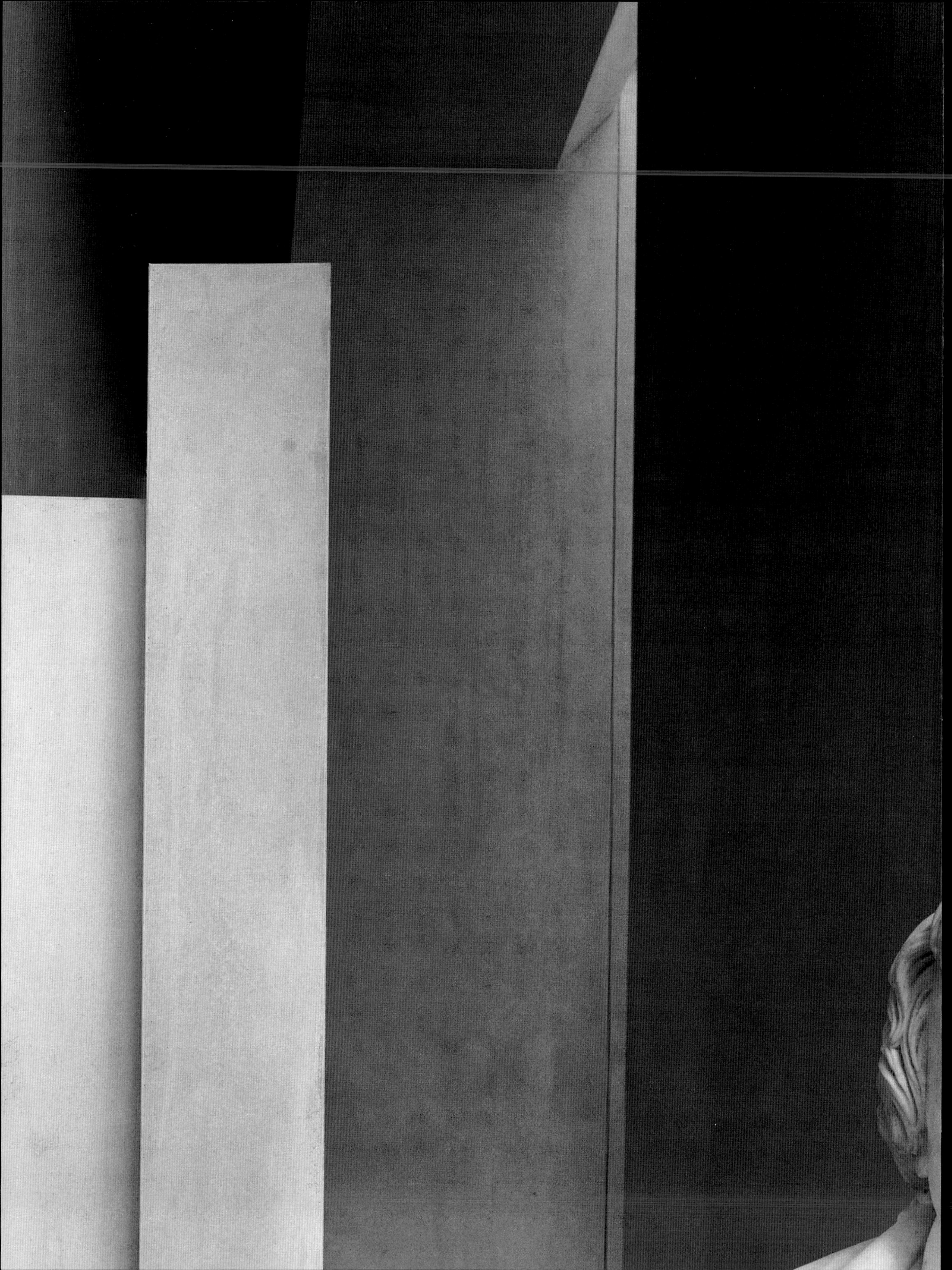

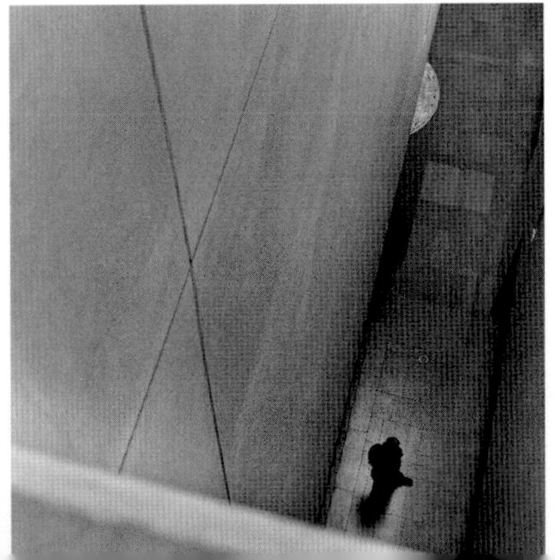

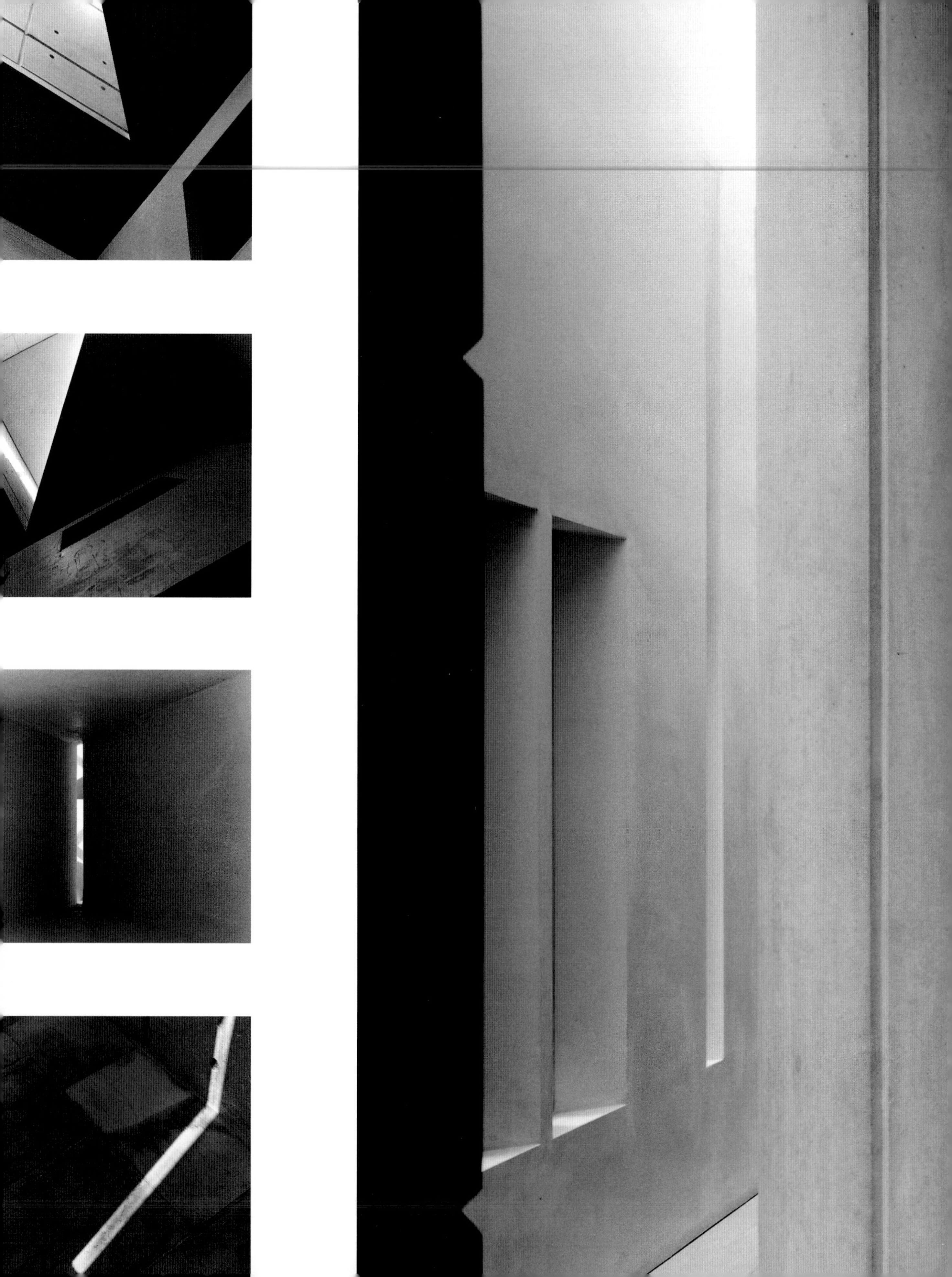

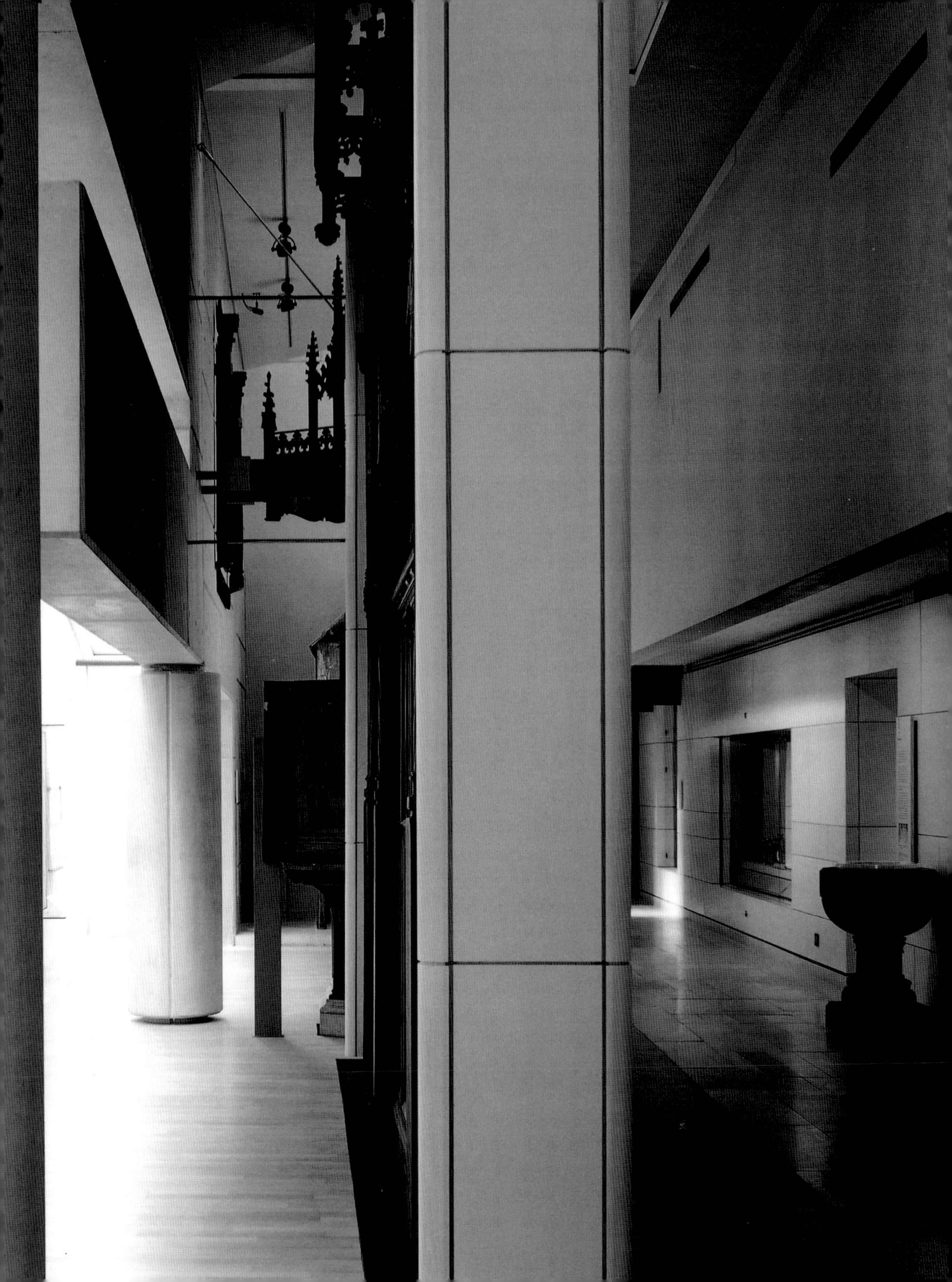

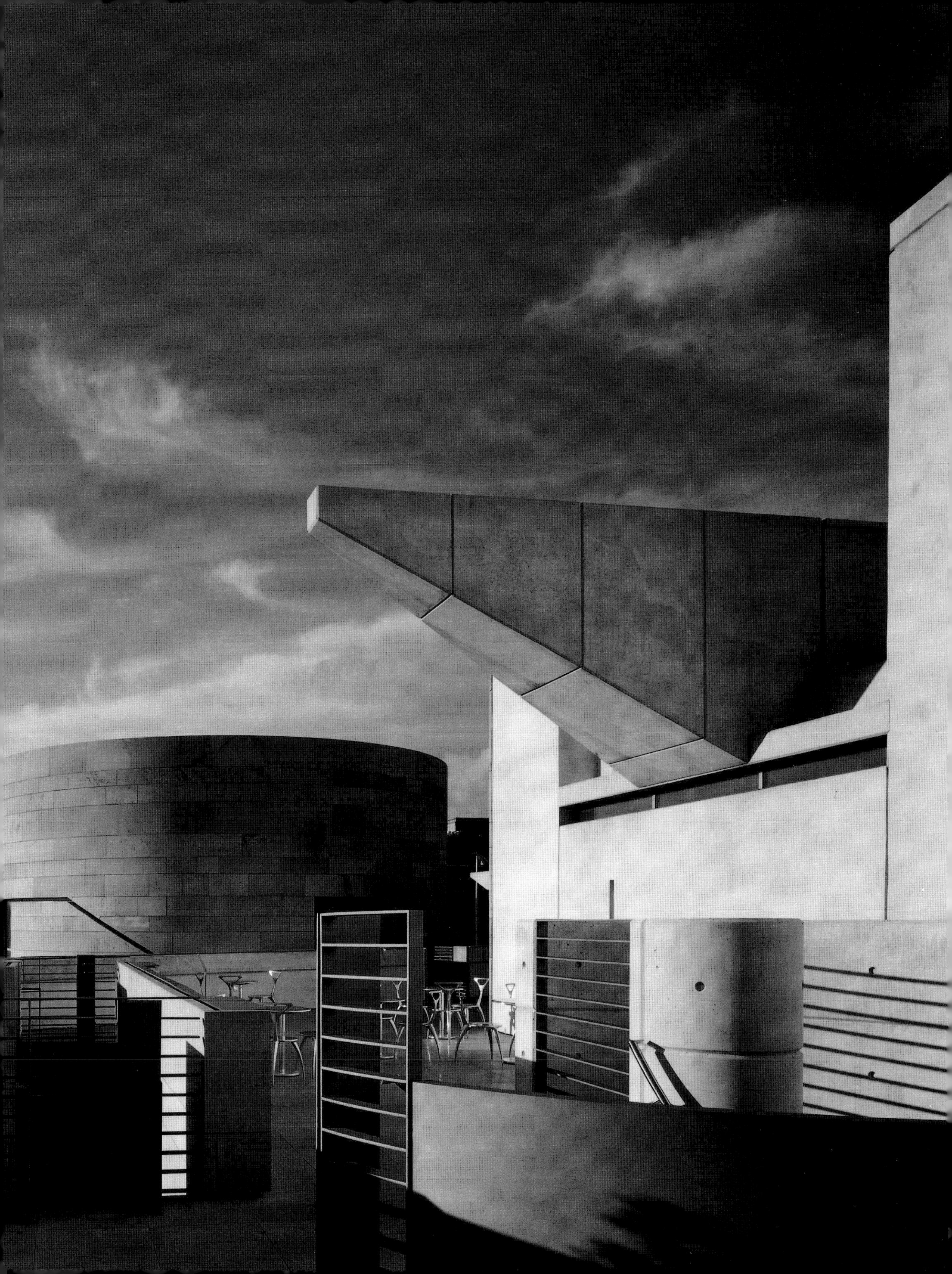

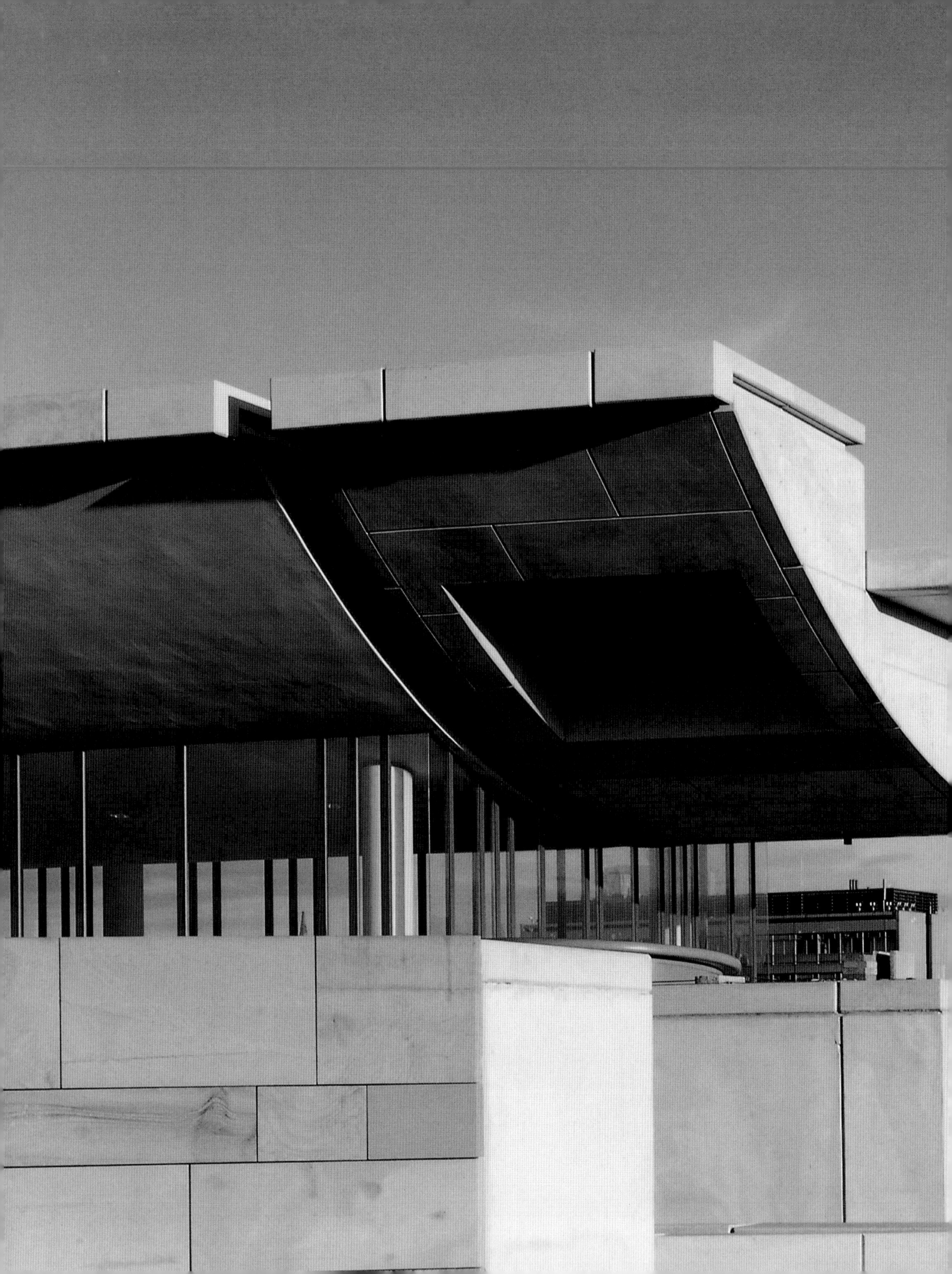

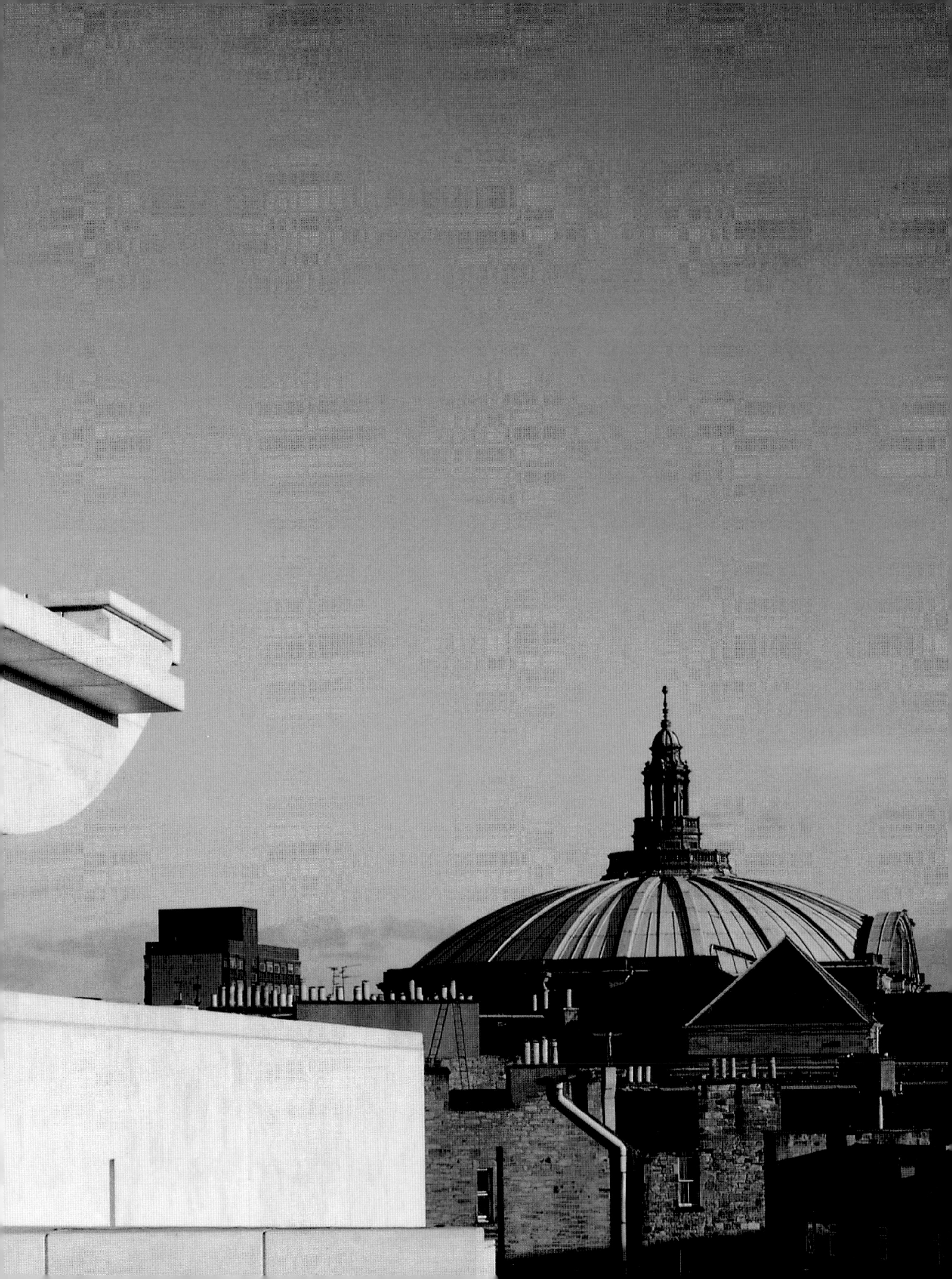

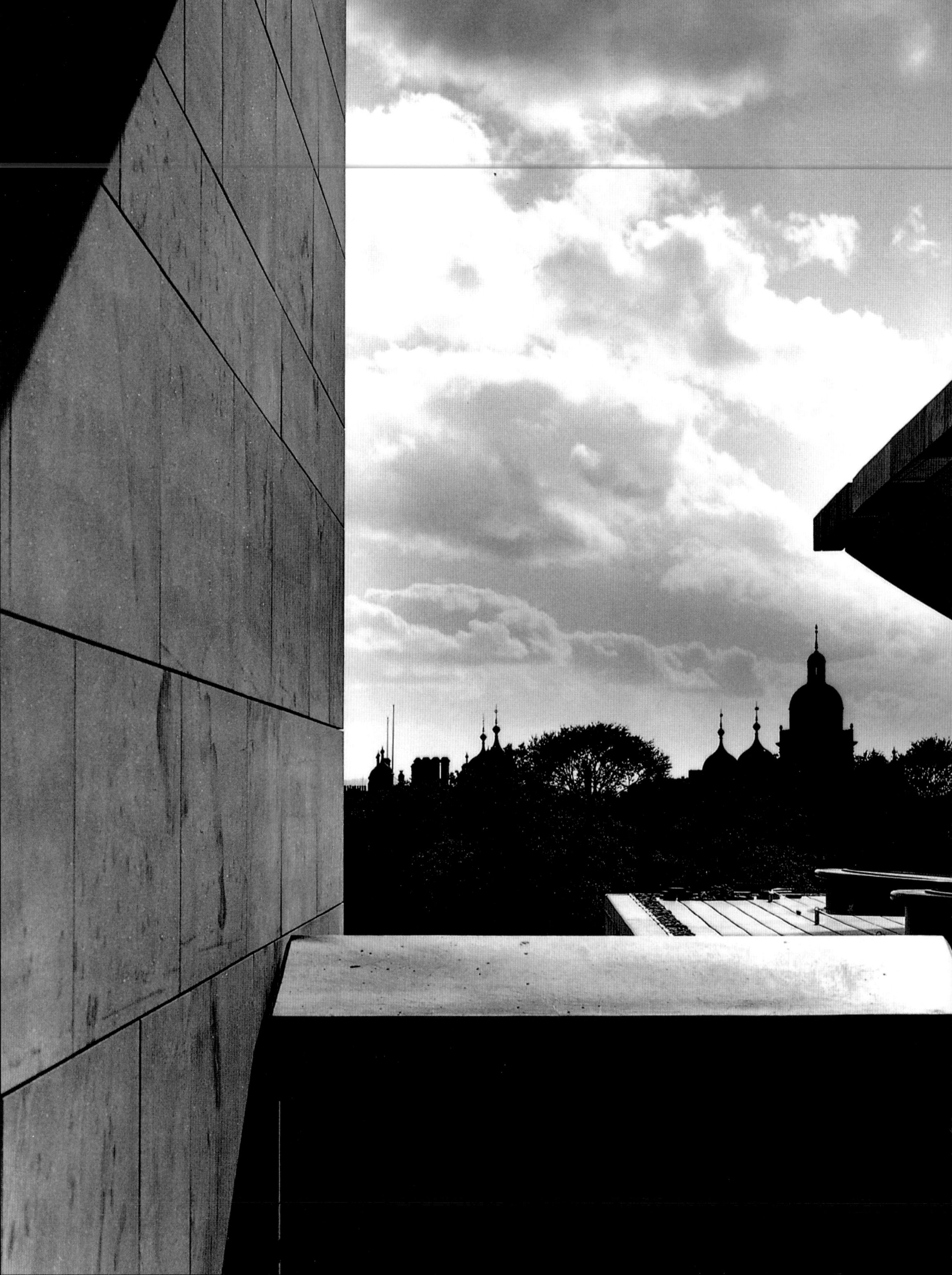

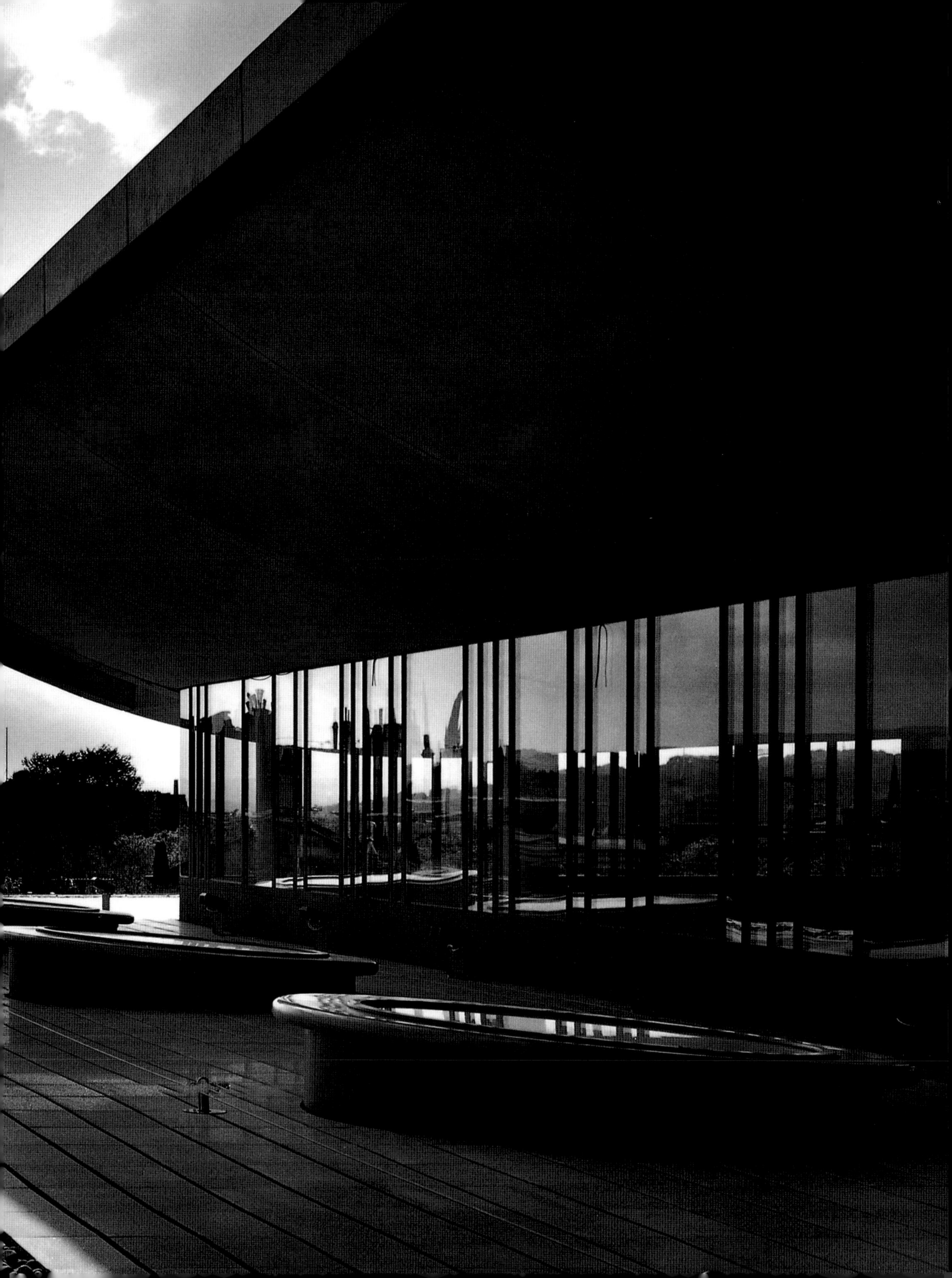

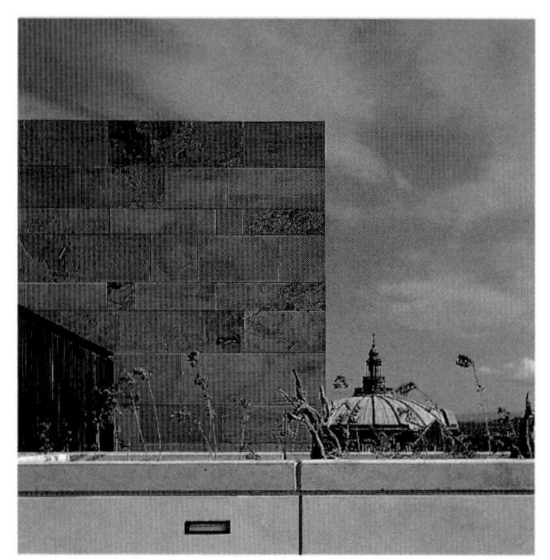

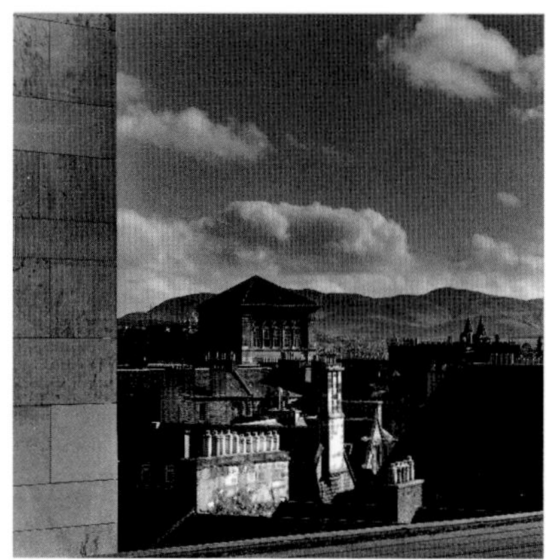

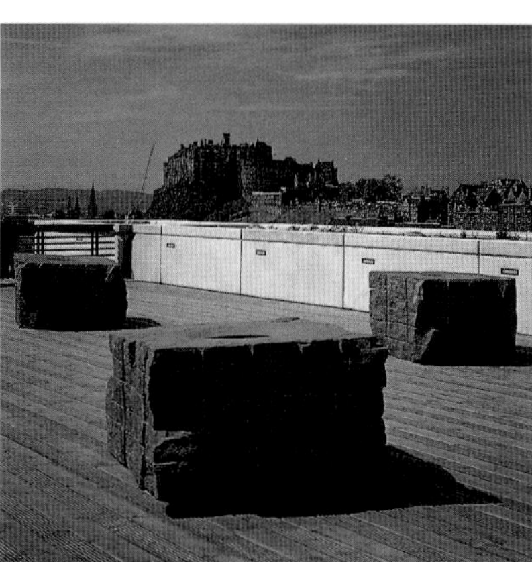

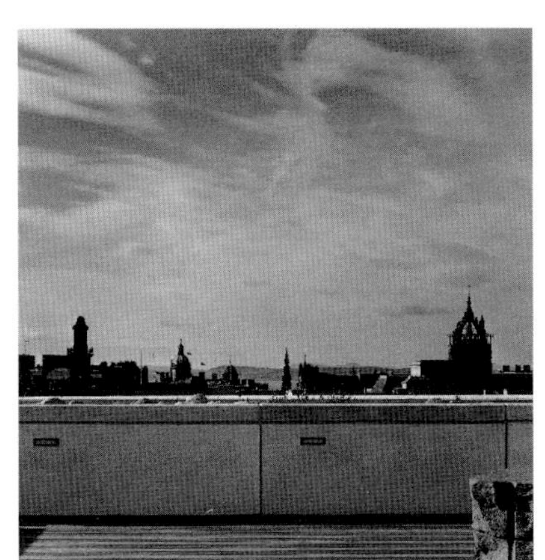

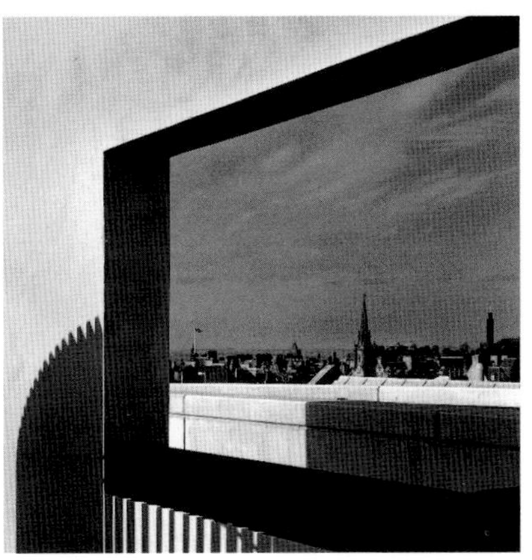

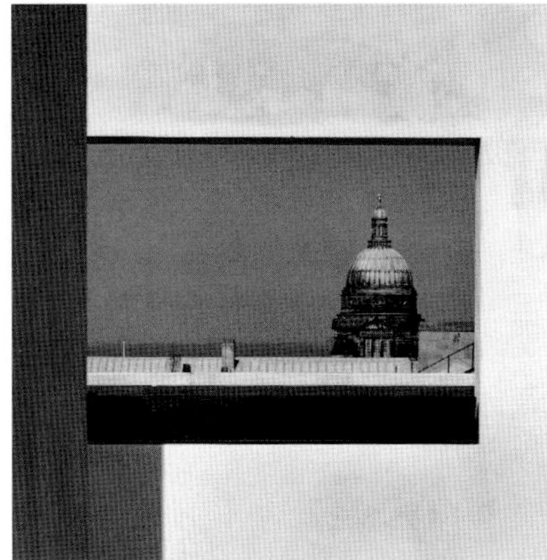

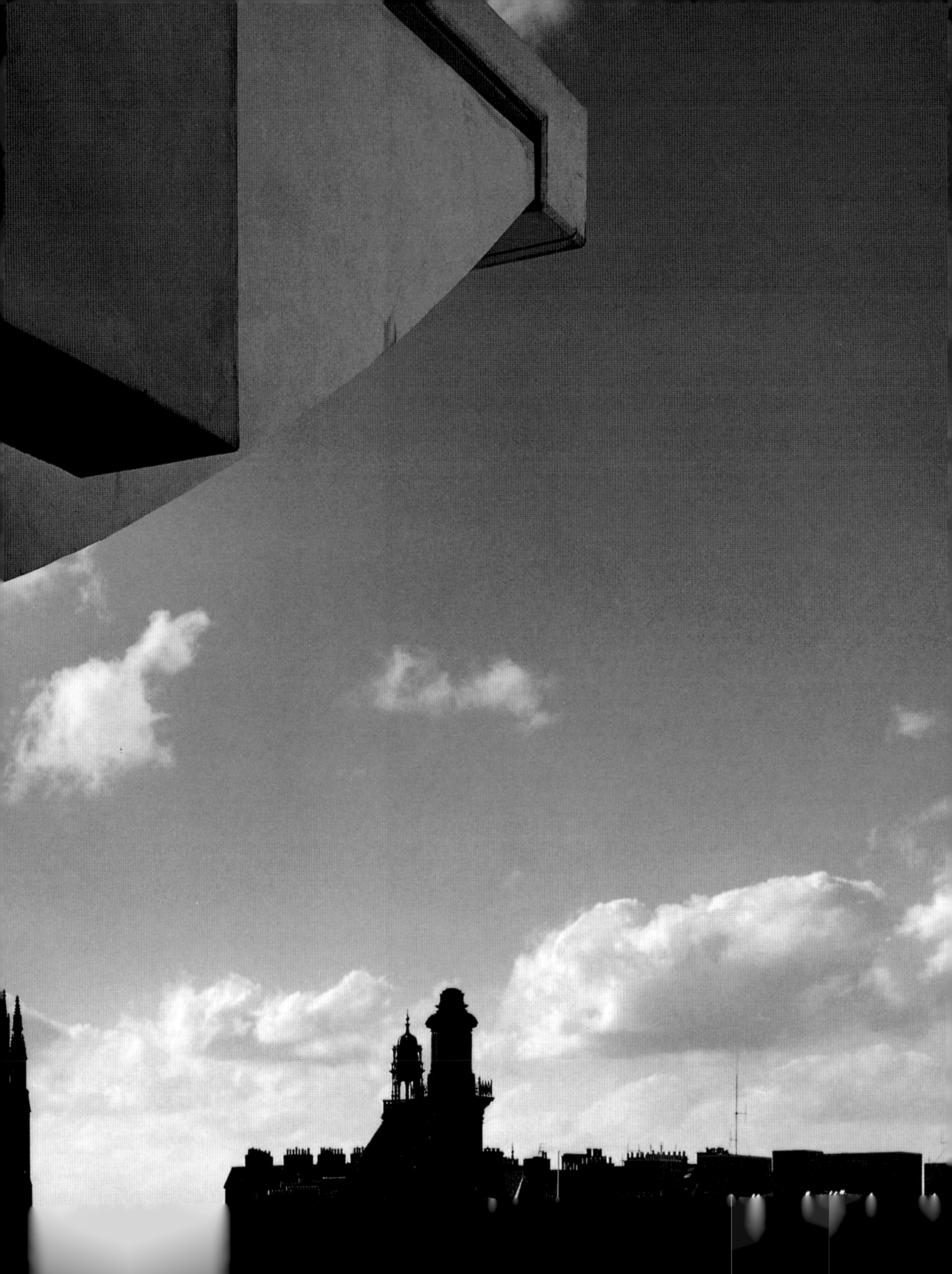

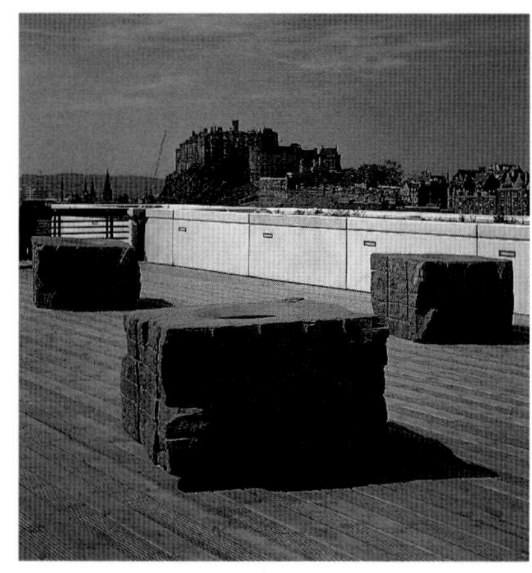

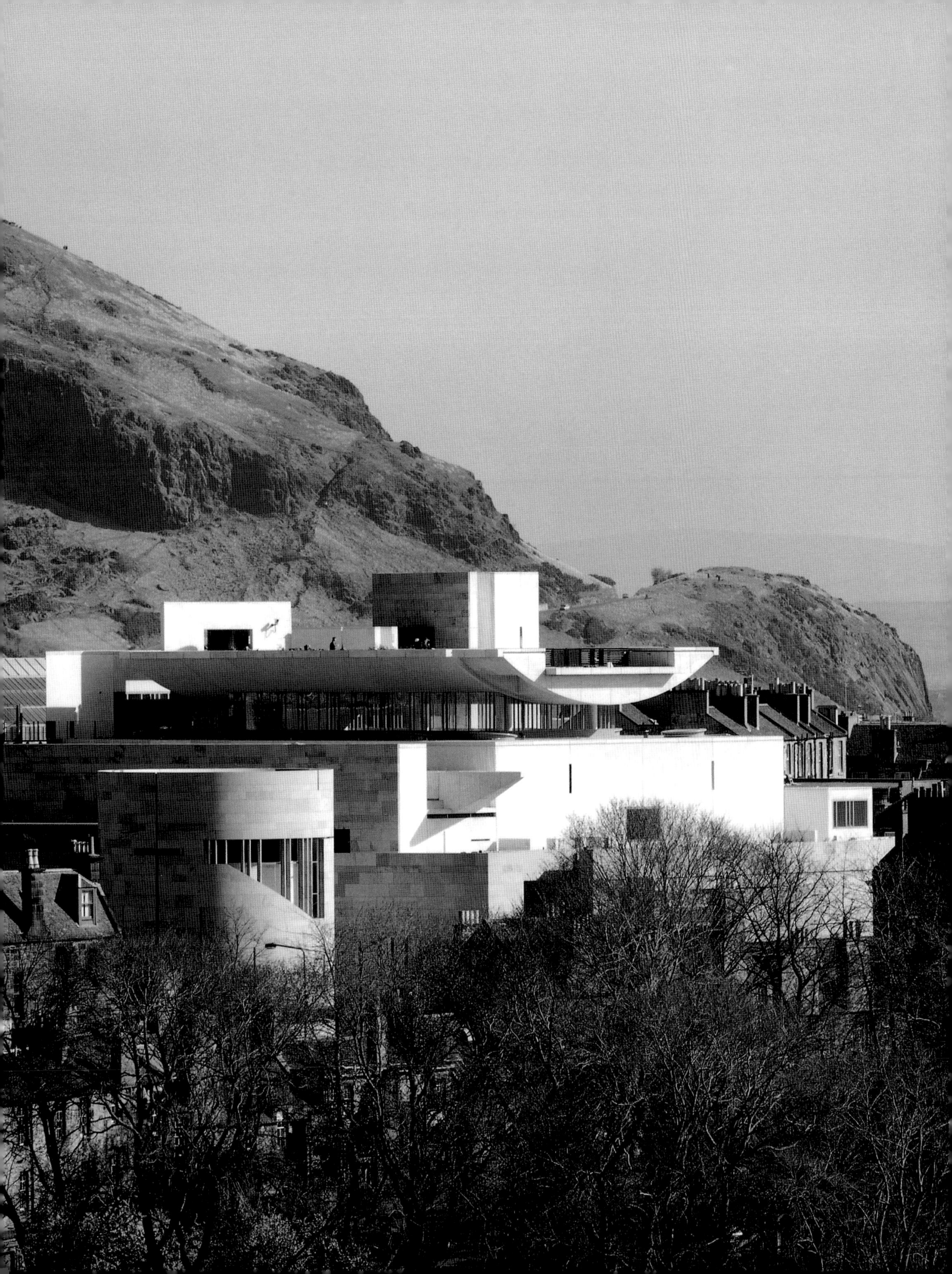

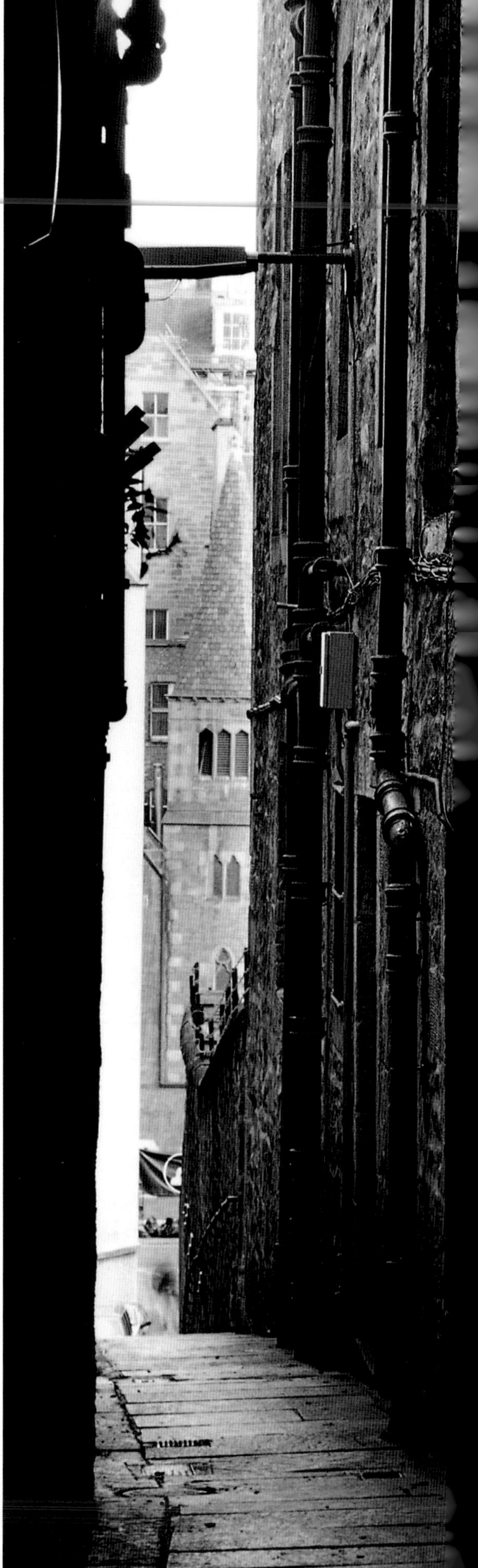

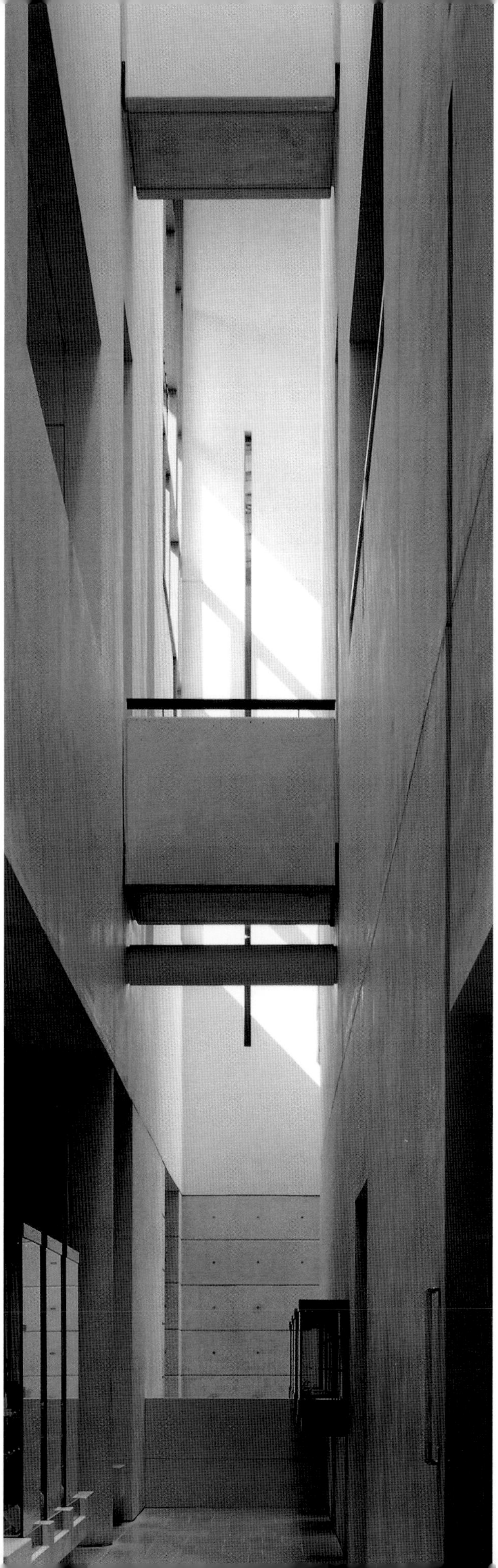

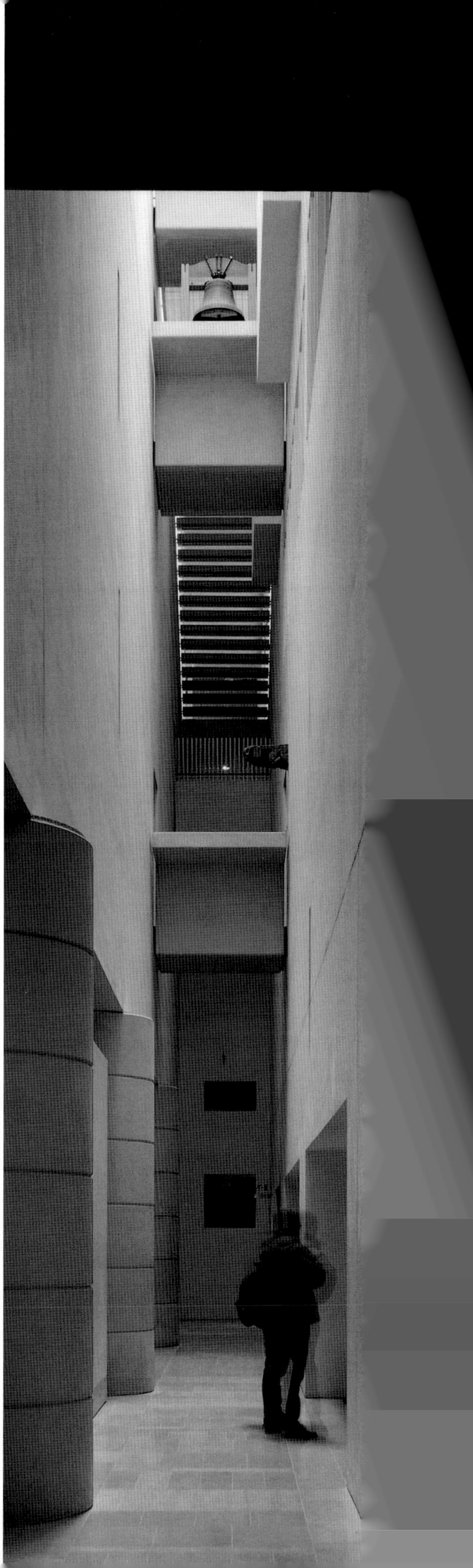

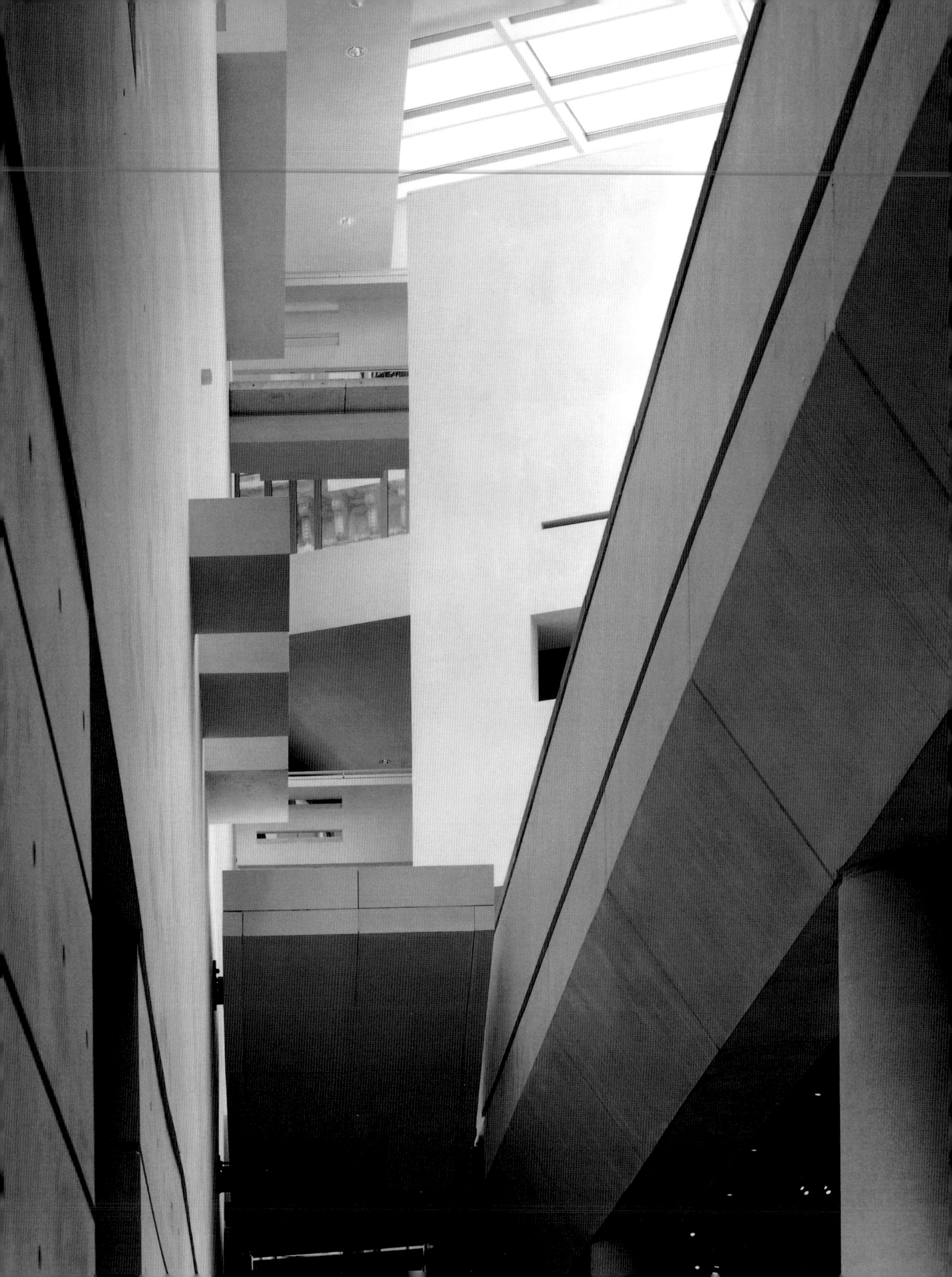

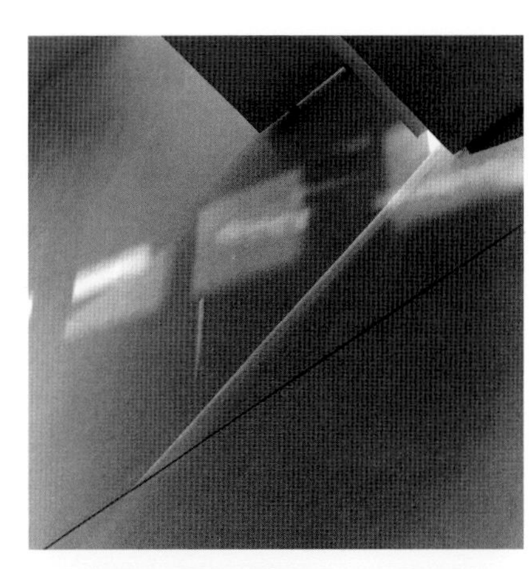

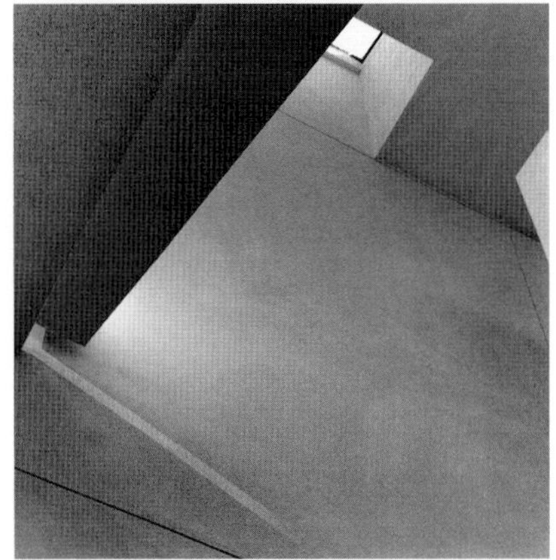

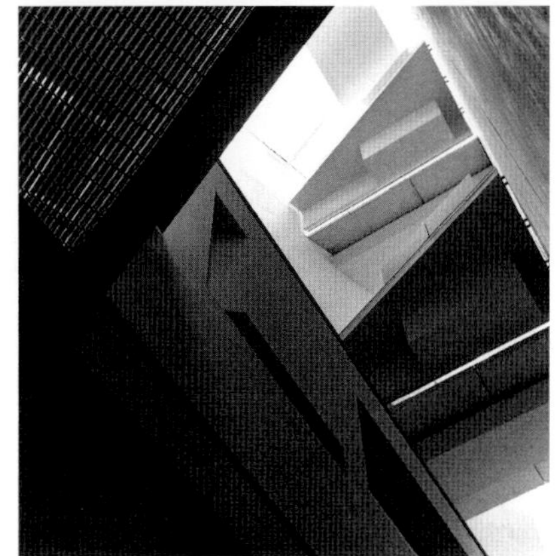

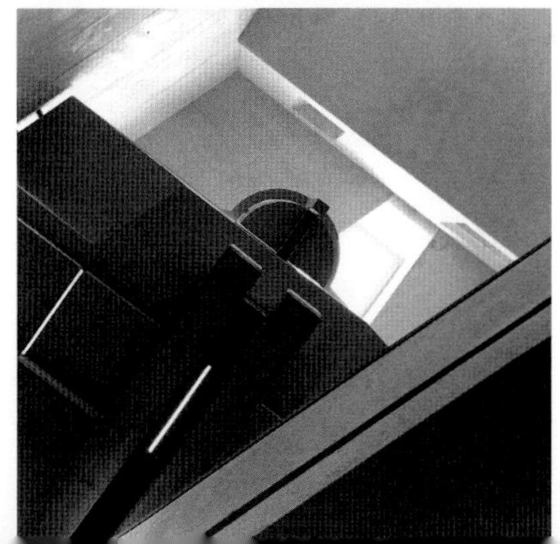

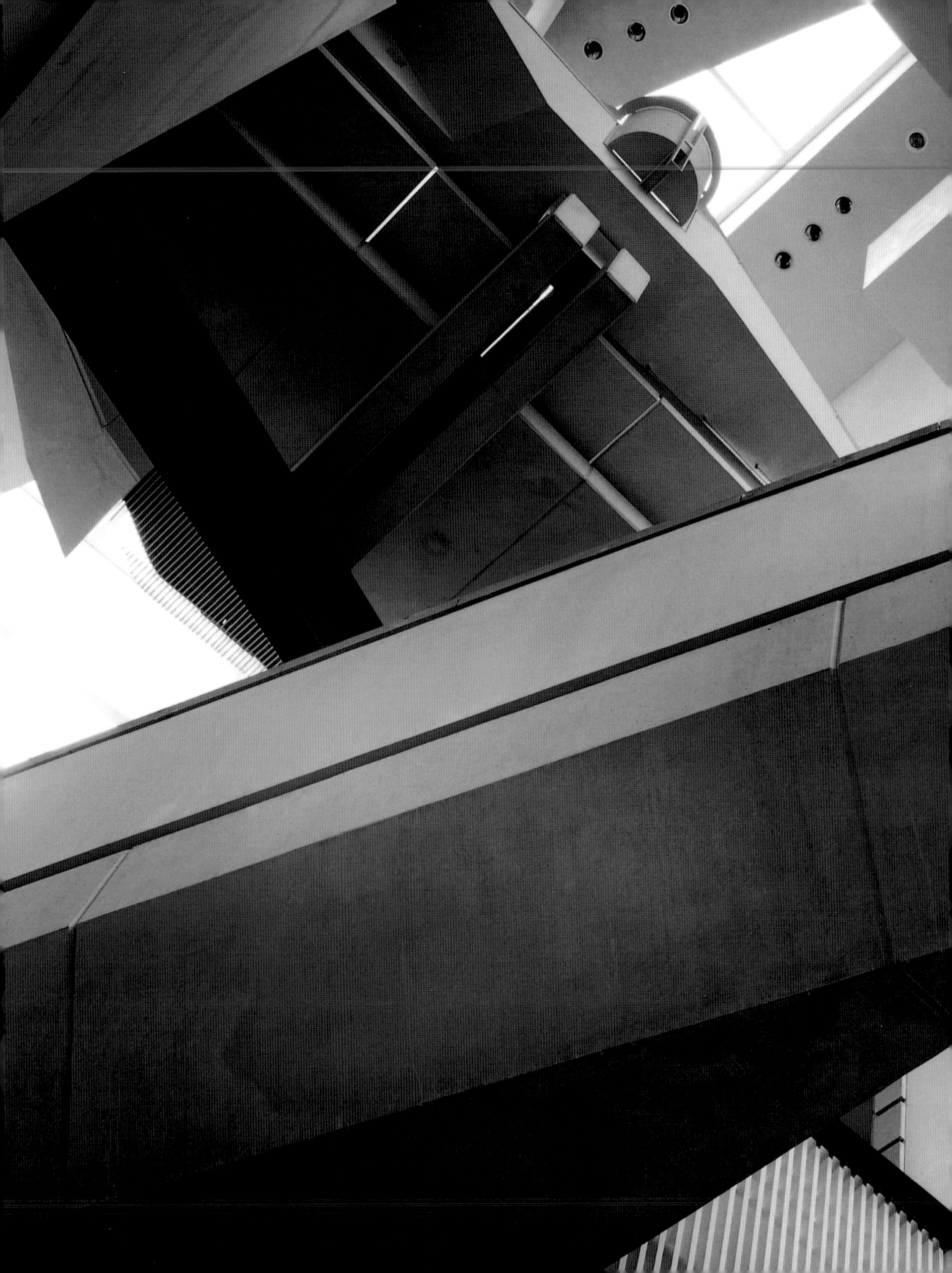

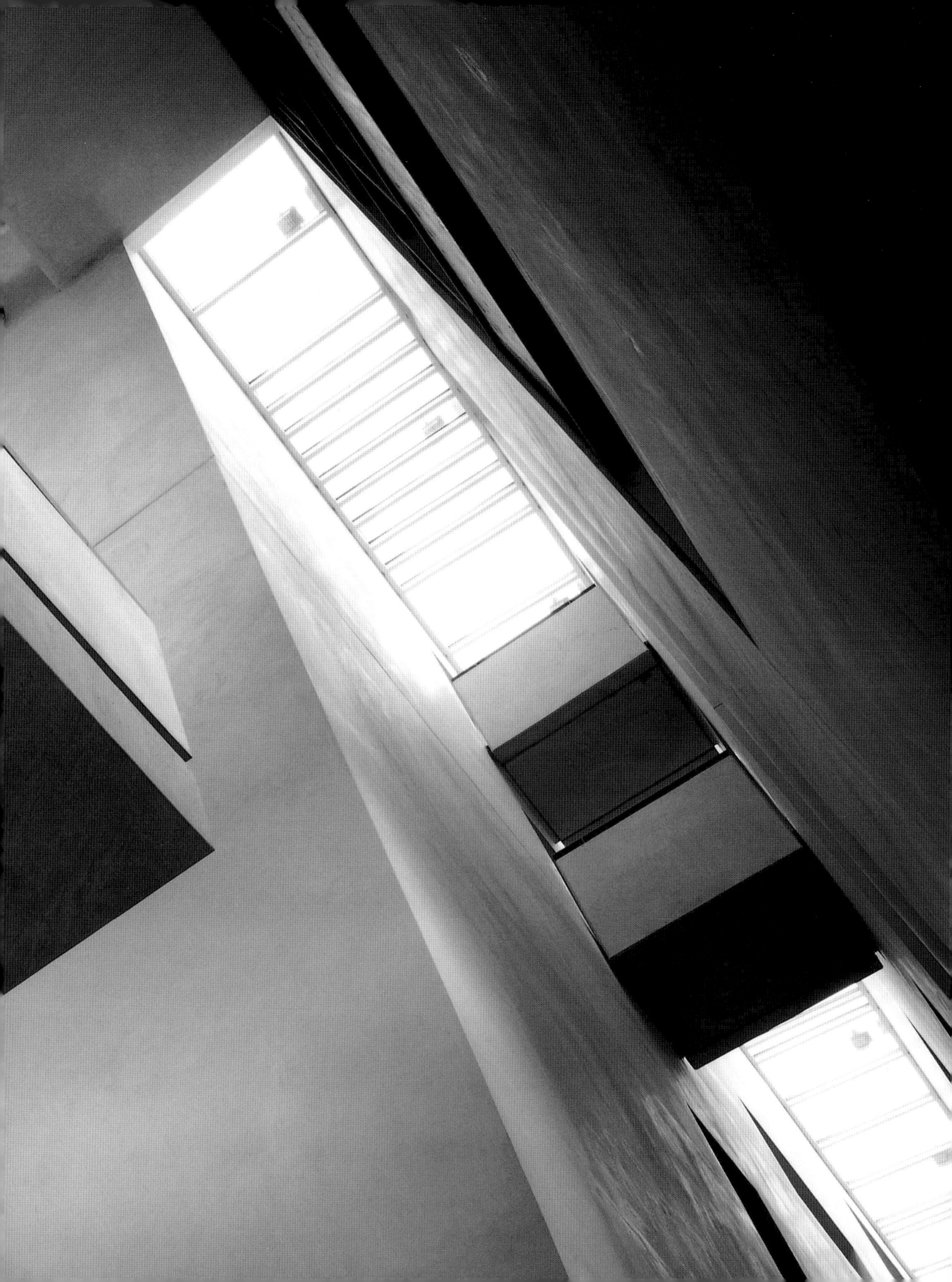

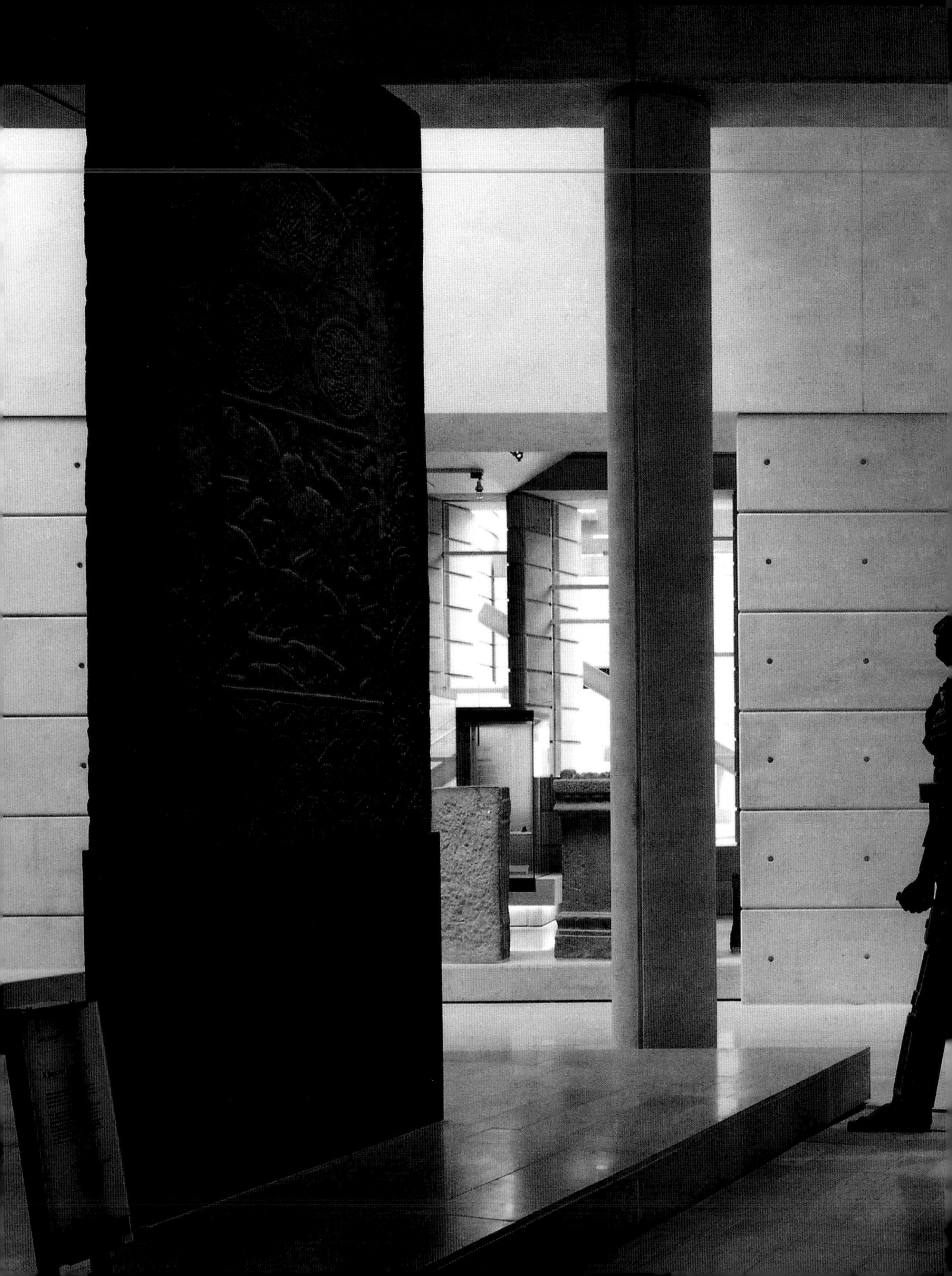

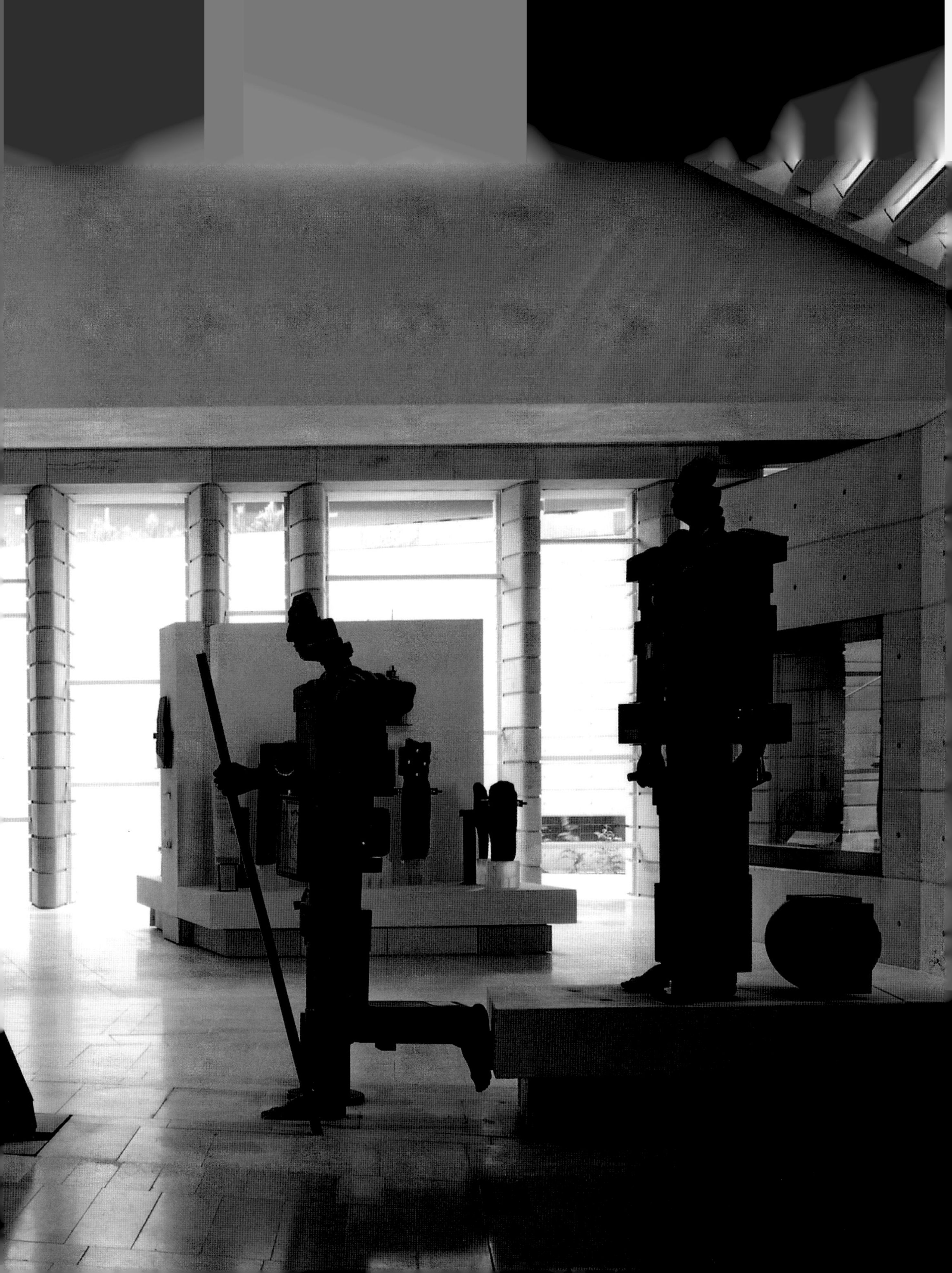

86

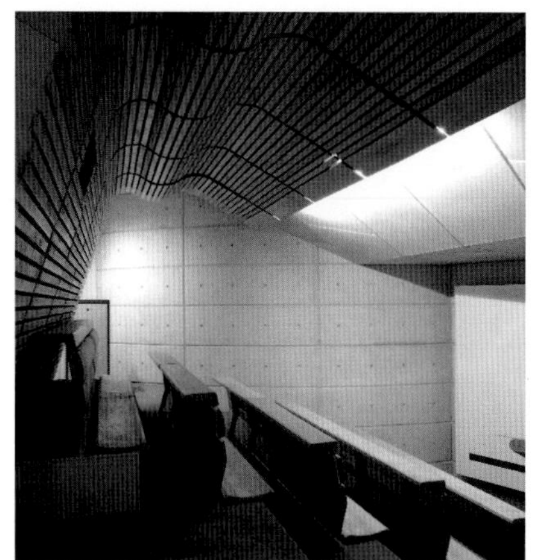

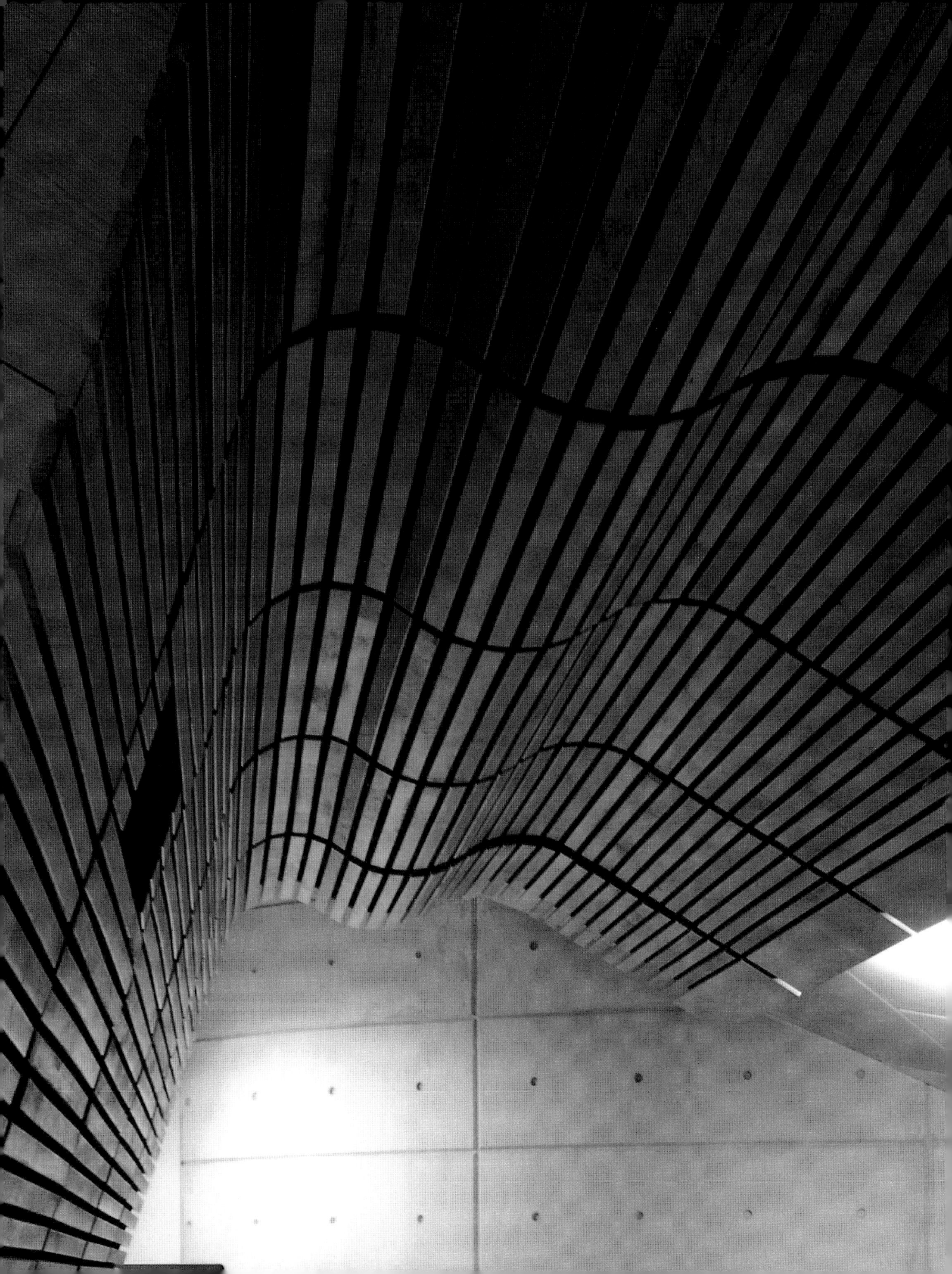

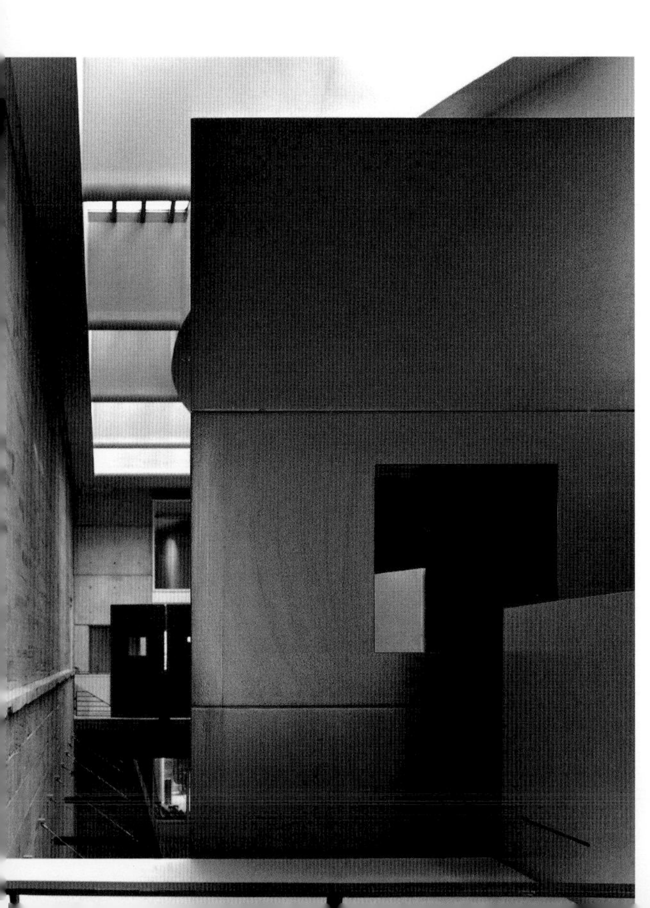

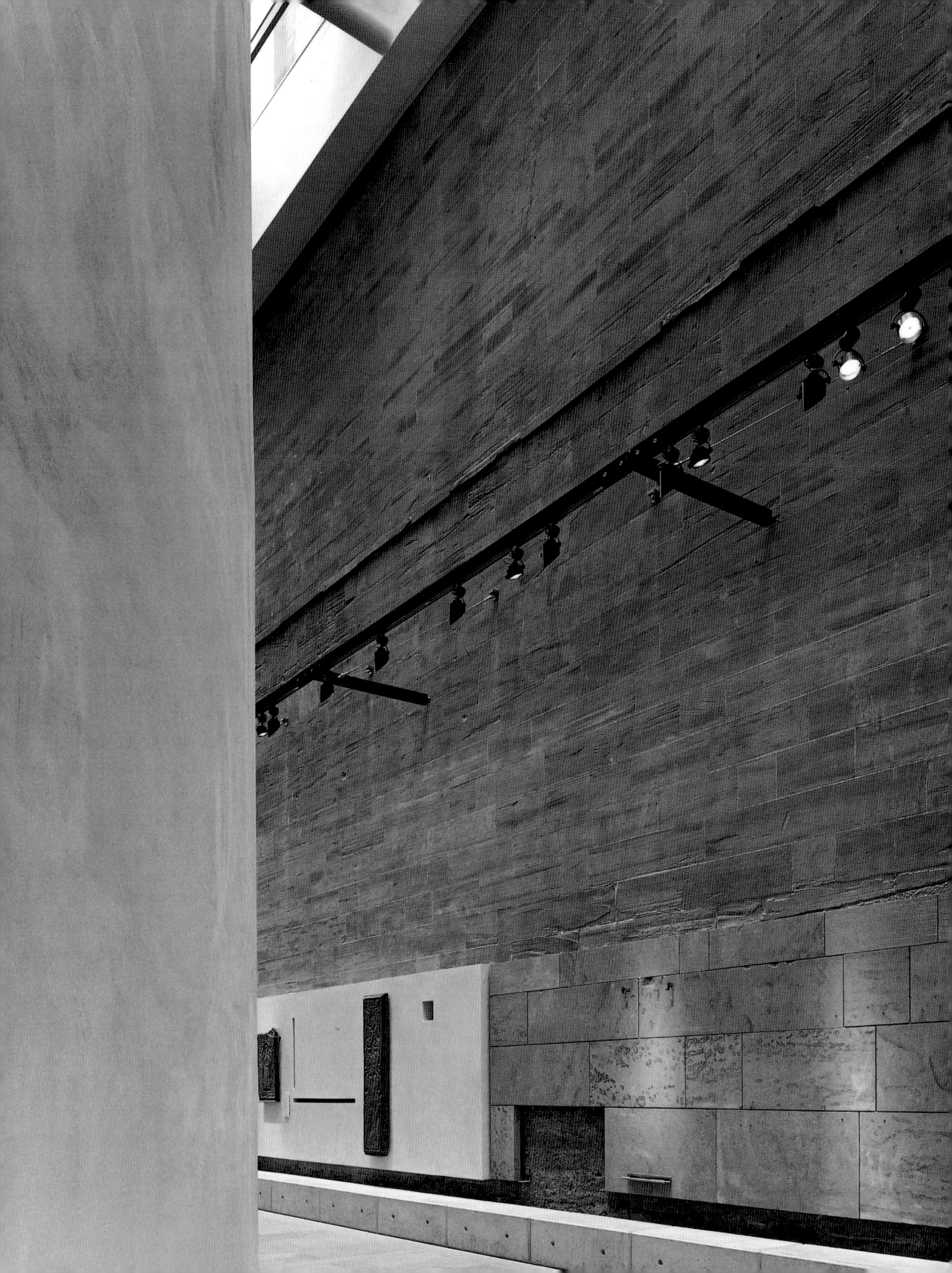

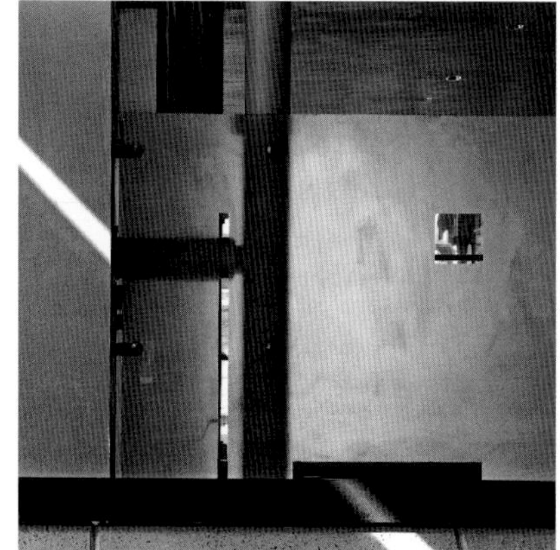

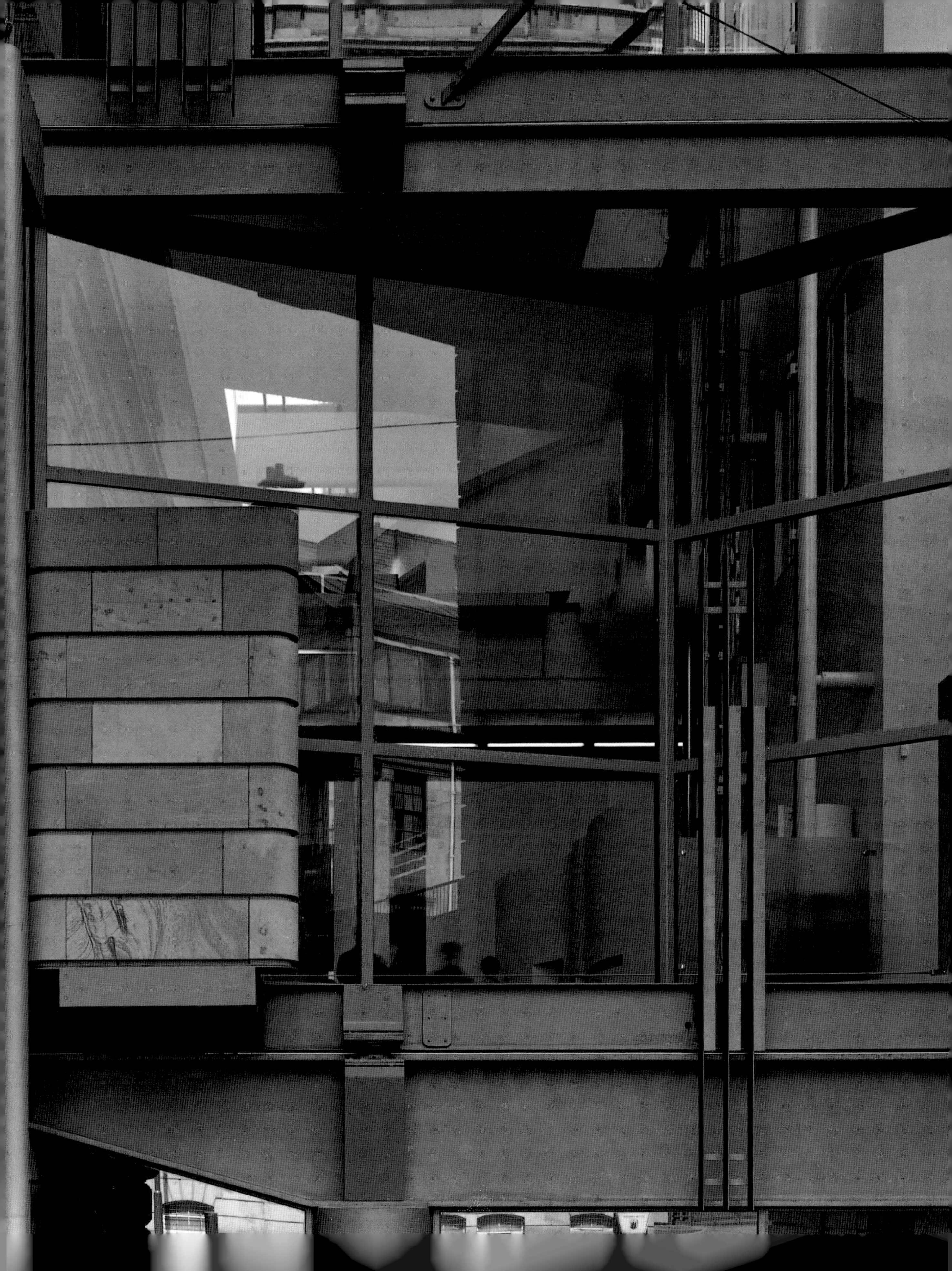

First floor

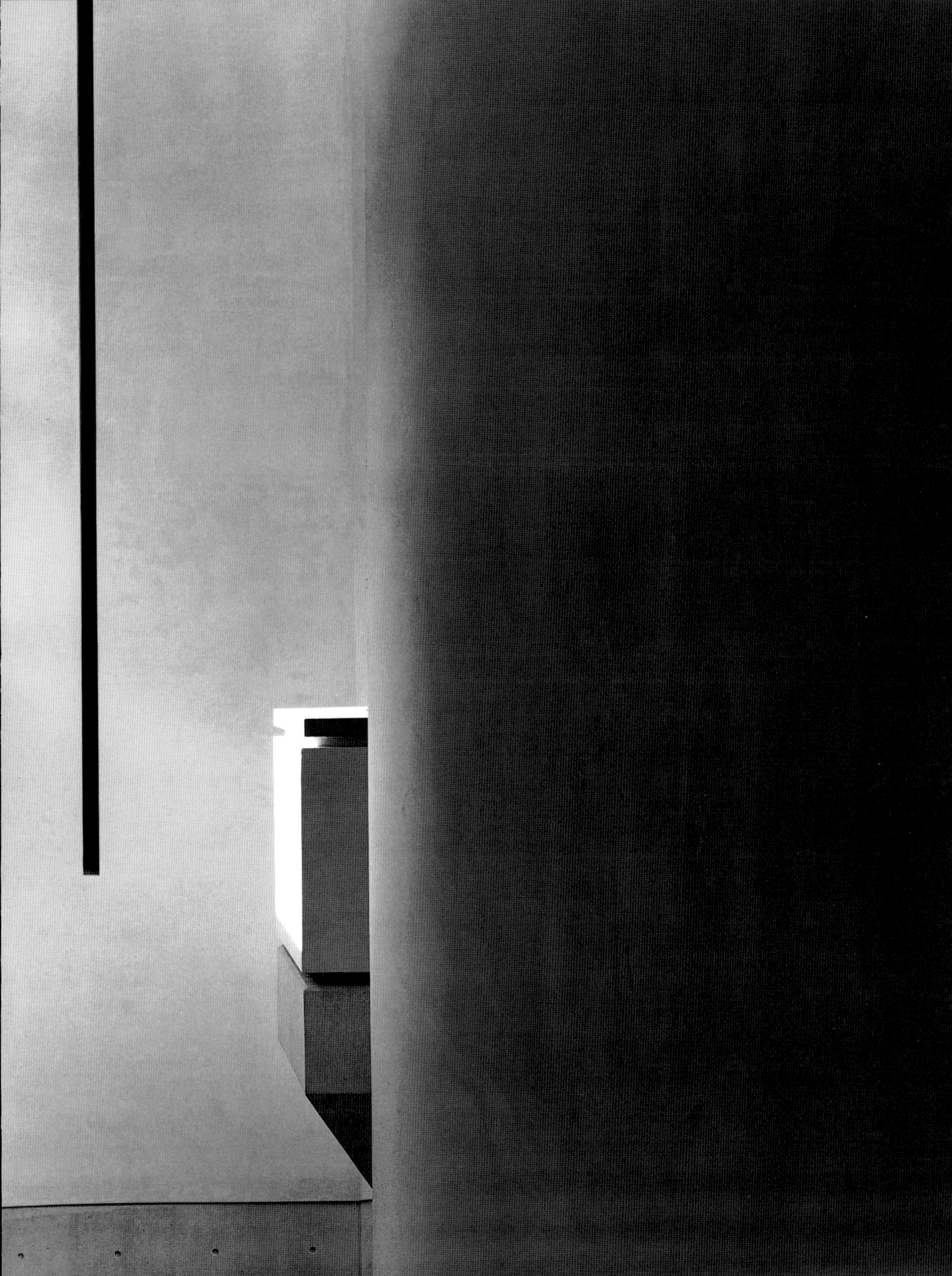

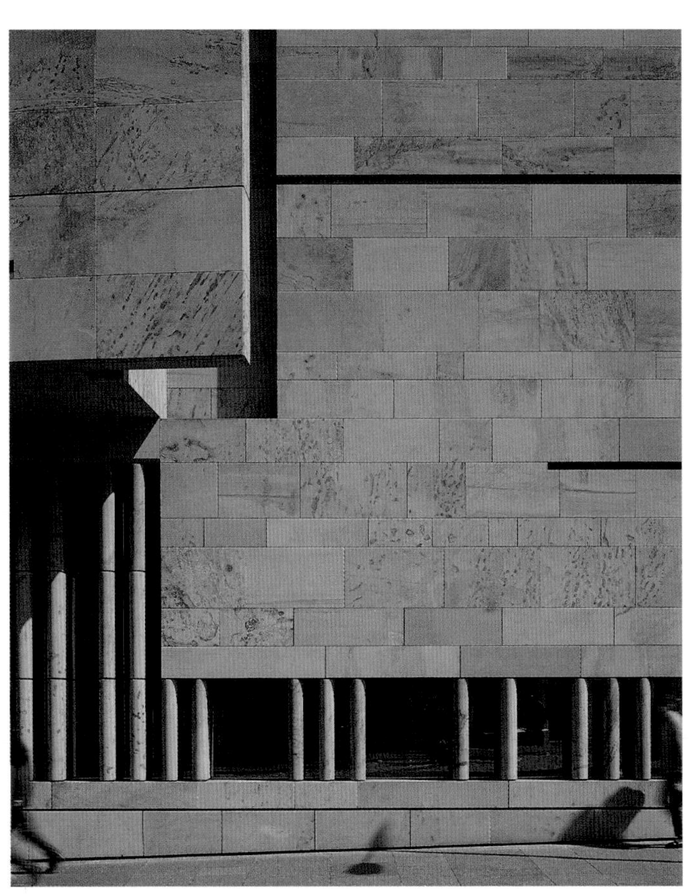

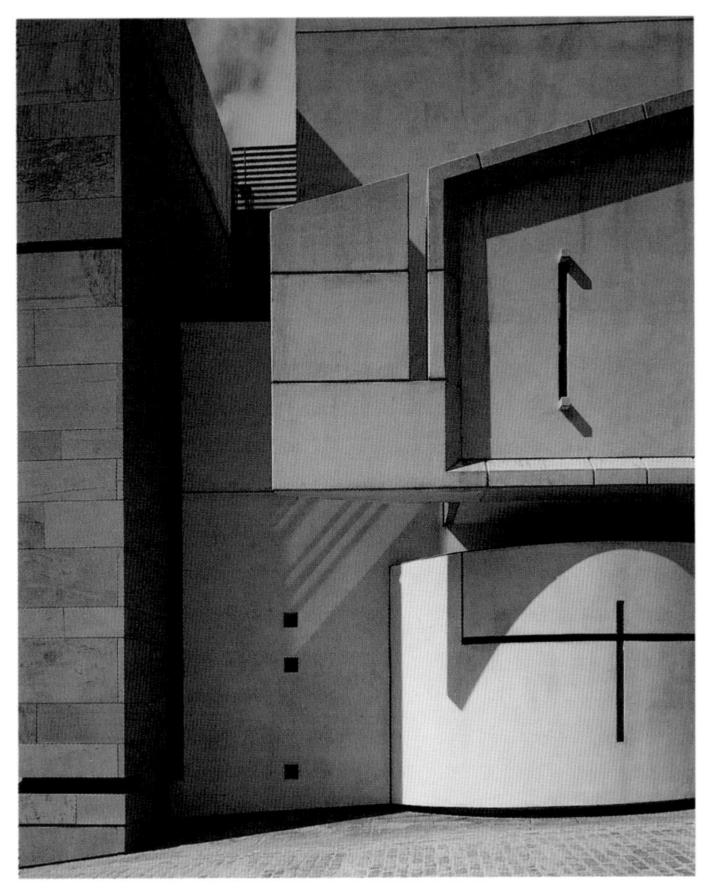

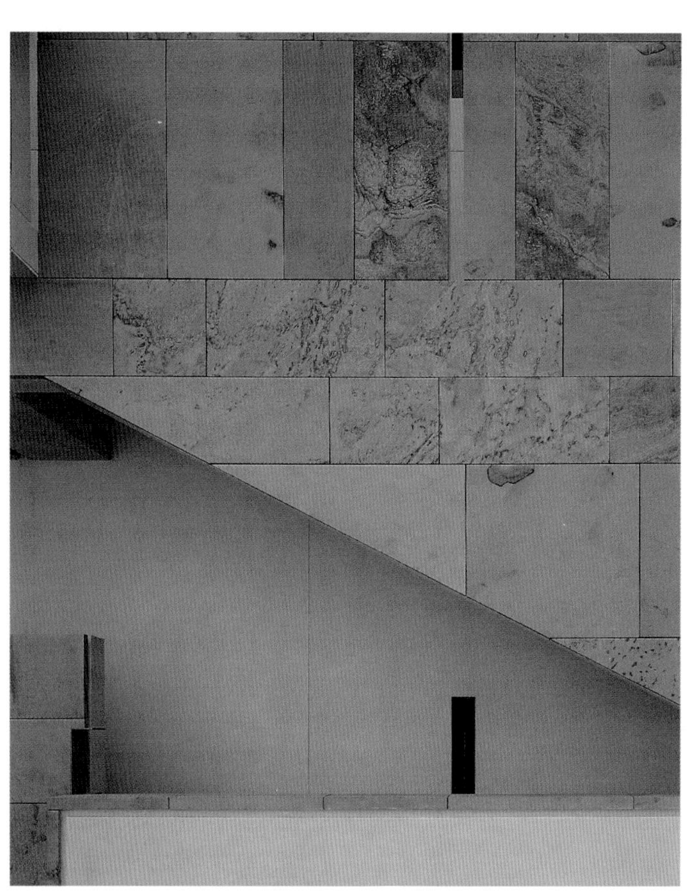

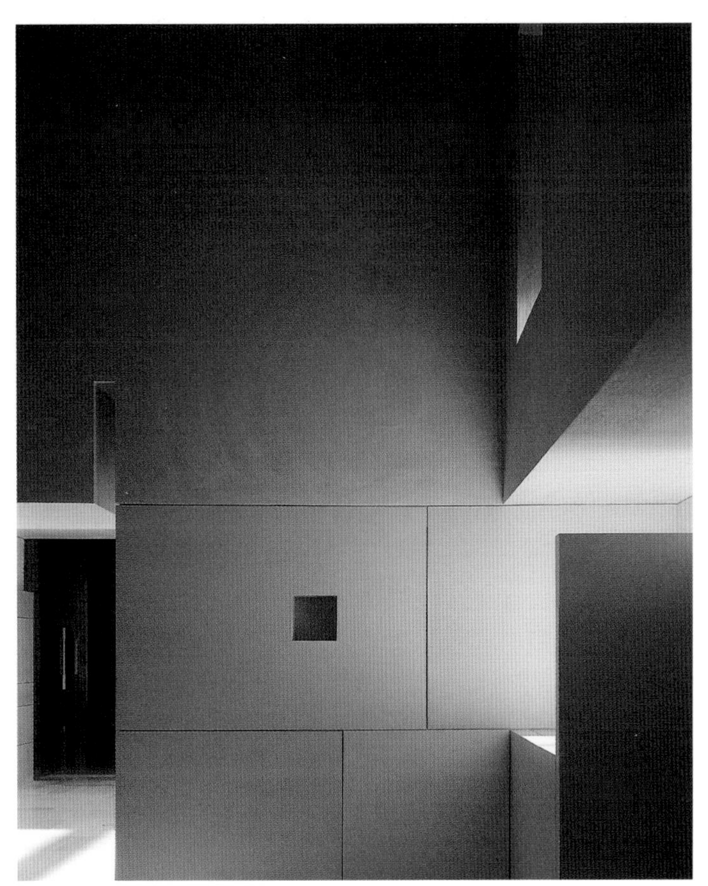

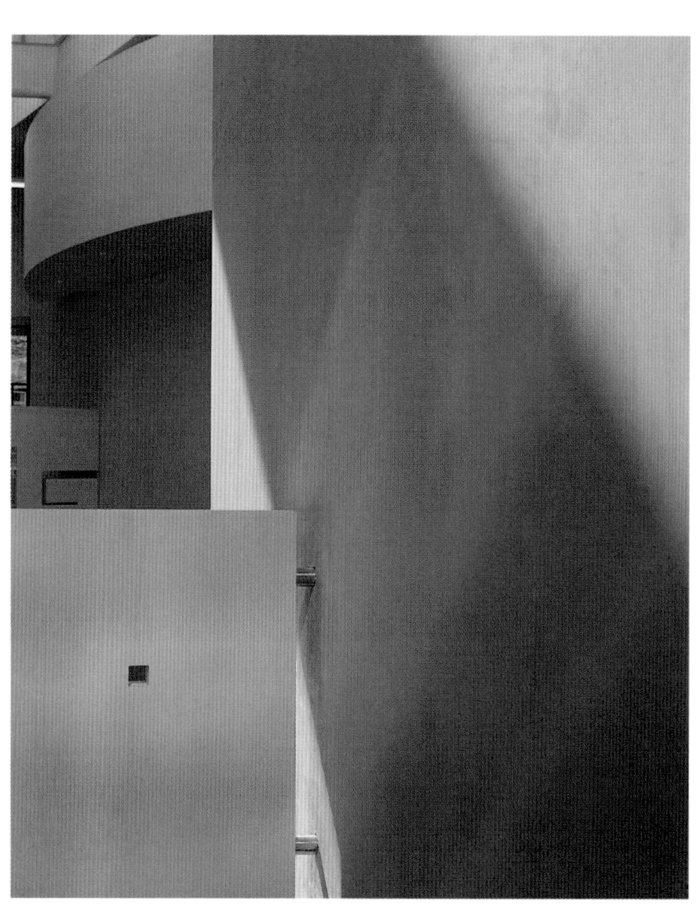

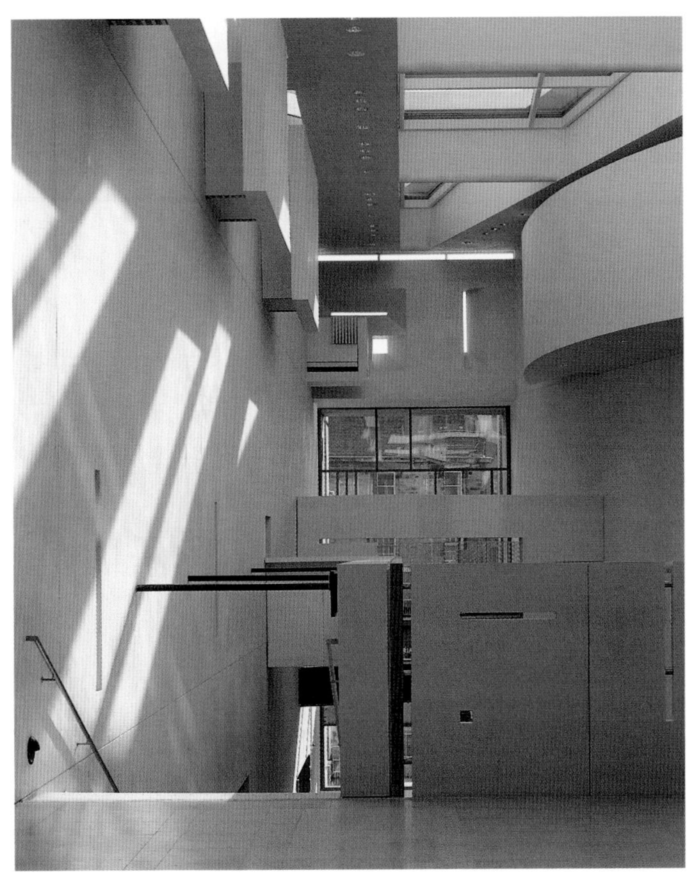

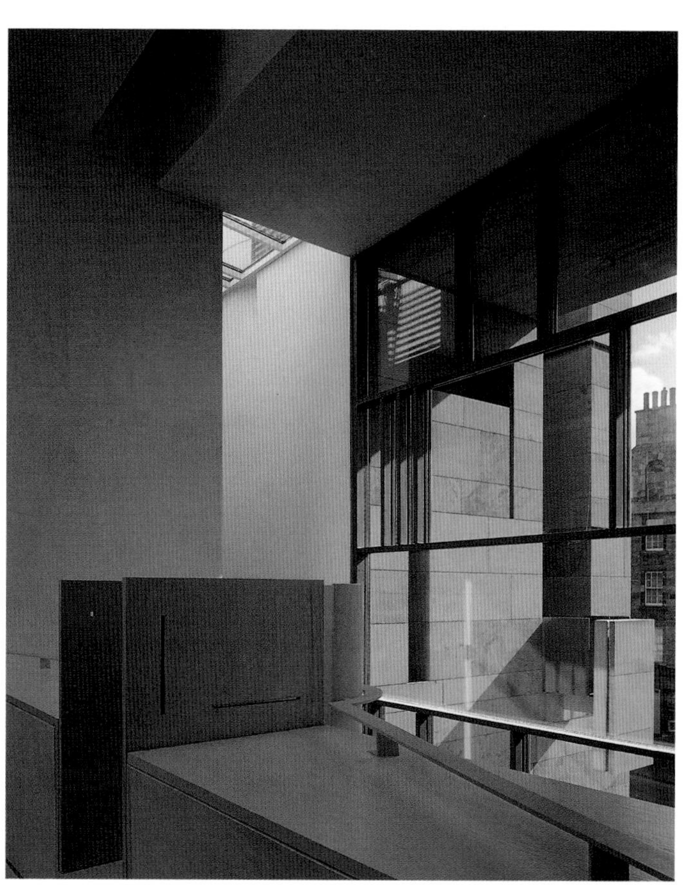

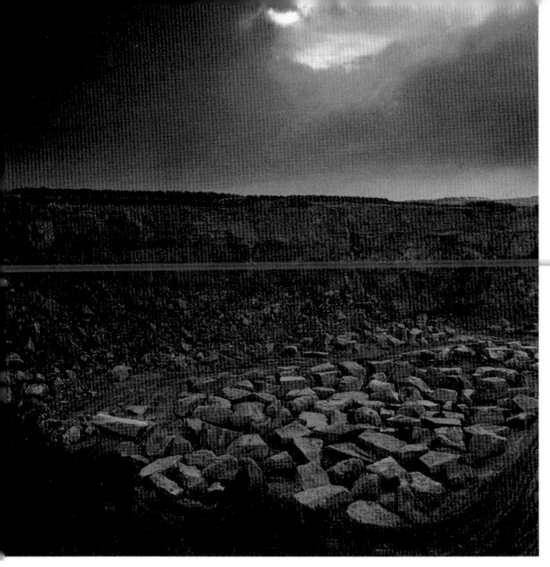

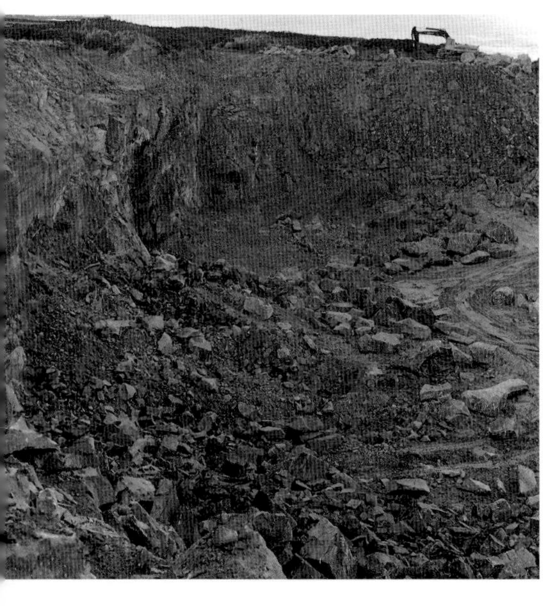

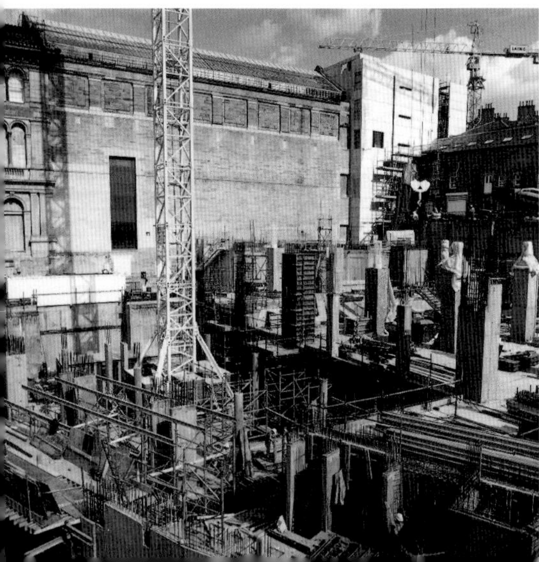

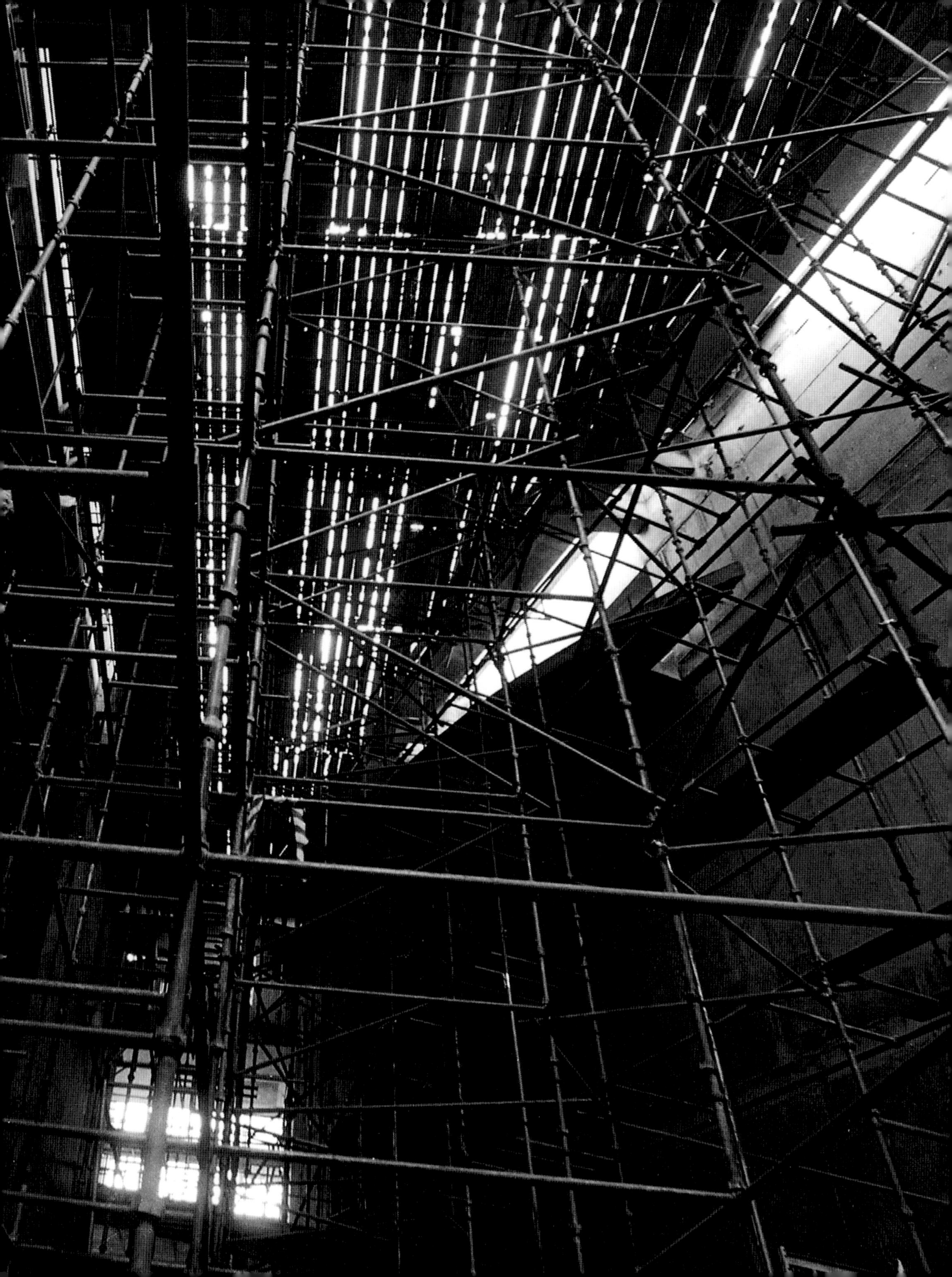

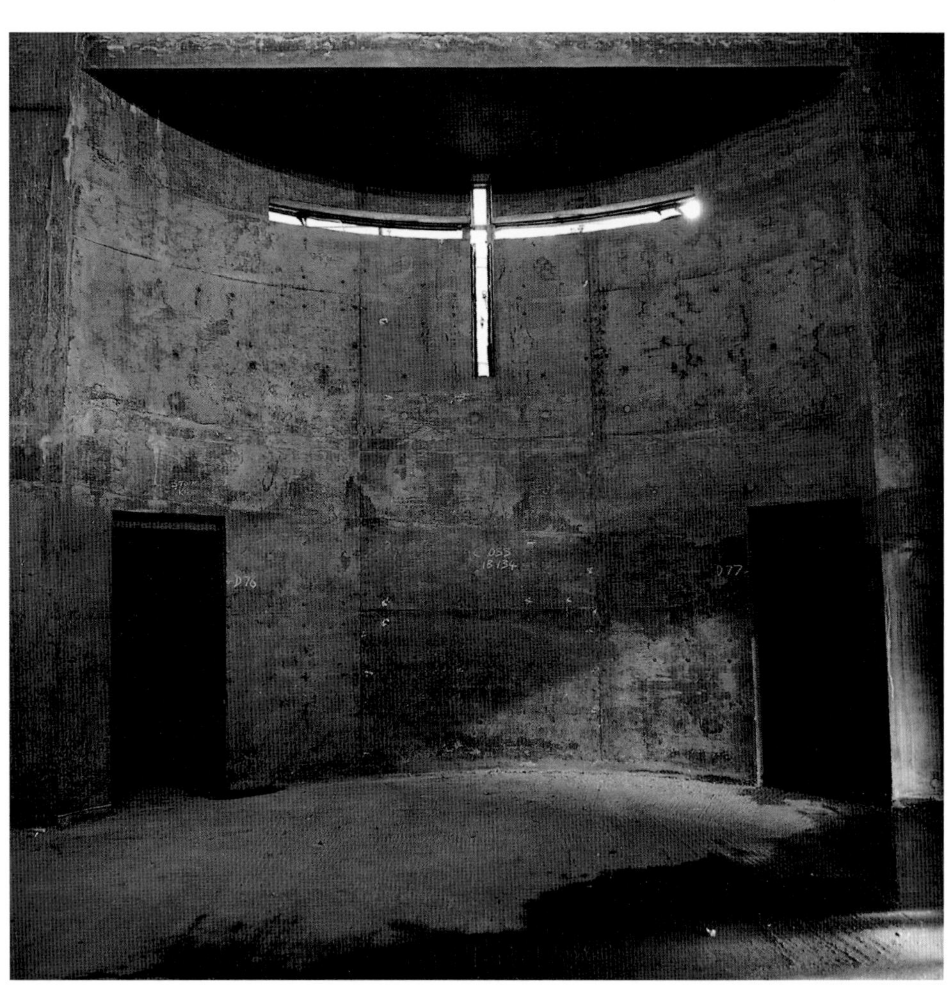

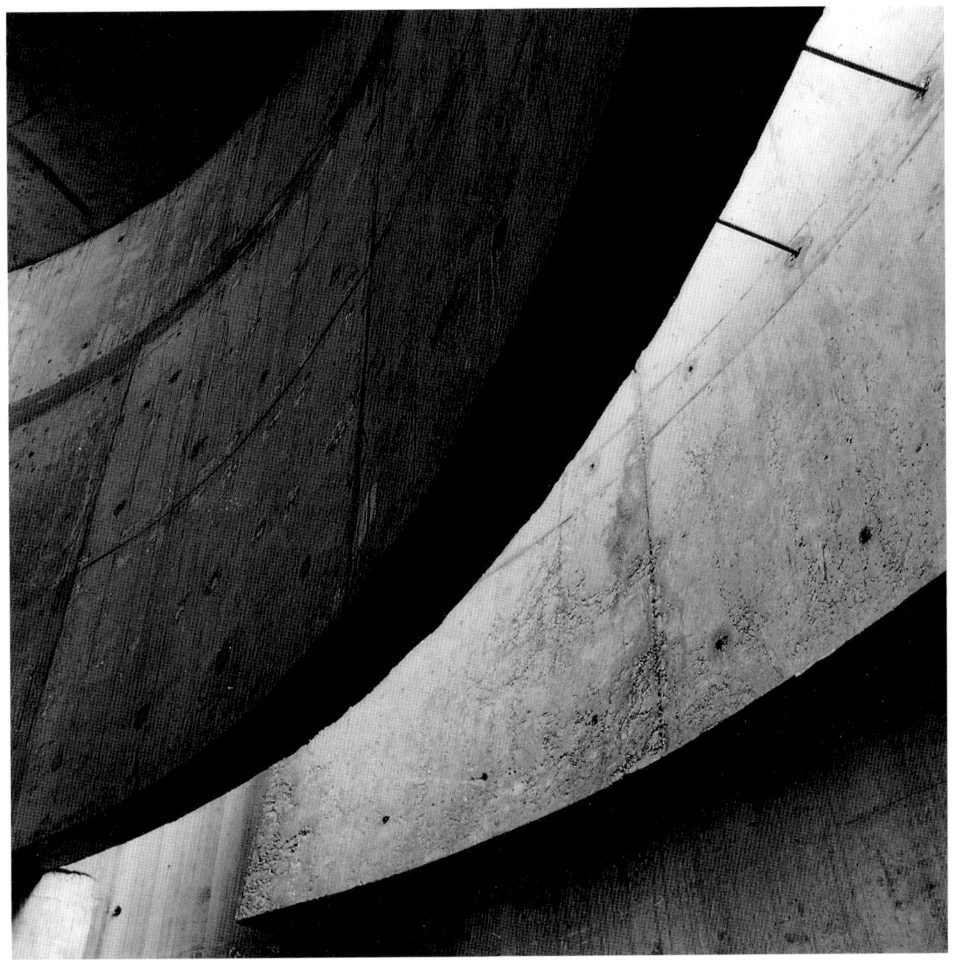

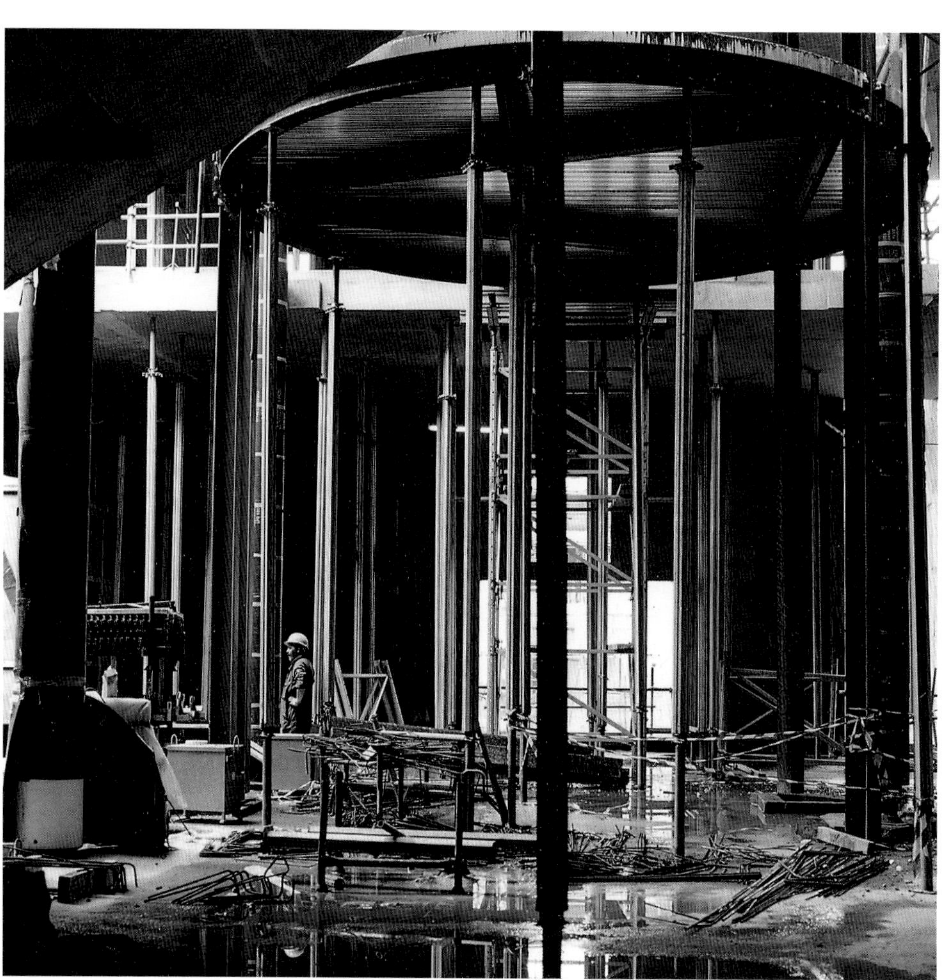

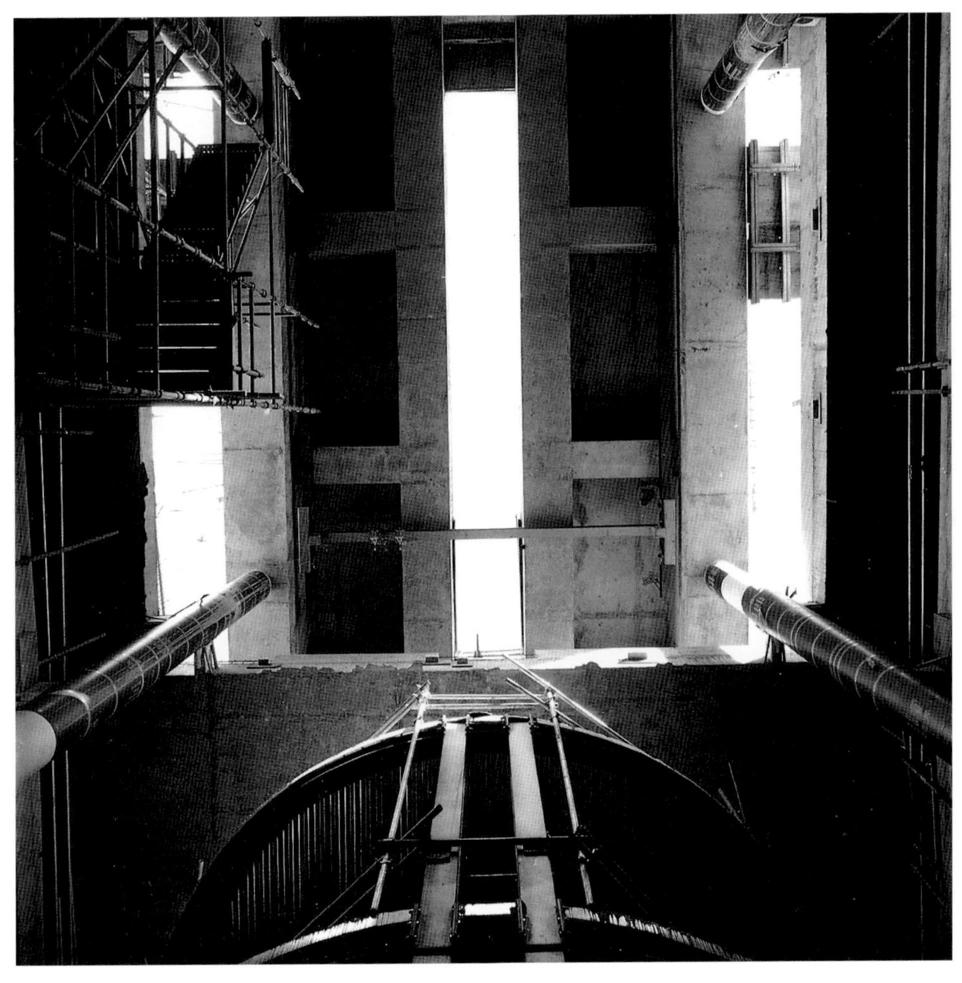

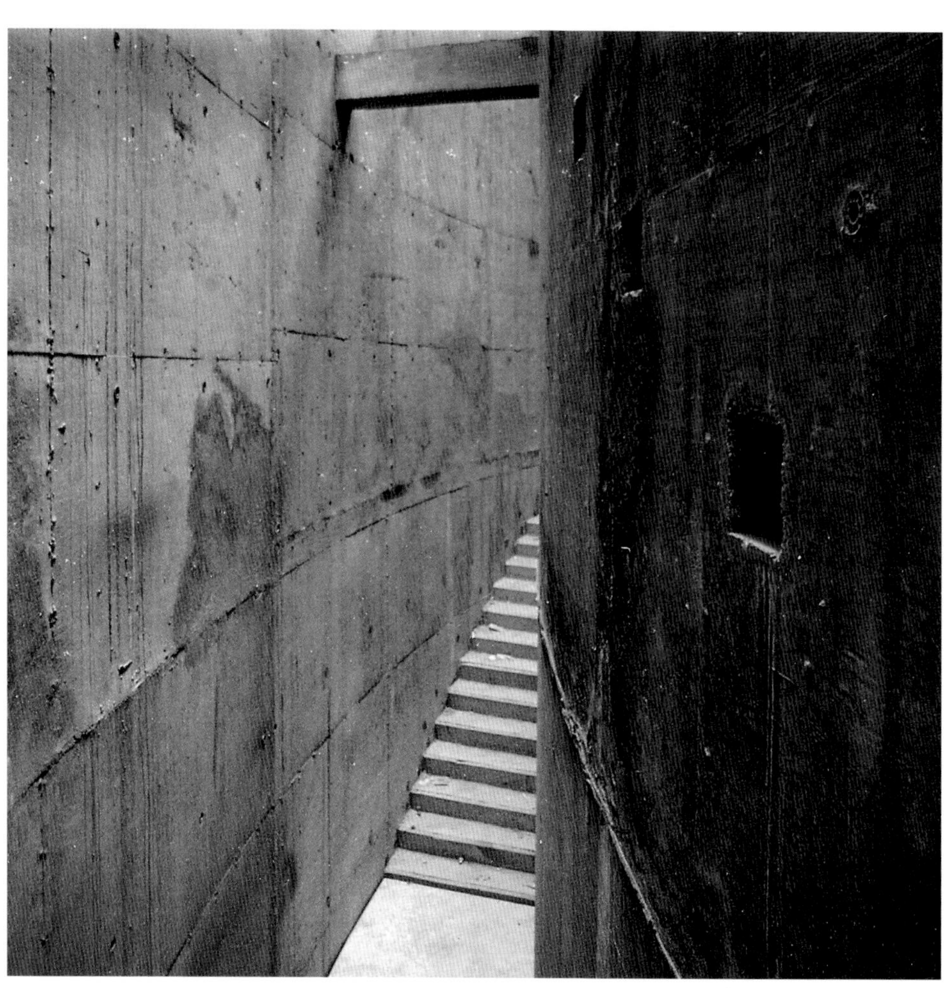

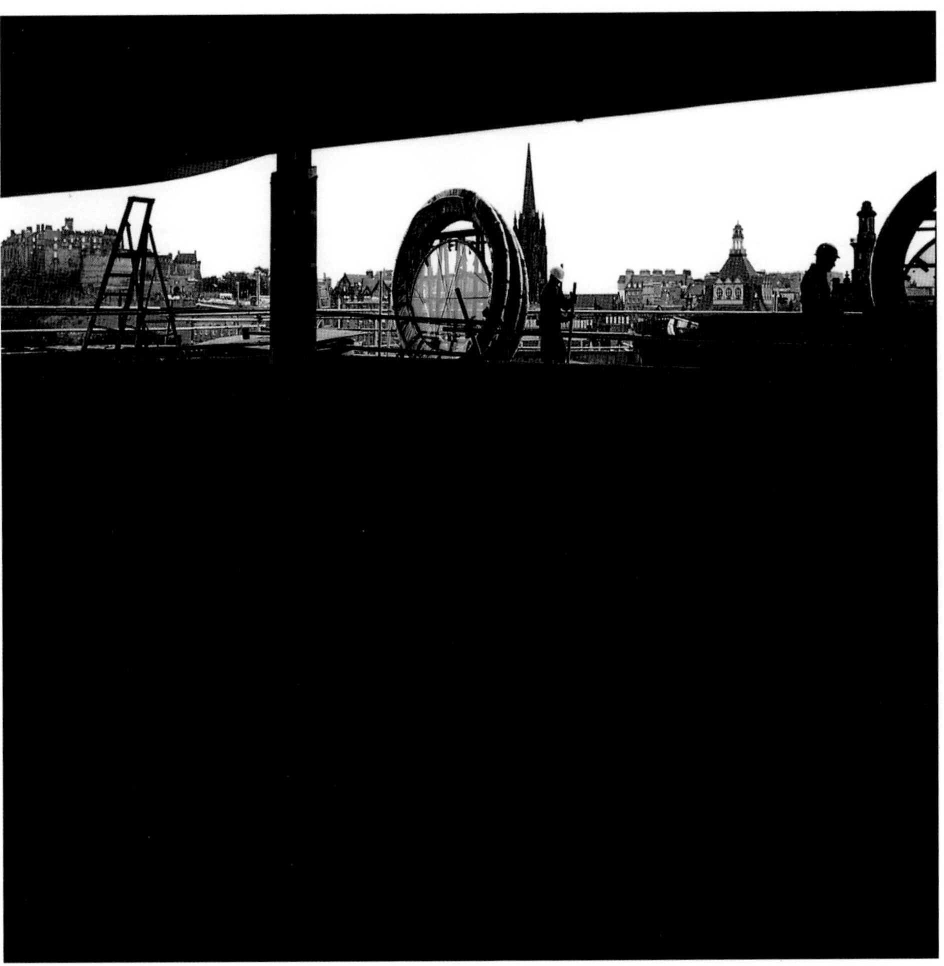

Museum of Scotland

Duncan MacMillan

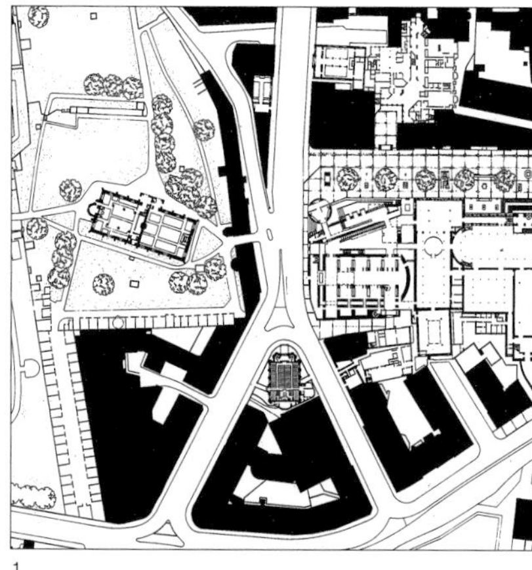

1

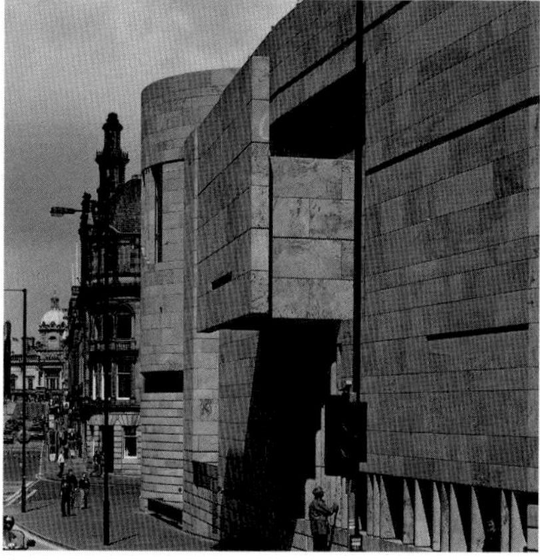

2

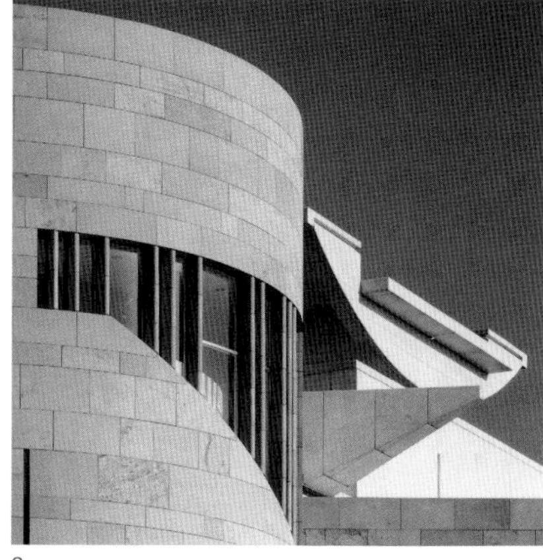

3

The Museum of Scotland is built at a crossroads. It faces north and west on a corner where no less than six streets meet. Layers of history are overlaid, one on the other in their converging lines, just as they are focused in the collections the Museum is designed to hold. This crossroads was the site of the Bristo Port, the main southern gate of the city, and the new building itself is defined to the south by the line of the old city wall in which the gate once stood. Bristo Port, the smallest of the six streets, a narrow cul-de-sac behind the Museum to the south carries its name. The adjacent Bristo Street follows the old main road south from the point at the Museum's south-west corner where the gate actually stood. Candlemaker Row, opposite, which climbs steeply up from the Grassmarket beneath the Castle Rock was once the only route from the High Street, the Royal Mile, to this gate. But George IV Bridge, one of Edinburgh's many street-bridges, replaced Candlemaker Row and opened the city's confined site to the development of new southern suburbs. Now the new building is approached from the High Street to the north along the level of this bridge. The actual site of the new building was once Brown's Square, built in the 1740s, the first terraced houses with their own front doors in this city of flats. In *Redgauntlet*, Walter Scott comments on how strange they looked when they were built.

But the Museum's main facade and entrance are on Chambers Street, a wide street that meets George IV Bridge at a right angle and that was built as part of a series of mid 19th century improvements designed to open up the narrow streets and closes of the old town to light and air. It was cut though Brown's Square. The sixth street, Forrest Road that leads off to the south-west, was the result of another later scheme of improvement. In this environment it is not surprising that the Museum's most important neighbours span the centuries from the 17th century Candlemakers' Hall and Greyfriars Kirk to the west to the recently constructed Law Courts opposite across Chambers Street to the north (1).

The nodal point where all these streets converge is now marked by the bold round tower of the Museum, a perfect cylinder that stands proud of the building's north-west corner. This tower is visible from most of the approaches, but only discreetly (2). For all its boldness it respects both roof lines and street lines. It is like a memory of the ancient city gate, for it is through it that you enter the building (3). You enter history perhaps, but there is nothing passive about this museum, nothing simply retrospective. The way its collections are knitted into the building and it into its environment suggests a more dynamic, a more engaged reading of history than you expect from a conventional museum. Mostly they set things apart, only offer a remote, detached perspective on the past, but this very modern building so much

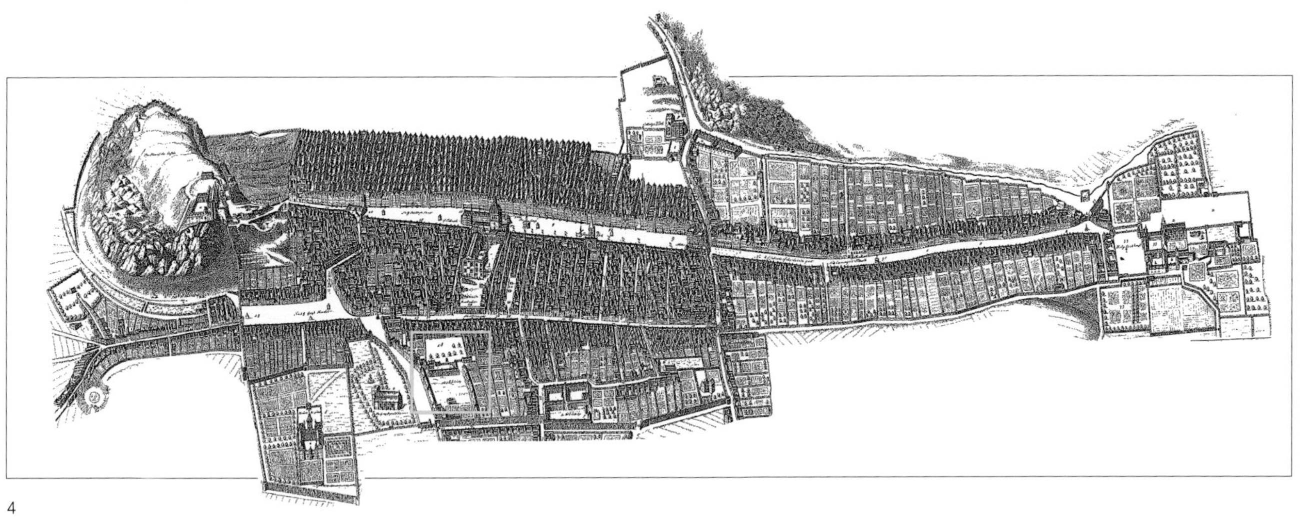

4

at home in its ancient context, its contents so much at home in it, suggests a different reading of things: the uses the past offers present and future. The Museum has after all been built at a crossroads in Scotland's history, too, and perhaps that in part explains this, but it is surely the building itself and the care with which it has been designed that really hold the secret.

And here the origins of the project are relevant. The proposal to build a new museum goes back to the early eighties and the Williams Report on the future development of Scotland's national museums commissioned by the Secretary of State for Scotland. Williams recommended the construction of a Museum of Scotland as a new and much expanded home for the historic collections of the old Museum of Antiquities – the museum of the Society of Antiquaries of Scotland founded in the late 18th century. Williams also saw this new museum as dynamic, a focus for national identity, not a popular idea among politicians at the time. He also specifically rejected the present site as too small to achieve this. Maybe this tempted the then Secretary of State Malcolm Rifkind to back the project. It seemed a generous gesture, but if it was too small, the museum could not actually carry any dangerous charge was perhaps the tacit thinking. And that is the measure of Benson + Forsyth's success. They have proved that thinking wrong and made a building on that site that really does work as a focus for the kind of cultural energy that has given Scotland back its Parliament.

Even if the site seemed small to Williams, this is nevertheless a very big building. But though it does not for a moment compromise its modernity and there is nothing retrospective about it at all and its formal language is purely abstract, it is nevertheless stitched into the surrounding fabric of the city with such subtlety that you are not conscious of its size. It sits at ease, suffers none of the insecurity that makes so many modern buildings assert themselves at the expense of their neighbours. The fabric of Edinburgh is stone, so here the main facades are stone-clad and nearby roof lines and window lines are subtly echoed "into" the stone work. Even the round tower is echoed in the rounded corner of a bank opposite. The channelled stone of the basements of this and other nearby buildings is also picked up in the channelled stone cladding of the lower part of the new building, and the window lines of nearby houses are drawn into the stonework of the western facade.

And though it is massive, castle-like even, this building is also transparent. From the street you can see through big windows directly to the displays within, but from the inside, correspondingly, there are constant links back to the surrounding city and beyond, ranging from stunning views of the castle framed in wide windows to subtle glimpses of passages of townscape

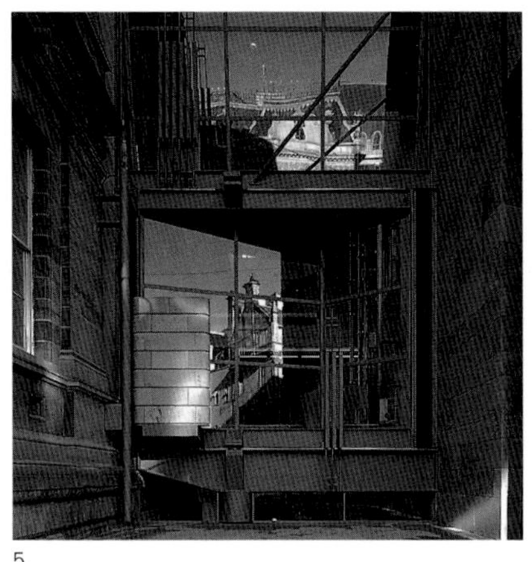
5

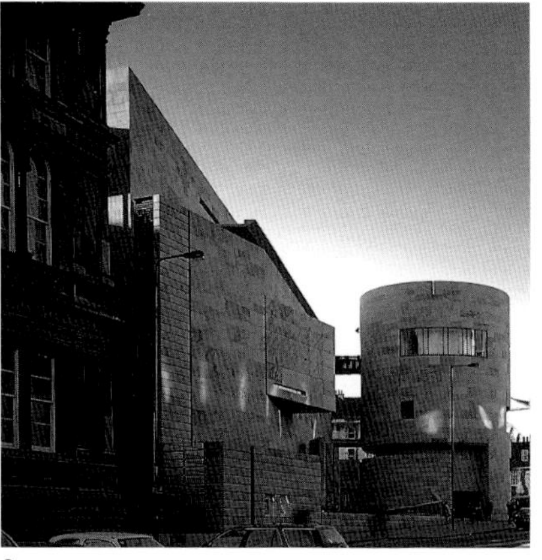
6

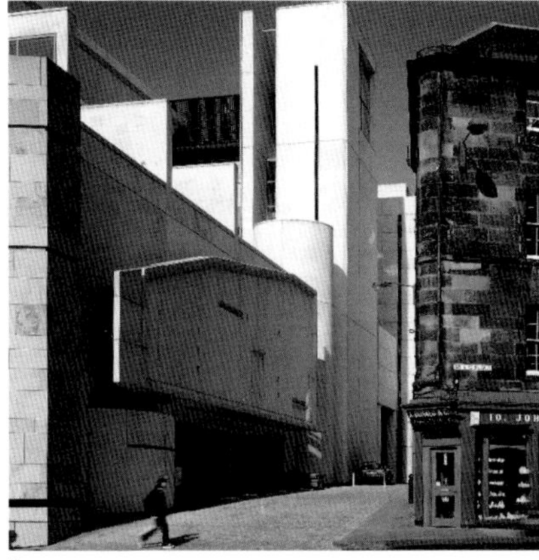
7

through tall windows narrow as castle fléchettes. This is a constant two-way flow, an intellectual and imaginative exchange between the building, its contents and its environment that is one of the Museum's most distinctive characteristics.

Such seamless integration was not easy on this site even externally. To the east, along Chambers Street, the north facade of the new museum stands up against the massive bulk of its partner and parent, the old Royal Museum of Scotland; what was its external west wall is now the internal east wall of the new building. Though it screens a magical, luminous interior of cast iron and glass, externally the old museum is a rather ponderous, overlarge Italian palazzo design, two wings and a long central facade above a high basement. But in contrast the new building's immediate neighbours to the west and south along Bristo Street and Bristo Port are modest, three-storey domestic and commercial buildings from the 18th and early 19th centuries. Most are ashlar, but some are harled. George IV Bridge and Forrest Road are on the same domestic scale.

The new building deals with these disparities very cleverly. First of all a very large window set back and apparently the full height of the building provides a caesura between the old and new museums (5). This is a practical device too, for though it weighs no less than seven tons, by an ingenious system of counterweights the lower part of the window swings open to provide both emergency ventilation and access for very large objects. Framing this window to the right, a stone screen stands forward on the line of the old museum. But the actual facade of the new museum is set back behind and above this, while above that again there is a high, stone-clad attic storey the height of the old roof line (6). Facade and attic begin together. But the attic departs from this junction at an angle with a sharp stone edge. The facade carries on the old line for a few yards, before also turning back at an angle. At first floor level a wide screen of stone swings out of the facade parallel to the line of the street to frame a big window facing west to the castle. From below, this and the free-standing screen together give the initial impression that the line of the old museum continues. But above, as they recede the separation of facade and attic creates a wide balcony which in fact serves as an open deck for the restaurant. Meanwhile round the corner, the western facade starts at no more than the domestic height of the buildings next to it across Bristo Port – the attic at this point is set right back out of sight – but because the ground slopes down to Chambers Street, when the two facades meet they are the same height. The fact that the stone-clad attic has disappeared at the junction is screened by the tower. This arrangement cleverly mediates between two very different scales, resolving a mismatch that had been left as a

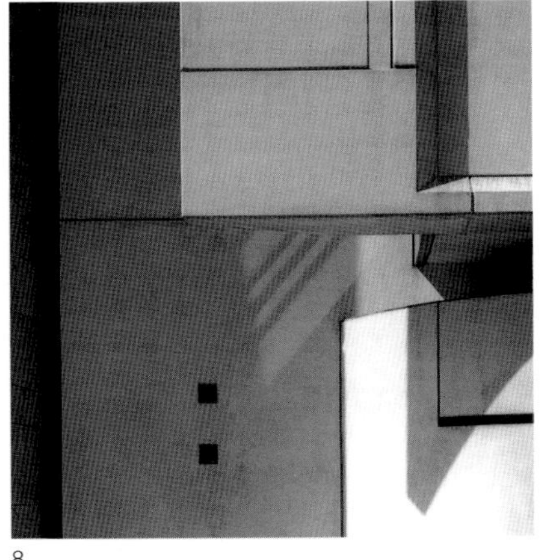
8

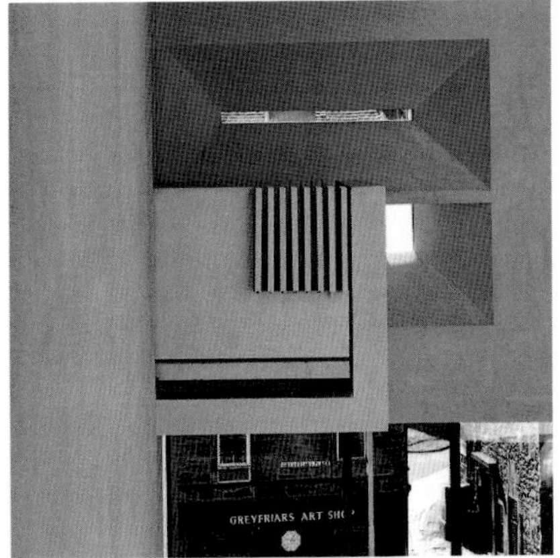

9

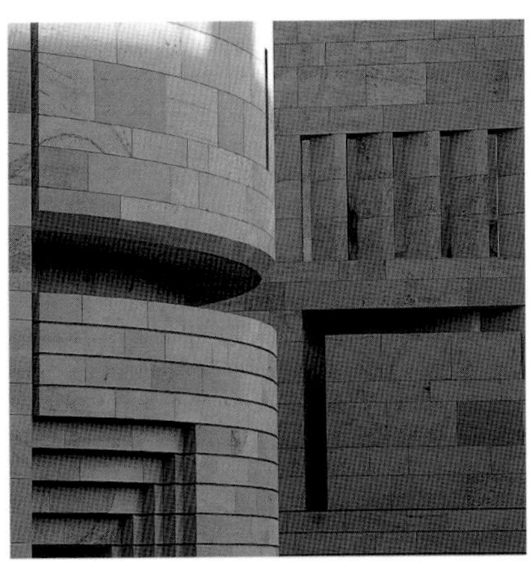
10

ragged edge for more than a century. But when the whole facade is seen from across the road, the tower flanked by two receding wings, it is a lively and balanced composition.

On these northern and western facades and on the tower the Museum is clad in beautiful, honey coloured Moray sandstone. It has a marvellous grain running through it, sometimes dark and gnarled as walnut, but really once windblown sand, now fixed for all eternity. Several windows have mullions in this stone too. But the remaining facade along the narrow cul-de-sac of Bristo Port to the south is white-harled, or white concrete which is pretty much indistinguishable, and so are the upper levels of the building that rise above and behind the main street facades (7). The junction of stone facing with harled walls is a common feature of traditional Scottish building and one that Mackintosh and Lorimer also regularly used. This partly hidden southern facade closed by a tall lift tower in the angle it makes with the old museum also uses apparently random windows and other details reminiscent of Mackintosh, but also of Le Corbusier and even suggests a link between them (8 & 9). The whole composition is topped by a white, boat-shaped hanging garden, another homage to Corbusier in its forms, but set back so that it does not weaken the impact of the street facades.

The round tower on the corner suggests castles and a deep basement area beneath the facade could be a dry moat. But this castle metaphor should not be misunderstood. First of all the shapes are still abstract. And the last time such a free-standing cylinder was used by an architect in Edinburgh with such stark and dramatic simplicity, it was by Robert Adam in the tomb he designed for David Hume in the Calton cemetery. So the tower invokes the Enlightenment as well as the castle tradition which Adam too was fascinated by. But there is no pastiche here, and also something important is invoked by the choice of castle metaphor. Scottish castles were not brutal war machines, the kind of static armour that Edward I built to secure his conquests, nor the dead weight of stone that George III used at Fort George to hold down the Highlands. They were fortified homes: quirky, asymmetrical, casually human. And here the stone of the facade laid in big blocks in courses of irregular depth echoes that informal asymmetry. Places where windows or doors cut deep into the walls give the impression of strength, but the windows, too, are irregular in shape and size. A stepped window in the tower, for instance, indicates a staircase inside following its curve. There are other cuts into the surface of the tower stressing its mass and volume (10). A tall narrow slot runs from roof to ground level for instance and a deep cut springs from the doorway to run round most of its circumference. The roof line continues this deliberate asymmetry – and Scottish castles

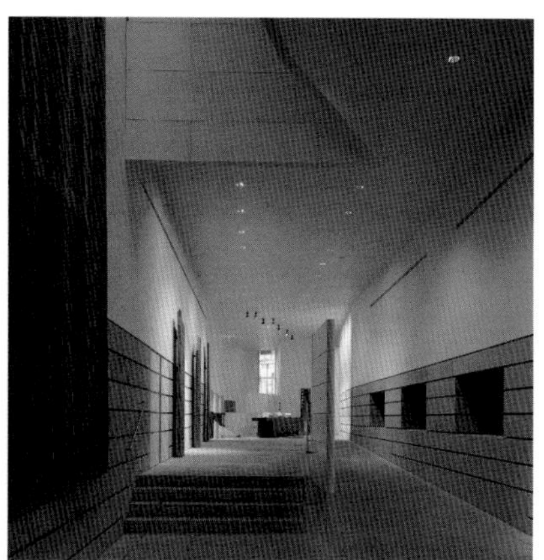

11

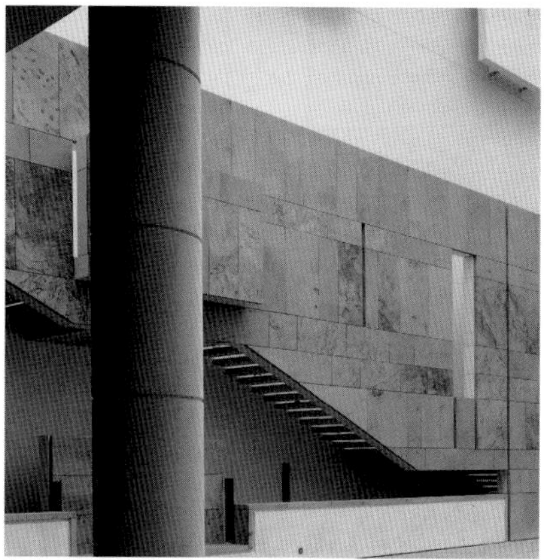

12

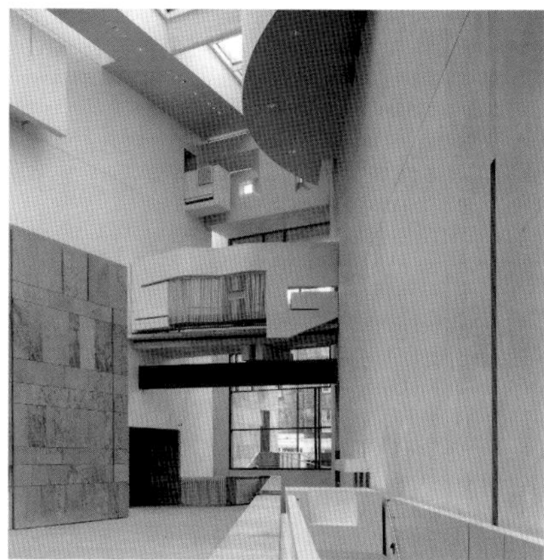

13

are often most architecturally complex at their upper levels – and also reflects the character of the spaces inside. They all declare that this is a building without a grid: it is not driven by any abstract argument, and so in spite of its size it will not impose conformity on you. It respects your human scale and will speak to you as an equal, be responsive, above all be sociable.

Gordon Benson and Alan Forsyth, by thinking deeply and imaginatively about the Museum, where it is, what it represents and what it has to contain, have created a truly modern building that really is sociable in a way that modern buildings rarely are, least of all built on this scale. And as it captures this quality in Scottish castles and townscapes, the Museum also invokes Mackintosh, for he did this too. Right at the beginning of the modern movement Mackintosh saw how these characteristics balanced sociability and individualism, and so here if the references are designed to emulate these qualities in traditional architecture, the language has an impeccable modern pedigree. But it is partly because of the former that there is such symbiosis between the building and the collections. Like this friendly architecture, they are not like some royal treasury filled with golden relics of forgotten delusions of grandeur, ill-gotten loot, or the spoils of war. They are much more human and domestic. Association is the key to them. So the language of the building reflects this. It does not just present them, it represents them, summarises what they stand for: the history of the nation that gave birth to the noble ideal of the democratic intellect, and a nation that for all its small size and apparent remoteness has historical links across the globe. That too is a message carried, not only by the collections, but by the transparency of this architecture and the creative exchange it proposes between national and international, between past and present.

It is in keeping with all this that from the entrance inwards you are put at your ease with the unobtrusive subtlety of true good manners. It is dignified, really grand even, but not assertive. You enter through a deep cut door in the tower. As it stands clear of the main building you then cross a bridge to enter a long lobby that runs back most of the length of the facade (11). As you enter, for a moment you look through an opening in front of you, across a space and through a far doorway into the heart of the collections beyond. Your curiosity aroused, you are invited in. Stone continues on the floor and the walls are channelled stone up to six feet or so. In this front block of the building on the floor above you is a 'discovery' display with views over Chambers Street and over to the castle. A long tapestry by Kate Whiteford hangs down from an enclosed balcony there. On the top floor, two floors up, is the restaurant with its open balcony high above the street and sweeping views of the castle.

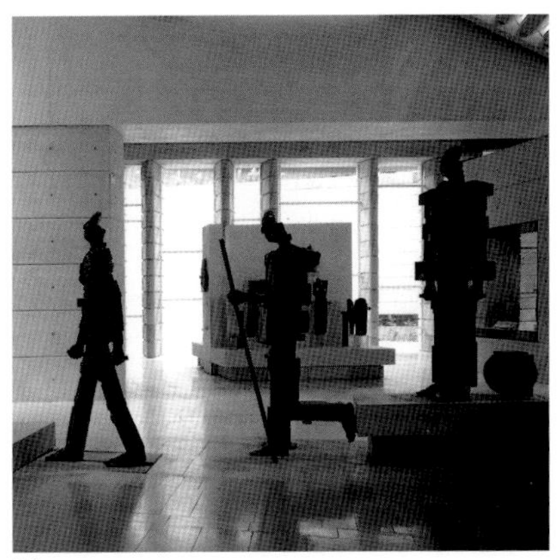
14

This entrance hall rises to take you from street level to the floor level of the old museum – the main floor of both buildings is continuous – just four steps, or a gentle incline with a screen divider. You pass the ticket desk and turn right into a dramatic open space (12). The first and largest of three principal spaces, it is a tall atrium that runs the length of the new building. Lit from the roof high above like the old museum next door, it is triangular. But partly it floats as on the two longer sides it stands clear of the walls to create light wells, lighting the basement, but lightening the structure too. A stair descends through the well on the outer wall. At the apex of this triangle at the western end is a tall window (13). The base of the triangle at the eastern end is the stone wall of the old museum, but it is screened by a lift tower and by bridges at two levels that link the tower to the discovery room and restaurant on the street facade behind you, to the central core of the museum in front of you, and though you cannot see it, to the first floor of the old museum beyond. As well as these bridges, windows and balconies look down from high in the walls. The top of the lift tower stops short of the glass roof to create an open viewing platform between two upper bridges. Another bridge crosses the atrium above the narrow western end. There may be memories of Piranesi here, and these details also make wonderful abstract compositions within this luminous space, but you see people on the bridges and balconies above you so the real point is constantly to restate human scale and human use.

At floor level the wall in front of you continues the line of the old building. Against it a stairway screened in stone leads to the first floor. The rest of the walls are natural coloured plaster, a soft, warm pinkish-grey – all the materials in the Museum are light-toned whether sandstone, limestone (used on some of the floors), plaster, limed wood or concrete. The floor here is sandstone, too. But this does not feel like an ordinary indoor space, more indoors-outdoors like the courtyard of a castle. Daylit and light coloured, it is airy, a comfortable place to make choices about where to go next.

The chronology of the collections is vertical, six levels from the basement upwards. If you want to begin at the beginning you go down by the stair in the atrium against the wall behind you: prehistory, Celts and Romans. Here are Eduardo Paolozzi's strange anthropmorhic display cases, some of the finest Pictish stones, the astonishing Roman lioness dredged from the mud at Cramond only a few years ago, and much else (14). But it must be said that this is the area where the display is least in tune with the architecture and so it lacks the lucidity of the rest of the building. The basement is the full depth of the building so it stretches back beneath both atrium and entrance to be lit by a big

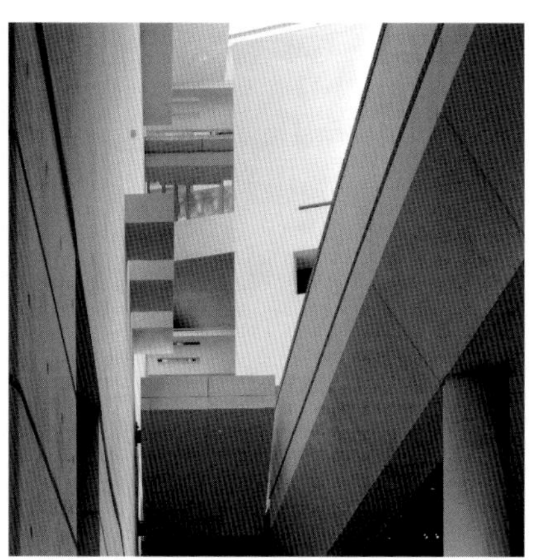
15

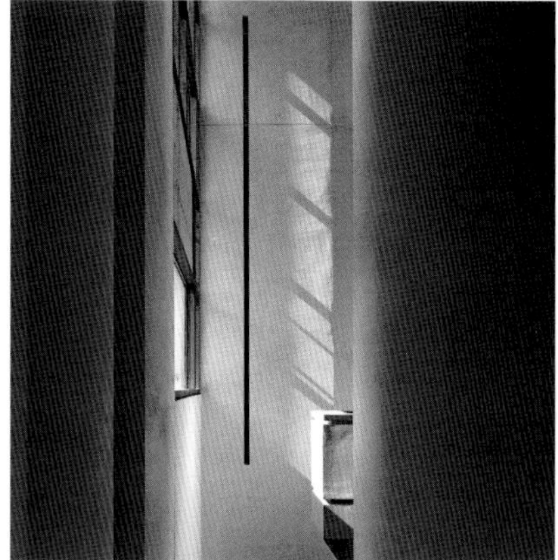
16

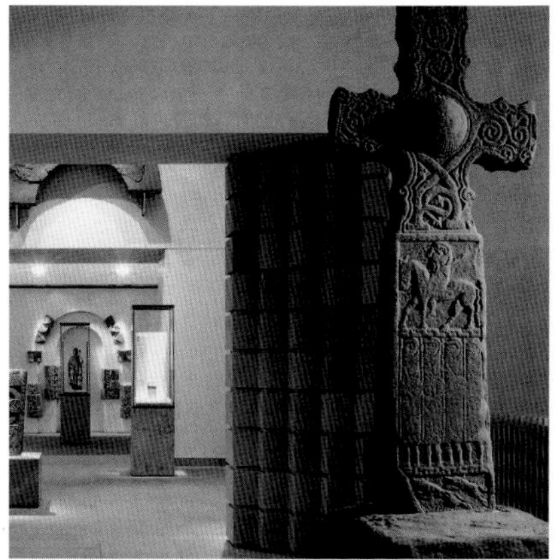
17

window onto the basement area, the dry moat on Chambers Street. It is also lit from above by the light wells (15).

Equally at this point in the atrium you could go up the stair to enter on the first floor: the 18th century and the Enlightenment, and in the two levels above it, the 19th and 20th centuries. But the real invitation is to go straight ahead through another deep-cut stone doorway stepped back into the wall of the inner tower. As you do so, if you look to your left, through a square doorway you can see the full length of the old building along its central axis. Continuing the castle metaphor, ahead of you the core of the building is like the inner tower of a castle. Indeed from outside to the west you can see it as a simple rectangular block with the facades wrapped round it like a curtain wall and the roof garden floating above. Inside long narrow light wells cut through the whole height of the building along its southern and western sides (16). Look up into them and they are criss-crossed by bridges that link the central core to the surrounding galleries, built at each level between it and that outer curtain wall. But above is the sky, daylight. It is a constant, a definitive feature of this building.

Defying the tyrannical darkness of the modern conservator, daylight reaches from roof to basement. Everywhere windows open from one space to the next, or link you back to the outside world, framing views. Daylight beckons to you round corners, leading you on, but helping you keep your orientation through complex spaces. The opposite of the disorientation of supermarket lighting, here the light keeps you in touch with reality, reminds you that the things you are looking at have meaning not because they are in a museum, but because they come from the daylit world outside.

At its eastern end the central core is defined by a curved wall that stands clear and separate from the wall of the old museum. A stair built in its thickness follows the curve of the wall as though in a castle tower or indeed a Pictish broch. (Elsewhere several turnpike stairs are cut into the walls.) So this inner core really is like a tower, almost free-standing, like an old building buried deep in a newer one, the historic heart of the matter; a metaphor for the process of discovery you are embarking on, for the onion layers of history.

Outside to greet you and to mark this principal entrance stands the Dupplin Cross, a massive free-standing Pictish Cross more than a thousand years old, a symbol of the independence and unity of the first Scottish kingdom. You pass it to enter medieval and Renaissance Scotland, the old Scottish kingdom (17). Great icons of early Scottish history greet you, the Pictish Forteviot arch cut from a single piece of stone, the Monymusk Reliquary that once held relics of St Columba. Phrases from the Declaration of Arbroath are written on the walls. There

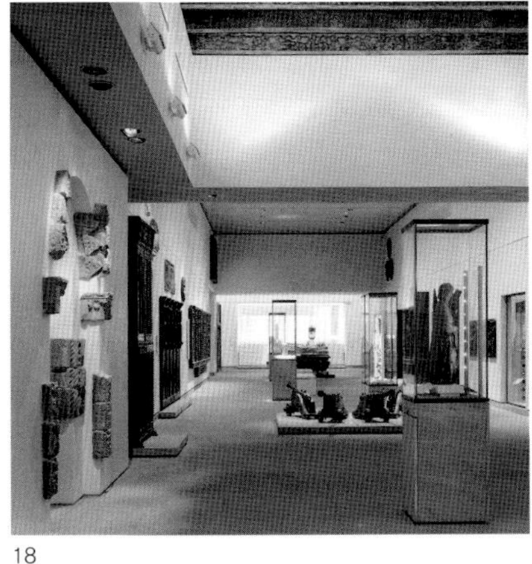

18

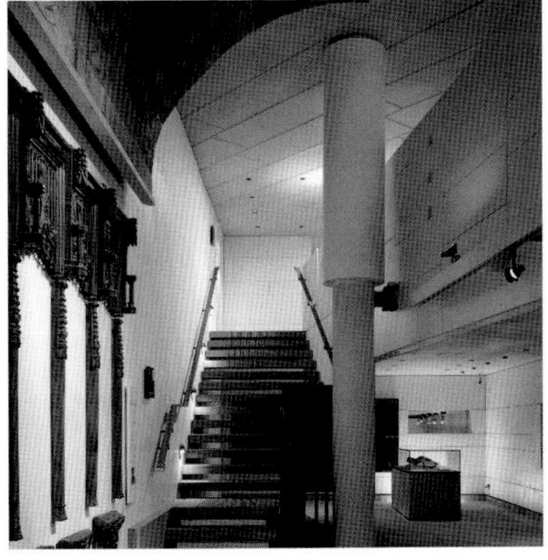

19

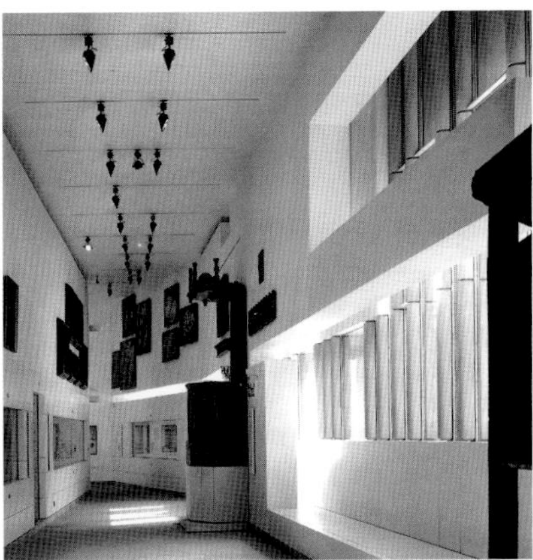

20

can be no doubt that this is a museum with a powerful emotional charge and that is constantly reiterated by the architecture.

To your right a long gallery opens onto the collections that represent the old kingdom of the Scots, medieval and Renaissance, the core collection of the old Museum of Antiquities. The second principal space, like a castle hall this gallery runs almost the length of the building, its castle character endorsed by the oak carvings that are one of the principal features of this display and the painted ceiling in the roof above the entrance. The walls are visibly thick like a castle's too, but there is daylight beckoning from a tall window at the western end (18). Varied, domestic scaled rooms run along both sides, deep display cases set into their walls: kings and queens on one side, the ordinary people of the towns and cities on the other. Openings cut through in the curved wall behind you open onto the old museum wall. The display continues there, and daylight comes down from above there, too.

A series of galleries devoted to the church is wrapped around the southern and western ends of this central tower. You cross the light well into a sequence of small spaces. The first is the medieval church. It is crypt-like, deliberately dark and low and opens to another level beneath so that at one point you are looking into the vault of a painted ceiling (19). This device is repeated on the upper level too so that at one point there you look into the carved detail of a wooden church screen. But as you go round here, these low spaces open into a beautiful and surprising circular room. With a memory of Ronchamp, but of the architects' own oratory in Cumbria too, narrow windows admit a mysterious light. Drama of architecture and drama of history enhance each other.

And this continues. As you turn the corner from the southern to the western outer wall, you move from religious gloom into bright daylight with the Reformation (20). Light floods in from a wide mullioned window that opens across the street to Greyfriars Kirk, site of so many of the Reformation's dramas, a visible link from the historic collections to the historic environment. But you can also look back across the intervening light well and along the Renaissance hall to the point where you began. Continuities count even in a revolution – and the Reformation was certainly that. History is a flow not a series of disparate events. But that flow is not the sweep of grand generalisations. Rather it is the sum of infinite particulars. It is that which gives all museums their imaginative force, but in this one by this brilliant use of space and light we can feel the dynamic of its flow as well.

From this point you can cross a bridge back into the Renaissance galleries and thence, by a door to match the one by which you entered, into the atrium and up the main stair to the first floor. The first floor, the third

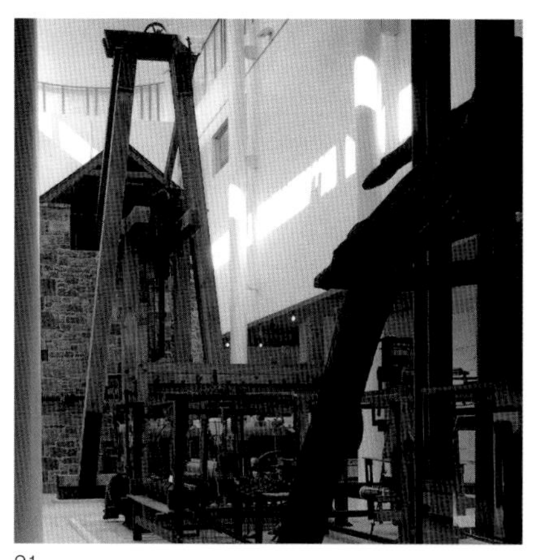
21

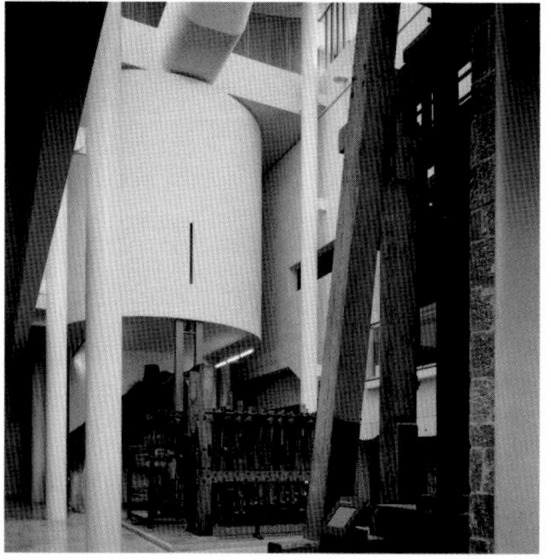
22

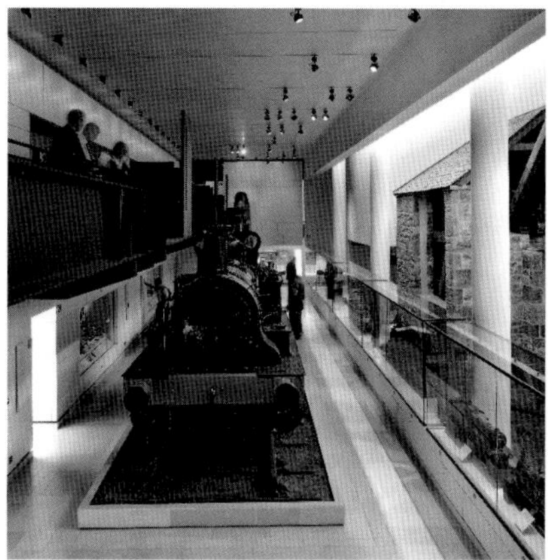
23

principal space in the building, is top-lit from a high clerestory that runs around three sides beneath the hanging, boat-shaped ceiling high above, the underside of the roof garden (21). This is supported on tall steel columns. The whole thing is like a cathedral of the Enlightenment, but is in effect an enormous light well cut into the centre of the core tower. The two uppermost levels of gallery line the space beneath the high windows. First domestic, scientific, engineering and social displays and displays devoted to the great individuals who drove it all and then above them on both sides the 20th century galleries, low rooms that run right around beneath the clerestory windows. Between them, hanging down into the main space, at one end is a cube, at the other a cylinder (22). Both have a small interior room, the lower ones devoted to pottery and silver respectively, the upper ones to interpretation.

Back at the first floor level, beneath the upper galleries the north side is a low enclosed gallery, the south side is open. Then at the next level this is reversed. The north side is an open balcony, and the opposite side is enclosed, except for a row of windows. This open gallery is wide enough for a small railway engine as well as a large whisky still (23). Above it is a narrow open mezzanine. Built in steel, its structure is a private homage from the architects to Scotland's industrial past. These two levels are linked by a small, informal auditorium, little more than an open stair. But the mezzanine is actually the main second level here. Carry on round and you enter the long, low, enclosed galleries devoted to 19th century design, or you can cross a bridge via the top of the lift tower to the restaurant. At this level there are still the surrounding galleries beyond the light wells to south and west, but when you go on up to the 20th century galleries, you are above the line of the outer curtain wall, so they are wholly contained within the central core.

The main first floor space is tall enough to house comfortably not only a thatched, peasant's cruck house but the two-storey stone building of an 18th century beam engine. Architecture within architecture, but quite at home. This was one of the early and definitive curatorial decisions, but of course the whole layout was based on close discussion between architects and curators. That has shaped the building.

A broad bridge here opens back across the atrium. You can pass through the lift tower to a second bridge across to the discovery level on the front of the building. Another linked bridge leads to the first floor of the old museum to the east and, as below, you enter it on its main axis. At the western end of this floor another bridge takes you to the tower, the one important part of the building that is not open to the public. Its two magnificent circular rooms are reserved for the Board of Trustees and the Friends of the Museum respectively. It is a pity, for they

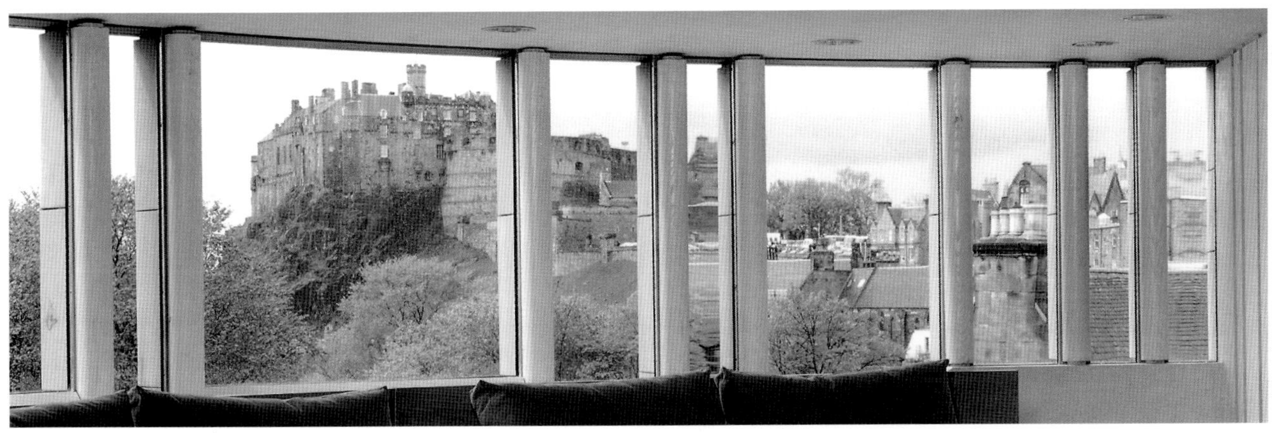

24

command spectacular views from their wide windows (24). But the most startling view is from the staircase built into the wall of the tower that links them. At a turn in the stair you move from dark to light and a tall window suddenly frames the Castle.

Like the light that comes through all these windows, such views remind you that this is all real. The things on display here do not have meaning because they are in a museum. It is the opposite. They are here because of what they bring with them from outside, our collective memory over generations. And if finally you go up to the wide roof terrace and garden, high above Edinburgh, you see that most vividly. Breathtaking views across the city to the sea: the man-made world framed by nature. This is a building wholly integrated with its place and with its function. But it will also be completely at home in the cityscape, for as you look around at roof level you see with what ease this great building has taken its place among its peers and companions, the Castle above, the medieval High Kirk of St Giles, the 17th century Parliament Hall, the 18th century City Chambers, the domes of Edinburgh University's Old College and McEwan Hall and many others all within a few hundred yards.

But among these, though not the grandest, perhaps closest of all in spirit is Geddes's Outlook Tower on the skyline beneath the Castle. In appearance it is no more than a lighthouse that has drifted accidentally into this cityscape. Patrick Geddes was a great champion of the dynamic possibilities of museums, not as dusty places where the past is locked away, but as resources of information, too. The Outlook Tower symbolised the way in which identity is forged from exchange, from two-way communication between our roots in our own community and our links with the wider world, and between our past and our present. It is not a static thing, but a constant process of mediation between fluctuating perceptions. Where this museum is so original is in the way it respects that fact, serves that need. And as here Geddes's thinking was rooted in the uniquely social vision of the Enlightenment, so this building not only gives a fitting home to the objects that reflect the history of which they were part and which shaped that thought, it reflects quality of the thought itself. Geddes would have loved it and understood too the care and imagination that have gone into it to make it the success it is.

Looking out from the roof terrace over Edinburgh to the natural world and the wider landscape of Scotland beyond, you see at a glance how the Musuem of Scotland is not a thing apart. It is a microcosm of all this, a brilliant distillation, and not just because of the collections it contains, but because of the way it reintegrates them with the world from which they come and embodies what is best in the traditions they enshrine.

In search of meaning: An architectural appreciation of the Museum of Scotland

John Allan

"Scotland in miniature" was, as I recall, the tourist tag used to describe the representative scenic completeness of Arran – that lovely island riding at anchor in the Firth of Clyde – whose exquisite silhouette remains etched in my memories of a childhood in Troon. "Scotland in essence" might serve as the equivalent sobriquet to be applied to Benson + Forsyth's new Museum of Scotland to suggest the range and authenticity of this educational and architectural experience. For even a day spent exploring this enthralling building and its contents will vouchsafe more insights and understanding of Scotland's story than might be gained in weeks of well-intentioned sightseeing.

As one of that numberless community of Scots who regarded 'home' as a place you leave (I graduated from Edinburgh in 1966 and have seldom visited since), I am hardly qualified to comment on the domestic or administrative history of this project, though it is clear that the role of the Williams Report in giving impetus to aspirations to rehouse the old Museum of Antiquities, the opportune funding of a former Conservative government, the precarious process of selection by architectural competition and crucial support of the winning scheme by the late Marquis of Bute must all be recounted to provide a proper understanding of its genesis. Nor can I speak of the strenuous and no doubt at times agonising grind of actually building the Museum, though like many others in my profession I have been following its progress with fascination and hope over these past few years. I intend to consider only the visible tip of this huge iceberg of thought and struggle, the building itself and its position in architectural discourse at this end of the 20th century.

The museum is one of the defining building types of our age. This ancient institution, once needed to protect totemic objects and valuable relics from pillage or dispersal and later overlaid by ideals of education, entertainment and cultural ambition, has come to epitomise modern society's ambivalence towards its past, a focus for debate over the role and meaning of "heritage". The museum is also a classifying device, as Thomas Markus has written[1], an instrument for the production of "visible knowledge", and in this instance its role in augmenting Scotland's self-knowledge and emergent sense of national identity is clearly paramount – if also unquantifiable.

Meanwhile another, increasingly explicit, function of the modern museum is as an instrument of economic competition in the civic rivalry of advanced European and American cities. And so when we consider the reinvented identities of Stuttgart, Barcelona, Berlin, Stockholm, Bilbao, Arles, Amsterdam, Los Angeles, we tend to think

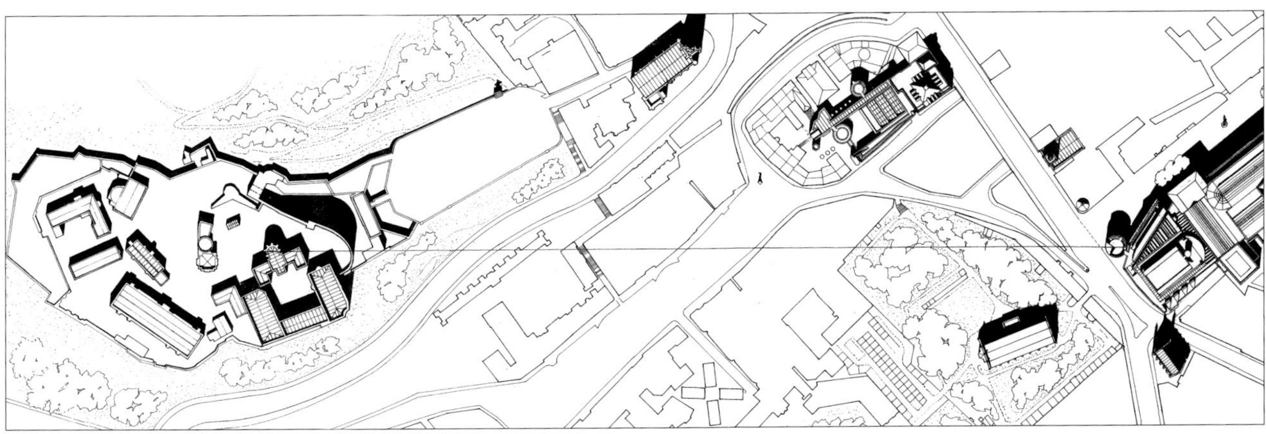

of their new museums by Stirling, Meier, Libeskind, Moneo, Gehry, Ciriani, Piano and Meier again.

Now Benson + Forsyth's Museum of Scotland enters this modern pantheon on equal or better than equal terms. With deep commitment and infinite care they have crafted a masterpiece of architectonic imagination, informed and sustained by tenacious adherence to a simple but central principle — that of casting the building itself in the role of devoted interlocutor. Like Coleridge's ancient mariner, this museum entreats and compels your attention to its story. As old Lubetkin used to say, quoting Pirandello, "facts are like empty sacks — they cannot stand up until we fill them with meaning". Here Benson + Forsyth have taken the "facts"of the collection (which, let it be said, are by no means of equal interest and quality) and filled them with all the meaning they needed, dramatising their presentation and binding the whole into Edinburgh's incomparable mise-en-scene with operatic intensity.

But though the architects have immersed themselves in the subject matter of the collection and found an architectural language to help communicate its messages, they have not succumbed to the design of scenery. The past is apprehended not through sampling but through metaphor. At no point in grappling with their task have they resorted to the architectural short-cut of using quotation marks, the emotional swindle of literal characterisation with which we have become so familiar through the "themed experience" industry. Nor, despite its overt expressionism, have they set out to make a "signature building" as such, exploiting the glamour of the commission to provide its own architectural justification. What they have achieved is far more difficult and far more subtle, in devising a response that is sui generis, undeniably contemporary, Scottish in spirit yet with a reach far beyond its obvious local significance to touch on matters of universal validity — man and nature, social progress, the vicissitudes of national identity.

The potency of this building lies not just in its function as a means of accessing the past, but in thereby suggesting that past's connection to the present — from which in turn a future is being constructed. "The past is never there waiting to be discovered", wrote John Berger, "to be recognised for exactly what it is. History always constitutes the relation between a present and its past. Consequently fear of the present leads to mystification of the past. The past is not for living in; it is a well of conclusions from which we draw in order to act. Cultural mystification of the past entails a double loss. Works of art are made unnecessarily remote. And the past offers fewer conclusions to complete in action."[2] (A fine example of how the mystification of which Berger speaks is avoided here is the treatment of the 'Forty Five' Uprising, which is de-mystified precisely by explaining the mythmaking that went into its aftermath.) Here the exhibits themselves are the material incarnation of the past and the building serves them as "commentary". It is impossible to recreate an earlier form of consciousness and, as Berger says, the past must always be mediated through the present, through commentary. In this process it may be illuminated, diminished, distorted or obscured and the Museum's ultimate value will reside in the quality of authenticity with which it endows its subject matter.

The architecture's palpable engagement with the story amplifies this authenticity, for it denotes recognition of the inescapable fact that it is also implicated in the historical process and is a participant in the story's continuation. The impulses it transmits will be absorbed both privately and collectively, for impossible though it may be to measure, one may be certain that in its ever expanding community of visitors a clearer image and understanding of Scotland will be cultivated. Thus subject and object are joined. The architects' rare contribution is to have interpreted their responsibility in this process in the widest possible way, bringing the whole city and its surroundings into the drama.

So much, for the moment, of the Museum's role; how is this served by its physical configuration? The strategic organisation of the building is the key. An almost square site footprint and the constraint of adjacent rooflines could easily have produced a deep bland volume — "the dumb box" so eagerly adopted by proponents of indeterminacy and flexible space, a volume that would become increasingly illegible and remote as you approached its centre. Instead, the architects have made a community of separate buildings and then exploited the opportunities thereby created to light, link, penetrate, enclose and characterise them in different ways. The range and sovereign control of spatial experience is nothing short of astounding — toplit courtyard, cavernous tunnel, vertiginous crevasse, pillared hall, cubic cell, spacious promenade, measured enfilade, apsidal chamber, and more. The building itself becomes a lexicon of different genres of Scottish space. Likewise the breadth of architectural characterisation — windows wide and narrow, deep and shallow, panoramic and oblique, doorways processional and secret. There are balconies, wells, outlooks, bridges, ramps, staircases — especially staircases, which are given a special role of their own in imparting the heightened frisson of discovery that accompanies the visitor from floor to floor, by allowing alternative wayfinding and a consequent sense of having made your own personal journey through the narrative. Thus sacred relics are hidden in a silent cryptic vault, industrial engines proudly displayed

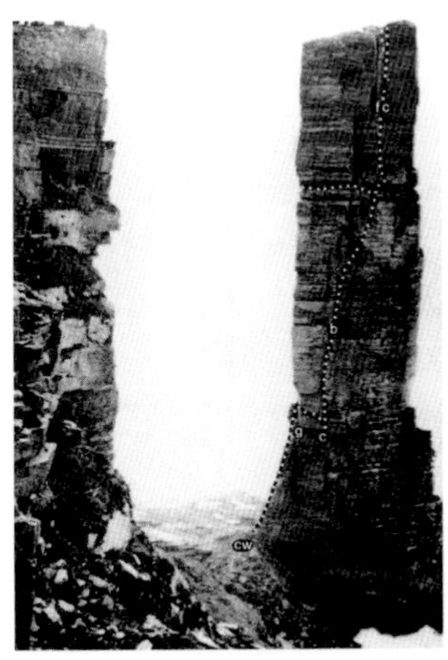

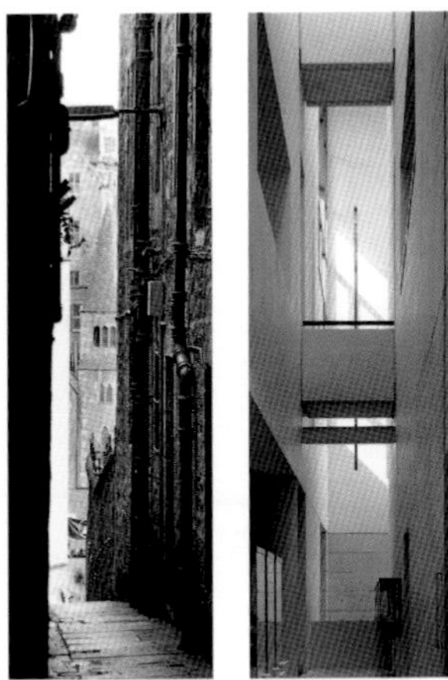

in a lofty machine hall, precious silver hoarded in an architectural jewel box.

Herein lies the paradox, for it might seem as the building feels so architecturally specific, so closely tailored to its current exhibits, that scope for future flexibility has been eliminated. Though developments will ultimately depend on curatorial policy, I would suggest that the Museum's flexibility is not to be sought in the conventional interpretation of neutral galleries and demountable walls — which by supposedly anticipating any eventual need tend to impose a permanent sense of the temporary — but rather in the sheer diversity of spatial and experiential typology that is built in from the start. What prevents this interior specificity from also being prescriptive is the way the actual materials from which it is conjured — ash panelling, bare plaster, concrete, render — are so consistently controlled as never to challenge the exhibits themselves.

No less bold are the architects' policies on structure and servicing. Instead of being vehicles for technical bravura as has become so common in current public projects of this scale and prominence, they are largely buried within the ample poche space that is also used to accommodate many of the cased exhibits. The only explicit manifestation of structure occurs in the wedged shaped basement and upper columned hall.

Old functionalists and engineers may question this relegation of their disciplines to playing merely enabling roles. But then for Benson + Forsyth neither structure nor services nor indeed technique as such have constituted the primary agenda. This is emphatically not the same as saying they lack conscientiousness in relation to these issues. It is rather that they scrupulously distinguish between form and content, between medium and message. As Arthur Drexler wrote in his elegy for the Ecole des Beaux Arts: "Until the advent of the utilitarian engineering style, architecture always and everywhere insisted upon the distinction between itself and building. The former is the domain of freedom of action, conscious choice, and ulterior motives; the latter is the domain of minimum effort in response to external necessity... The effort to decide what is important — to declare value — is something about which we have no choice. It is a function of human intelligence, and to suppose that its difficulties can be avoided is to advocate that we make ourselves stupid. Making our choices intelligible demands a flexibility of architectural speech that accepts the distinction between form and content: the medium is not the message, except when we no longer know what we wish to say."[3]

What is never in doubt here is Benson + Forsyth's acceptance of the architect's responsibility to declare value and to locate that value in the story being told. Of course,

Drexler was writing nearly a quarter of a century ago, before the depredations of post-modernism had converted the abstinence of old modernism into its exact opposite — a self conscious enciphered dialect that constituted its own reference system and which, by suggesting that any utterance betokened significance, effectively dissolved the power of articulate speech. This recent debasement of architectural rhetoric, from which the profession has barely recovered, has left yet another layer of difficulty for architects like Benson + Forsyth concerned to restore architecture's capacity for conveying meaning.

Take the facade for instance, perhaps the most persistent and problematic element in 20th century architecture's quest for aesthetic validity. In the pioneer years its dematerialisation was as much a badge of historicist rejection as an exploitation of the freedom of frame construction. "Facade treatments do not form part of the common theory of the Modern Movement as our elders and betters have it", wrote Reyner Banham in 1954 in mock didactic vein. "In the pure theory the problem of the facade does not exist; form follows function, and when the problems of the interior have been correctly resolved, the exterior form will be found to have crystallised into an unarguable solution."[4]

Yet it was precisely the continuing inhibition of modern architects from allowing an elevation to express anything more than the vertical expression of its plan or the constructional necessities of its materials that produced the vacuum so opportunistically and embarrassingly exploited by post-modernism. With Benson + Forsyth undaunted by these failures, the facade emerges again as an articulate instrument of urban negotiation, connecting the Museum with its neighbours in place and time. Their primary differentiation of the outer ring of building from inner core allows the former to participate in the anecdotal circumstances of the site boundary while the latter stands white and clean, defined by its gridded clarity. A castle and its keep? The new unfamiliar present emerging like a seed from the old shell of the past? A giant wrapped in a mighty stone plaid, pinned at the shoulder by the circular brooch of its entrance tower? The search for suitable metaphors only testifies to the density of latent meanings in a vocabulary fully recharged.

And how, incidentally, is it possible for a building clad in million year old material to appear so contemporary? By the way it is done, of course. Even the technically uninitiated can sense that this stone wall is a modern thing. Quite apart from the absence of historical mouldings and cornices, the ubiquitous open joints, incised with meticulous precision and demonstrating that no single stone

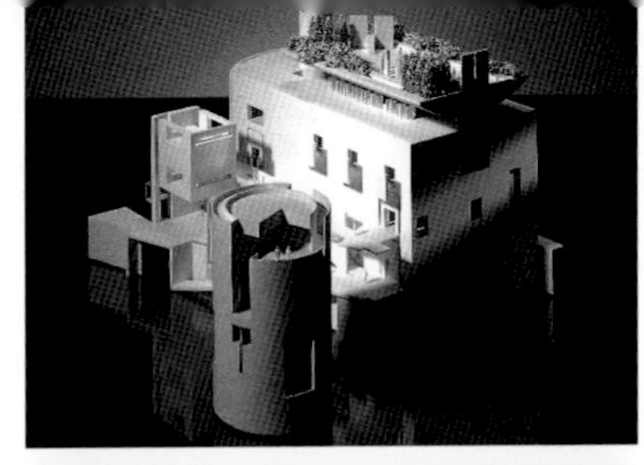

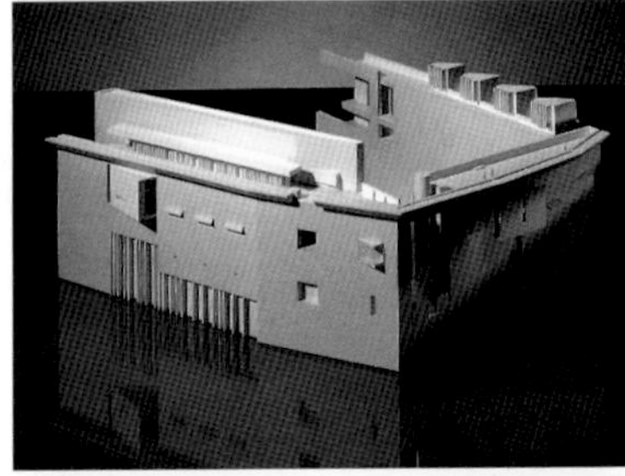

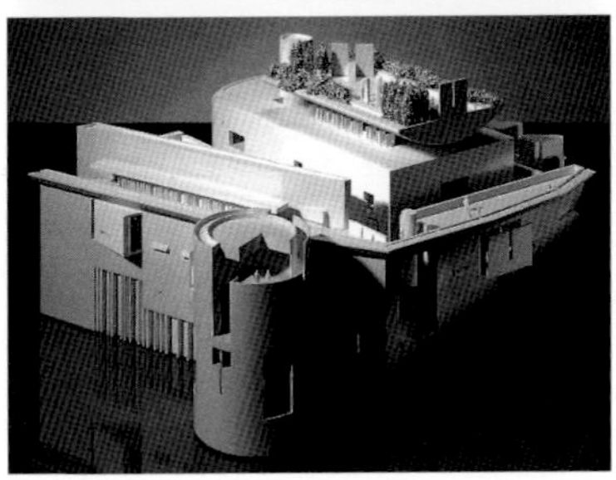

touches another, tell you that it cannot be a traditional compressive structure. As Marcel Breuer wrote in 1937, "the basis of modern architecture is not the new materials, nor even the new form, but the new mentality."[5]

Such thoughts of the building's response to its site surely lead on to a consideration of the Museum's place in Edinburgh as a whole. It is here, to my mind, that Benson + Forsyth's search for meaning yields its richest rewards. Their achievement is not only to convincingly embed this huge new institution in an ancient city but to do so in a way that offers new perspectives on the city itself. As far as its contribution to urban improvement is concerned, modern architecture's reputation has not been good. Even before Jane Jacobs exposed the inadequacies of modern city planning it was evident that contemporary buildings and infrastructure, through their preoccupation with the solution of immediate programmatic needs, tended too often to neglect the larger civic and social obligations of their setting.

But "History builds the town" declared the modern pedagogue Arthur Korn, and there must be few places to which this injunction could be more readily applied than Edinburgh. In 1969 the Edinburgh Architectural Association astutely observed: "The most acute problem which Edinburgh sets to today's architects and developers is not that of character...but simply of opportunity and its proper use. Small sites in established areas may offer an interesting challenge, but it is the strictly limited number of larger developments which will decide whether the present century will establish itself in a great and continuing city."[6]

After thirty more years of building this cautiousness seems well justified in the light of many of the large but inconsequential developments of modern Edinburgh — bland corporate headquarters, meretricious hotels, nondescript commercial and public buildings — which readily avail themselves of Edinburgh's scenic resources while offering little or nothing in return. To be sure, Edinburgh owes its unique identity more to its innate topography than to any single building within it. But even this indigenous drama can lose its potency through being employed passively as mere scenery rather than being cross-examined for its meanings. Now the Museum's determined engagement with its surroundings begins a whole new chapter in Edinburgh's self-explanation. Indeed it is in making these connections that the architects articulate the significance of geography and history through their representation in the horizontal and vertical axes of the building.

Let us start with the dramatic splay in the Chambers Street facade. This is readily grasped as a means of making space for the cylindrical corner tower which so satisfyingly marks the confluence of surrounding streets.

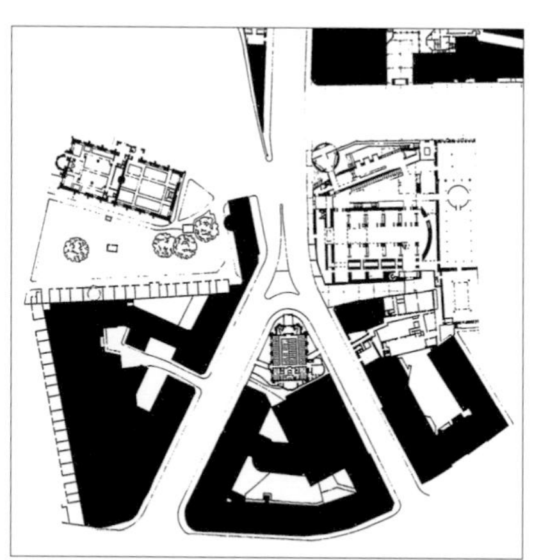

Also well-noted in published commentary to date is the rapport established between this tower and the Castle Half Moon Battery half a mile to the north-west. But there is another more subtle and perhaps more profound consequence of this oblique geometry, which begins to make itself felt as you contemplate the Nolli plan. It is the almost exact reflection of this splay in the splayed orientation of Greyfriars Church, as if both buildings had been set out symmetrically from the extended centre-line of George IV Bridge. The effect of this manoeuvre is to join the three otherwise disparate principal buildings at this end of the street – Greyfriars Church, The University Chaplaincy (as I still think of it), and the Museum itself – into a coherent ensemble to counterbalance the Bank of Scotland at the other end.

From being simply an important feeder road to the Southside, George IV Bridge is raised to the status of an axis, a spatial vector in an urban forcefield, which in turn now projects a still more powerful beam north-west towards the New Town. The ramifications gather momentum as you begin to see how the ripples of this pebble spread across the city plan. Instead of only reading Edinburgh's urban grain east-west as one always has – the medieval line of High Street and Canongate being repeated by the triple corridor of the New Town – you now begin to revalue the significance of the north-south connections, the Bridges, Lothian Road and the crucial central link – Hanover Street and George IV Bridge, joined though the sinuous docking mechanism of The Mound. One's consciousness is directed northwards and one appreciates again the role played by the Forth in containing the composition, absorbing the energy transmitted by this axis as it attenuates across the hinterlands of Goldenacre, Trinity and Newhaven.

With the Museum having prompted this reappraisal of the city's laylines, one looks afresh at the monuments punctuating the central area, registers their historical signatures, their material testament to the priorities of their makers, and becomes aware of the legibility their cumulative presence imparts to the whole town – a legibility which in strength if not in scale can surely match that of any of the great cities of Europe.

In the optimistic preface to his epic book *Design of Cities* Edmund Bacon invoked the image of "the city as an act of will", expressing his hope of dispelling the idea "so widely and uncritically held, that cities are a kind of grand accident, beyond the control of the human will, and that they respond only to some immutable law." "The building of cities is one of man's greatest achievements," Bacon contends. "The form of his cities always has been and always will be a pitiless indicator of the state of his civilisation. This form is determined by the multiplicity of decisions made by people

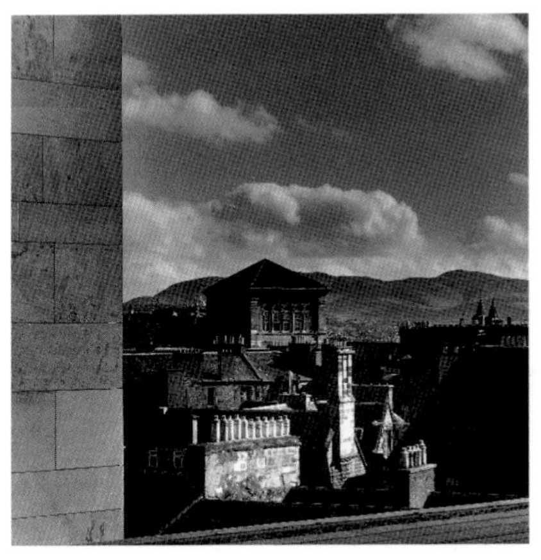

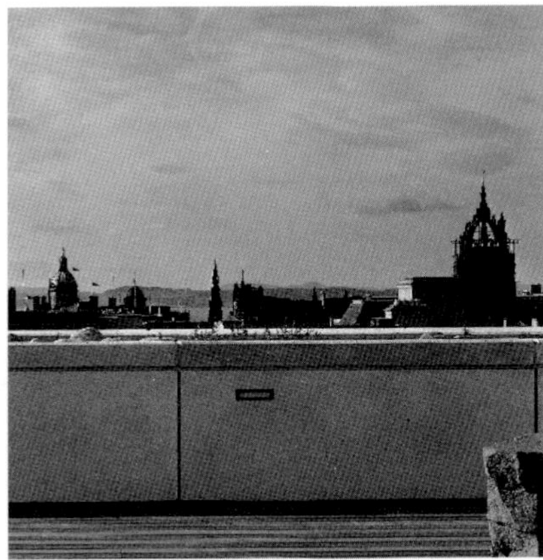

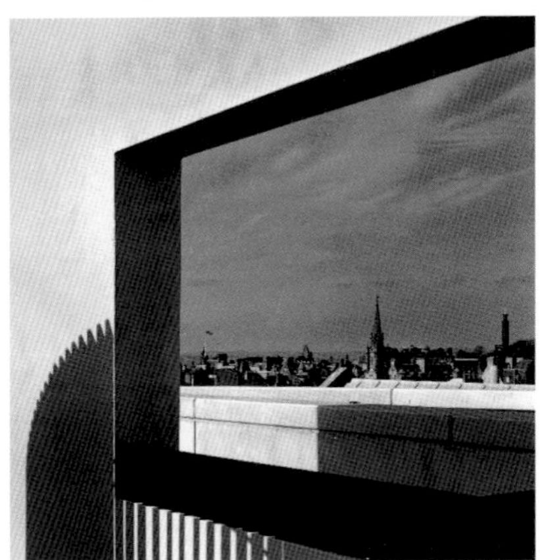

who live in it. In certain circumstances these decisions have interacted to produce a force of such clarity and form that a noble city has been born."[7]

In Edinburgh's case its prestige as "a noble city" has seemed so secure for so long as to obscure the realisation that its process of formation was just such an act of human will, neither inevitable nor immutable, but sustained over centuries and still ongoing. That the building of the new Museum of Scotland might suggest a renewal of this understanding could hardly have been expected, but such is the domino effect of Benson + Forsyth's intervention.

And we have still to reach the roof garden, which adds yet another dimension to one's appreciation of the city. This seemingly gratuitous, but actually fundamental gesture, raised aloft and presented to Edinburgh like an honorific quaich, completes the time loop that began in the basement with Scotland's primordial rocks. The long ascent from sedimentary compression to this aerial release, placing the visitor himself in the larger showcase of Edinburgh and its environs, reveals the central force of nature – and specifically Scotland's landscape – as the constant factor in the story. Looking back towards the Museum from the Castle Esplanade, seen against the backdrop of Arthur's Seat, surely nobody can fail to grasp what this lapidary building is trying to show us. It is vital that the Museum authorities exploit and maintain these upper outdoor levels – they are an integral part of the building's message and of the educational experience the Museum exists to provide.

This brief appreciation of the Museum of Scotland would not be complete without some concluding reflections on its position in contemporary architectural culture at the millennial "bend in the road". I have perforce used the term "modern" or "modernism" at several points in this essay with increasing uneasiness, realising that its connotations and its products are becoming ever more historic.

In 1980 the art critic Robert Hughes wrote: "When one speaks of 'the end of modernism'...one does not invoke a sudden historical terminus. Histories do not break off clean like a glass rod; they fray, stretch and come undone, like rope; and some strands never part. There was no specific year in which the Renaissance ended, but it did end, although culture is still permeated with the remnants of Renaissance thought. So it is with modernism, only more so, because we are that much closer to it. Its reflexes still work, its limbs move, the parts are mostly there, but they no longer seem to function as a live organic whole. The modernist achievement will continue to affect culture for decades to come, because it was so large, so imposing, and so irrefutably convincing. But our relation to its hopes has become nostalgic."[8]

Architecturally the Museum of Scotland is rooted in modernism, of that there can be no doubt. It is predicated upon the modern principle of abstraction. Its forms are refined until purged of literal references, leaving only a series of timeless echoes. The echoes of Le Corbusier and Mackintosh are clearly audible. But then so are those of Soane, Hawksmoor and Piranesi. The architects neither suppress nor recycle architectural tradition. They metabolise it. Yet the search for influences is ultimately not the point, for as Telemann reputedly observed "no influence is beneficial unless it is transcended", and such transcendence is abundantly evident here.

The issue is less one of stylistic provenance and more to do with architectural values, with whether a cultural statement of this kind offers directions to the future. In this other sense the Museum of Scotland is not 'modern' at all, but deeply traditional. The belief that architecture's capacity to convey meanings is still a relevant or progressive attribute is itself under attack. Indeed it is argued as being the ultimate betrayal of the pioneer modernists' self-imposed mission which, according to this polemic, was precisely to liberate architecture of its monumental art-historical burden to become a life-sustaining instrument of service, valued only to the extent and for as long as that service might be needed. By this criterion it is not such projects as the Museum of Scotland that signpost architecture's future, but the ubiquitous and burgeoning big sheds, distribution centres and service complexes of the post-industrial age.

Such iconoclastic visions are nowhere more cogently argued than by the critic Martin Pawley in his recent study of "terminal architecture" – a deliberate double-entrendre signifying both the mortality of the architectural discipline as traditionally understood, and the urgent priority of future building to accommodate the systems, networks and controls that underpin our current social existence. "The architectural profession that survives into the 21st century," writes Pawley, "has the opportunity to become the producer of instruments, not a creator of monuments. It need no longer be enslaved by ideas of value drawn from the 'treasure houses' and museums of antiquity. Instead it will be free to exploit the products of research and development in every developing field of technology, living like a parasite upon the body of all productive industry, from aerospace to biotechnology – a paperless profession that will travel light, relying on electronic brainwork instead of voodoo symbolism and the tribal taboo of the past."[9]

The strength of this proposition is undeniable, but it is surely not universal, and it certainly does not cover the sorts of problems with which the Museum of

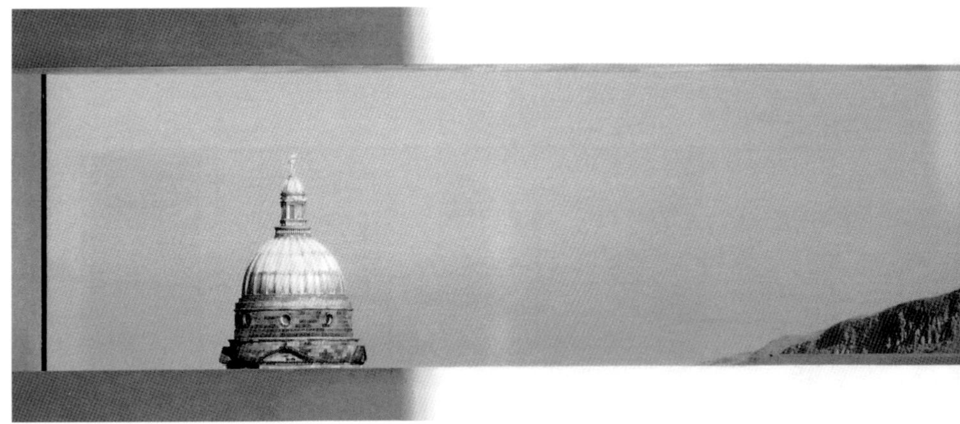

Scotland has to contend. Worship of information transmission instead of information content may simply be another form of idolatry. The tabula rasa upon which the fulfilment of Pawley's vision apparently depends is only imaginable in a geographical and historical vacuum, and as the modernists themselves soon discovered, no such vacuum exists. "Voodoo symbolism" and "tribal taboo" are at least as powerful as the Internet and virtual reality. They too occupy a sort of cyberspace in collective sub-consciousness, hard-wired onto the cultural home page of their originating society. Specifically, what a thousand-year-old carving has which even the brightest digitised image of it has not, is aura. And therein lies the essence of the museum as an institution. It is the act of confronting the artefact and sensing its materiality that connects us with its maker and his humanity. And it is ultimately the continuity of that humanity with our own that is the only constituent of the past that does not date.

In taking its stand on the "traditional" side of this argument, the Museum of Scotland also flies in the face of much of the new wisdom that departmentalises design as a sub-set of procurement strategy, project management and product delivery. Perhaps such marginalisation is only to be expected in the vapid development that the modern world predominantly requires. Projects like this one will always be the exception and never the rule. But it surely cannot be denied that this degrading of architecture as a creative agent of the future slowly and steadily reduces the resonance of the built environment and reinforces its gathering undertow of alienation and meaninglessness. After all else, it is for its glorious and defiant resistance of this apocalyptic and perhaps avoidable prospect that Benson +Forsyth's Museum of Scotland must be celebrated and cherished.

Notes

1. Markus, T. *Buildings and Power*, Routledge, 1993 p.171
2. Berger, J. *Ways of Seeing*, Pelican, 1972, p.11
3. Drexler, A. (Ed) *The Architecture of the Ecole des Beaux Arts*, Secker & Warburg, 1977, p.42
4. Banham, R. 'Facade', *Architectural Review*, vol. 116, 1954, p,303
5. Breuer, M. 'Architecture and Material', *Circle*, Faber and Faber, 1937, 1971, p.194
6. The Edinburgh Architectural Association, *Edinburgh – An Architectural Guide*, 1969
7. Bacon, E. *Design of Cities*, Thames and Hudson, 1967, 1978, p.13
8. Hughes, R. *The Shock of the New*, Thames and Hudson, 1980, 1991, p.376
9. Pawley, M. *Terminal Architecture*, Reaktion Books, 1998, p.208.

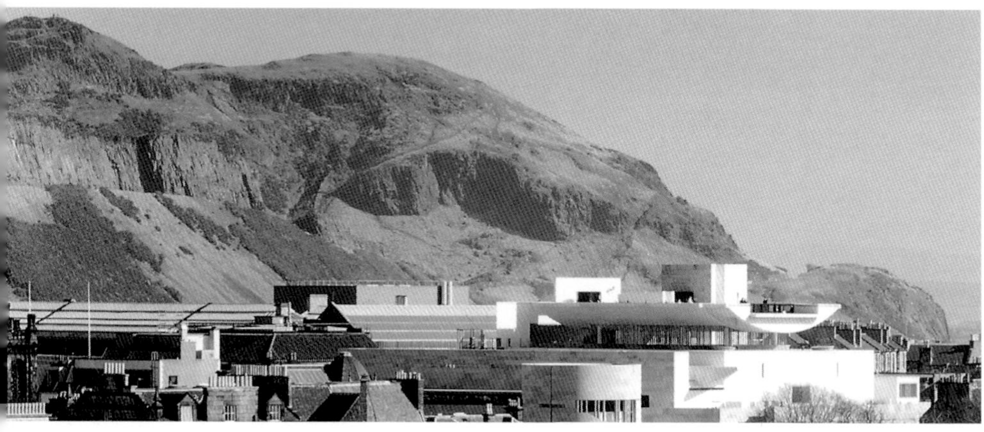

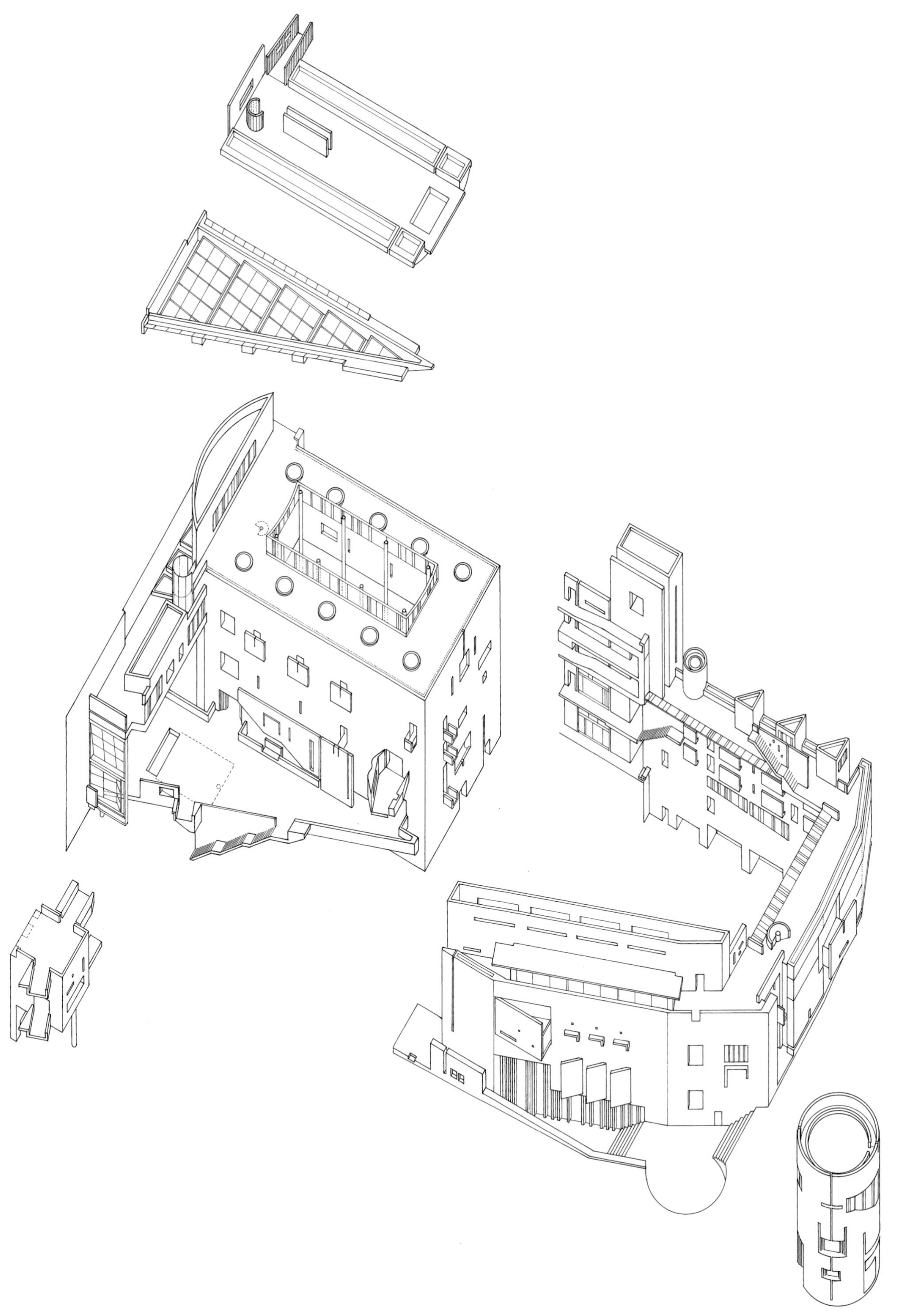

Ground floor

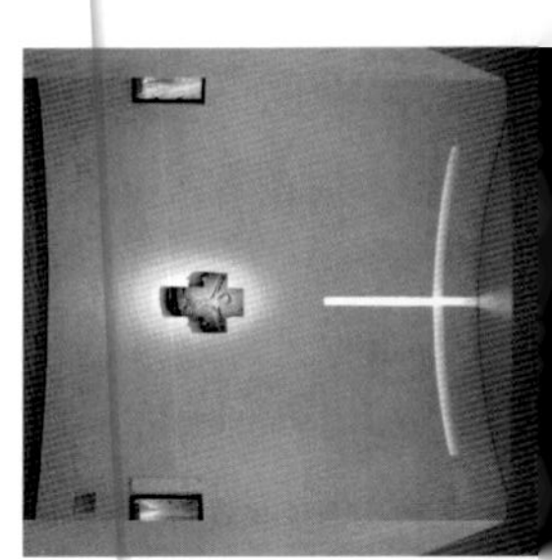

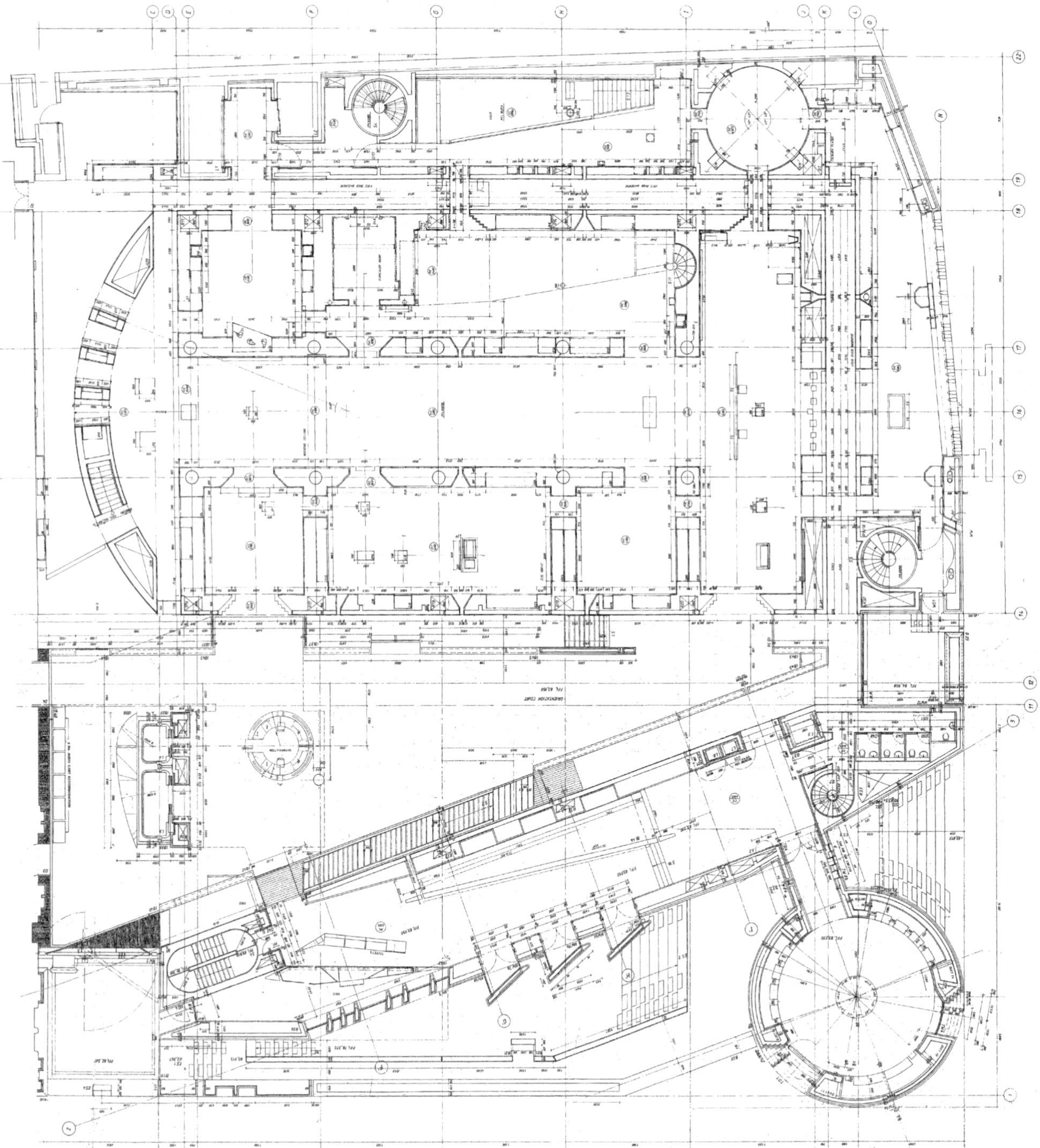

First floor

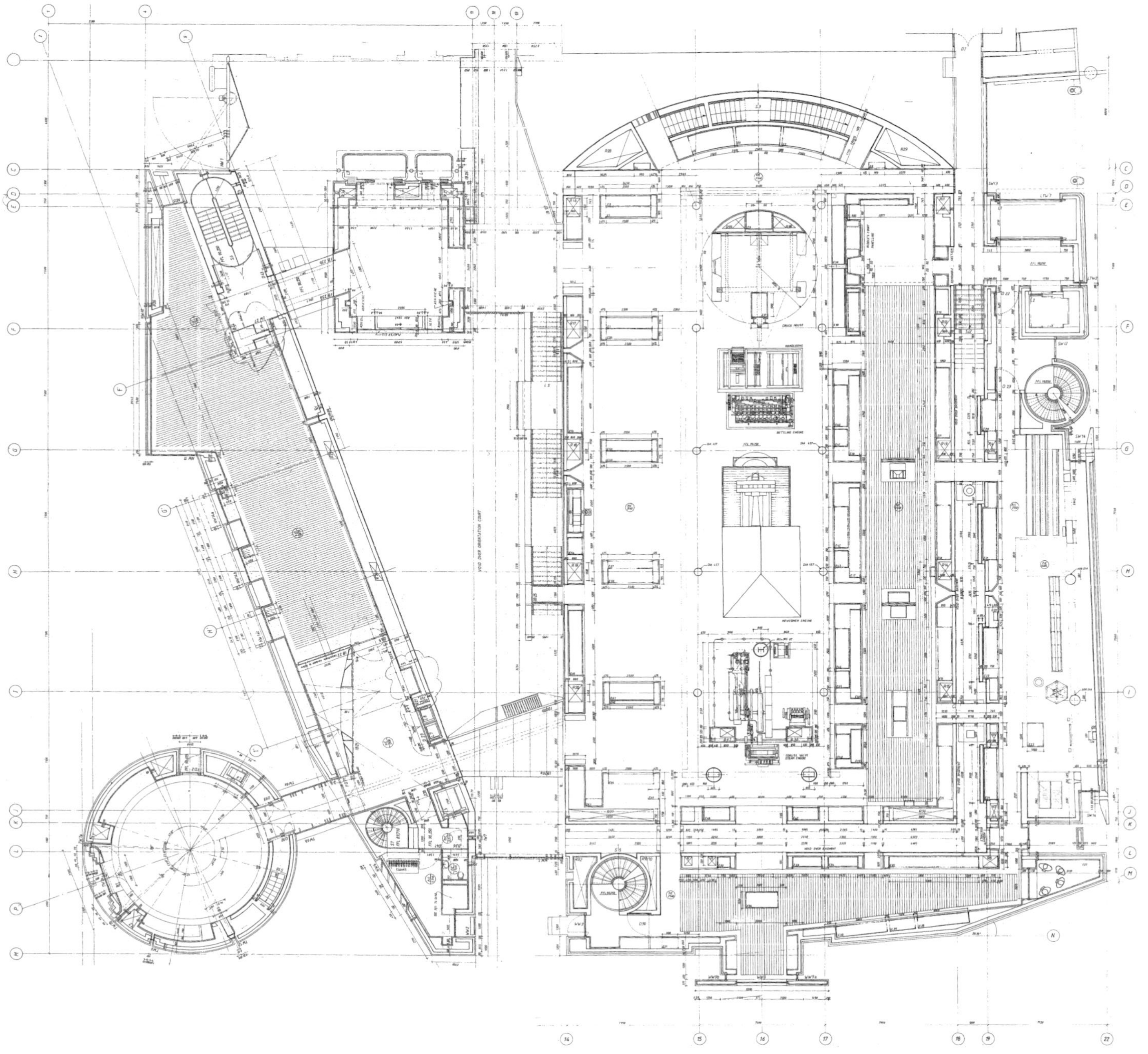

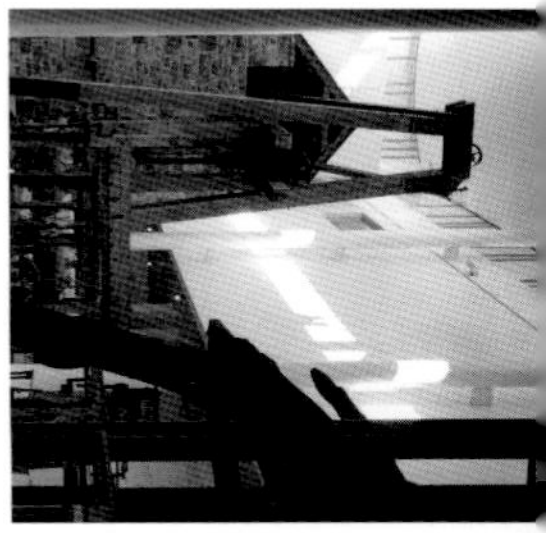

VOID OVER ORIENTATION COURT
C
D
E
F
G
H
I
J
K
L
M
N
P
14
15
16
17
18
19
22

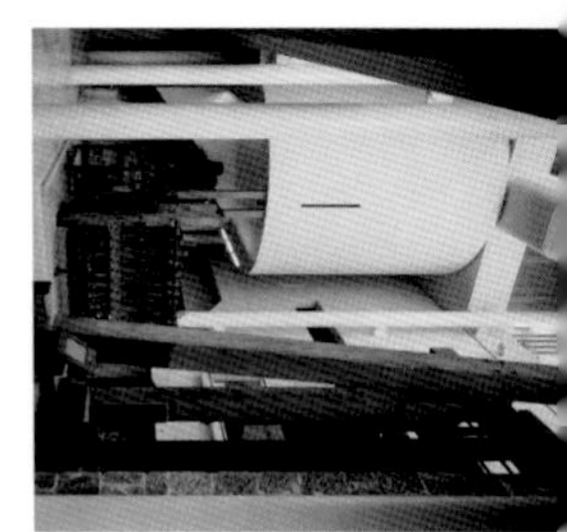

Tower section

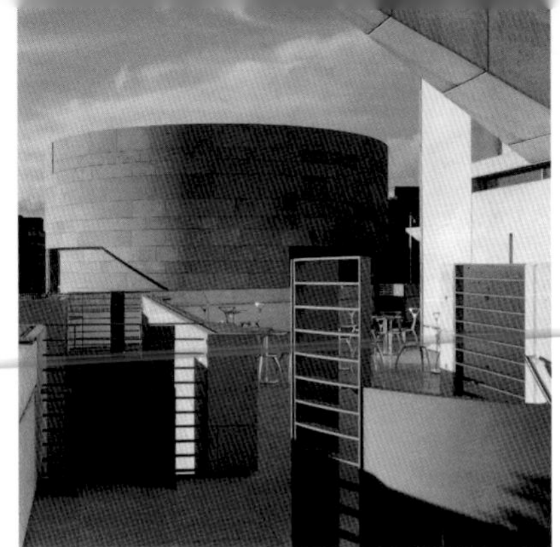

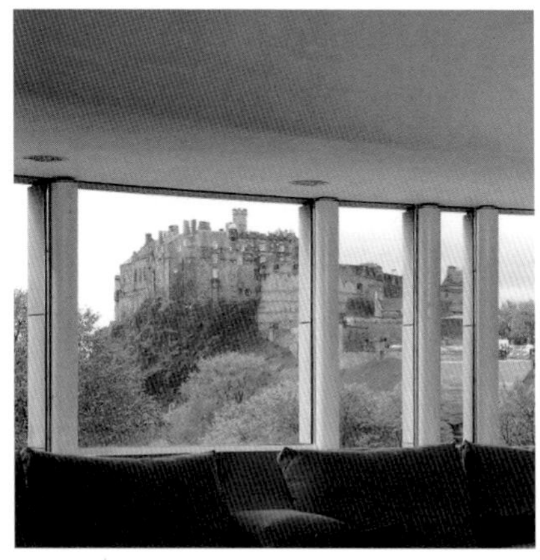

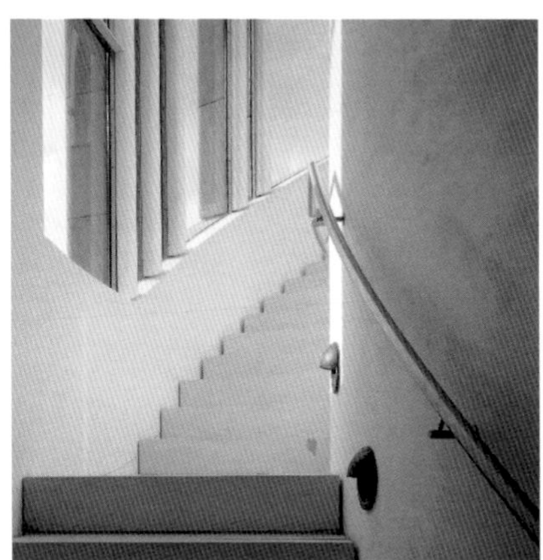

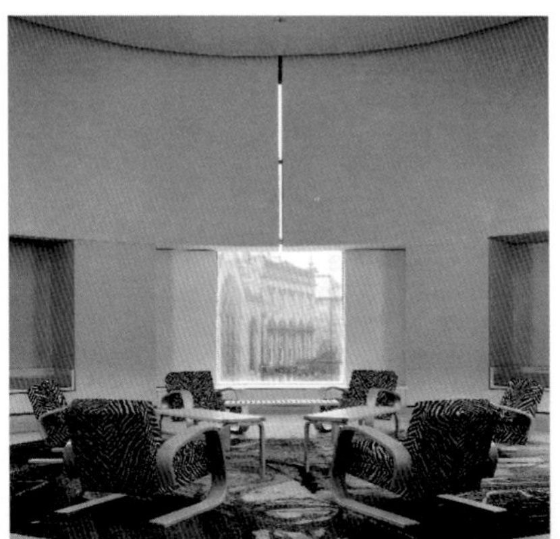

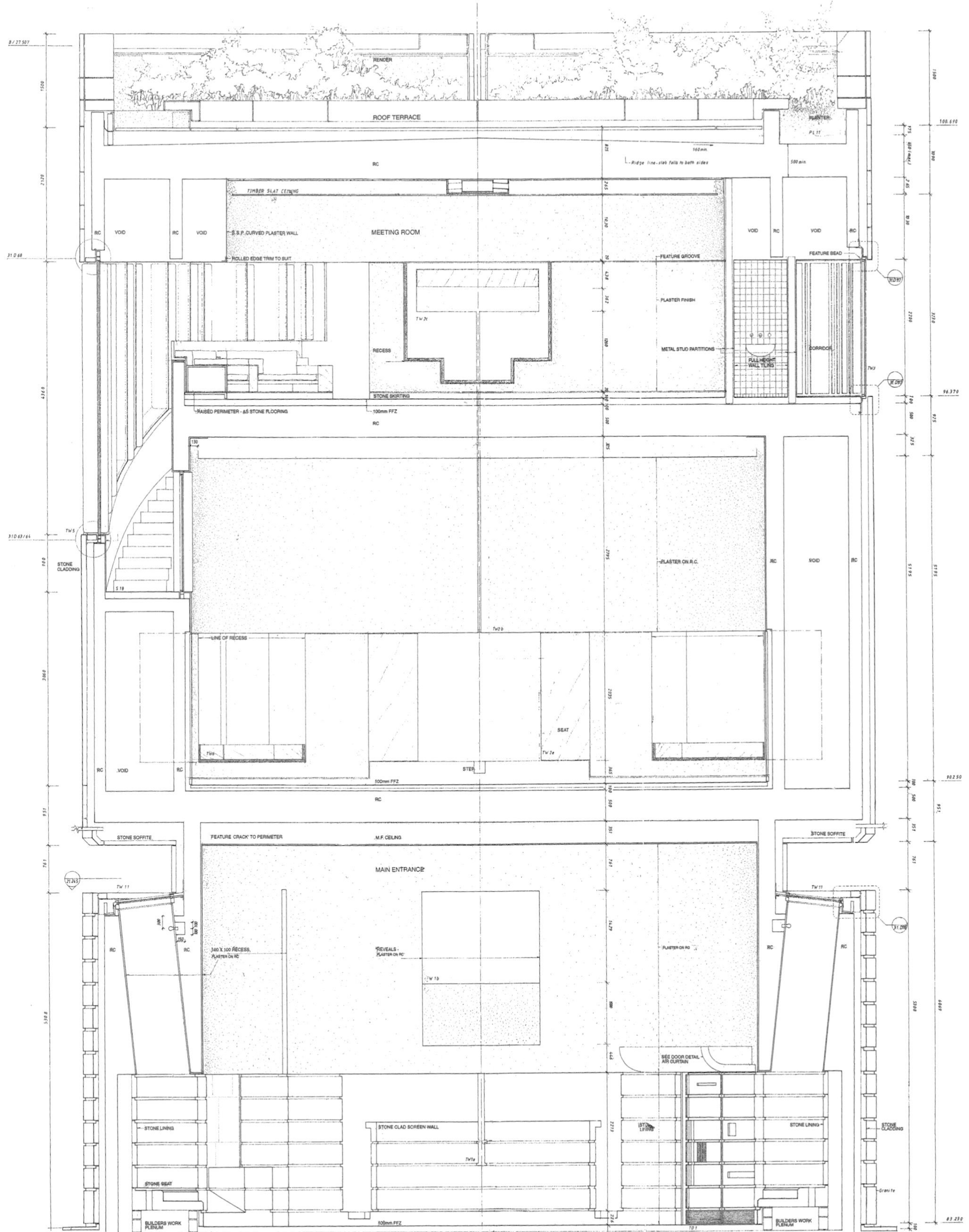

Tower plan

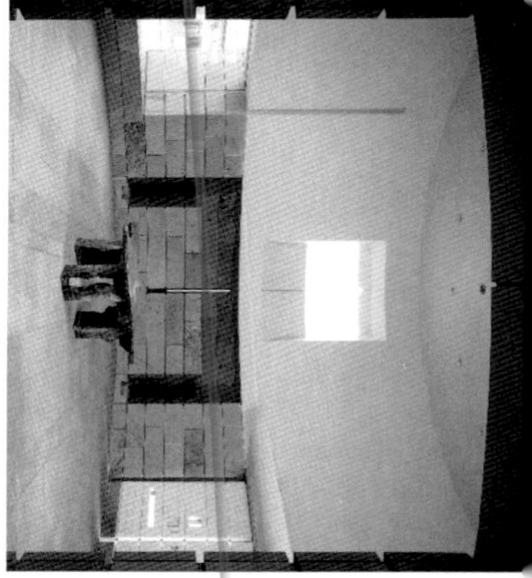

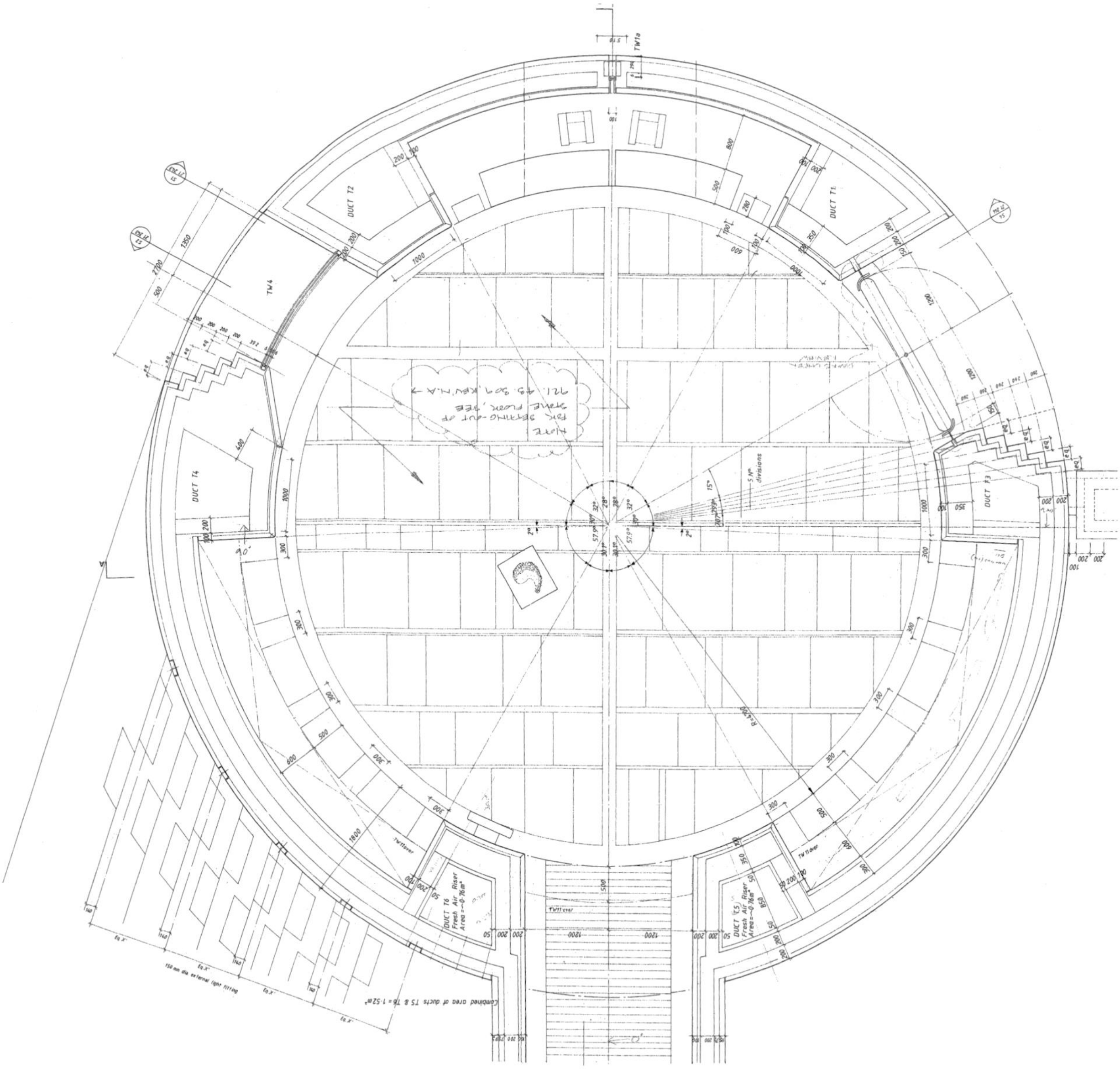

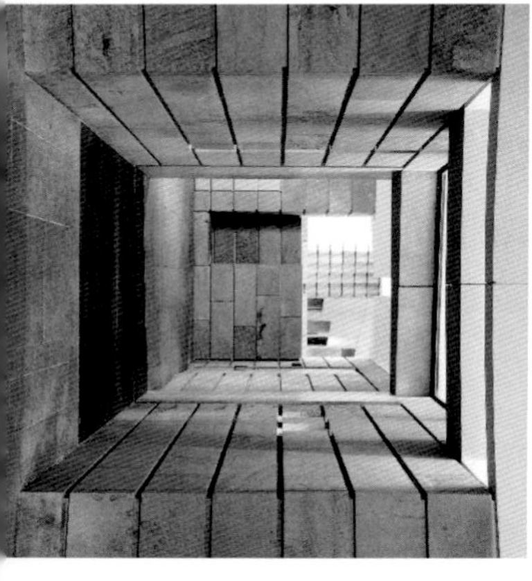

Tower details

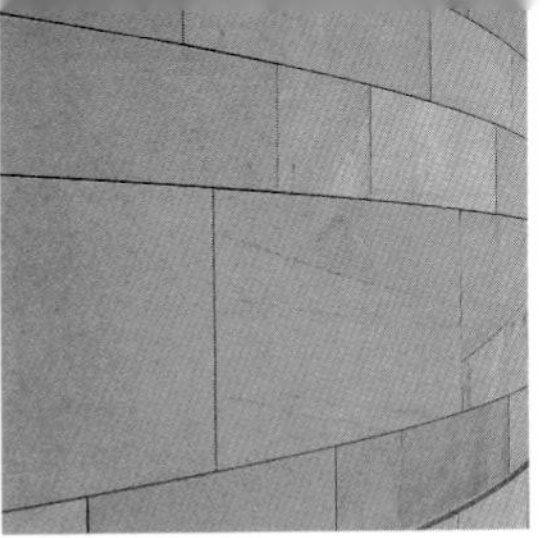

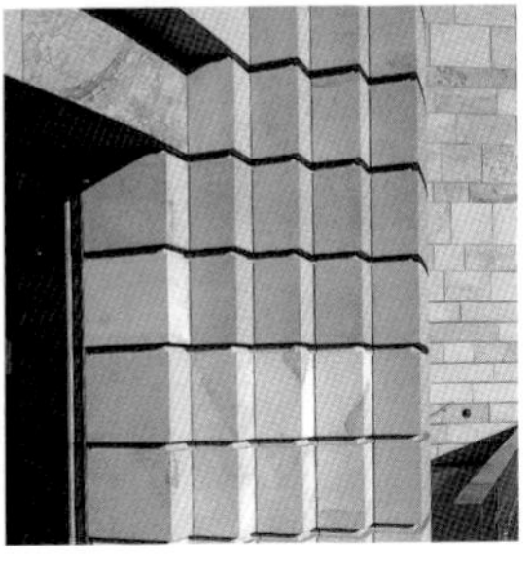

PLAN 6

PLAN 3

PLAN 2

PLAN 1

PLAN 7

SECTION 1

SECTION 2

SECTION 3

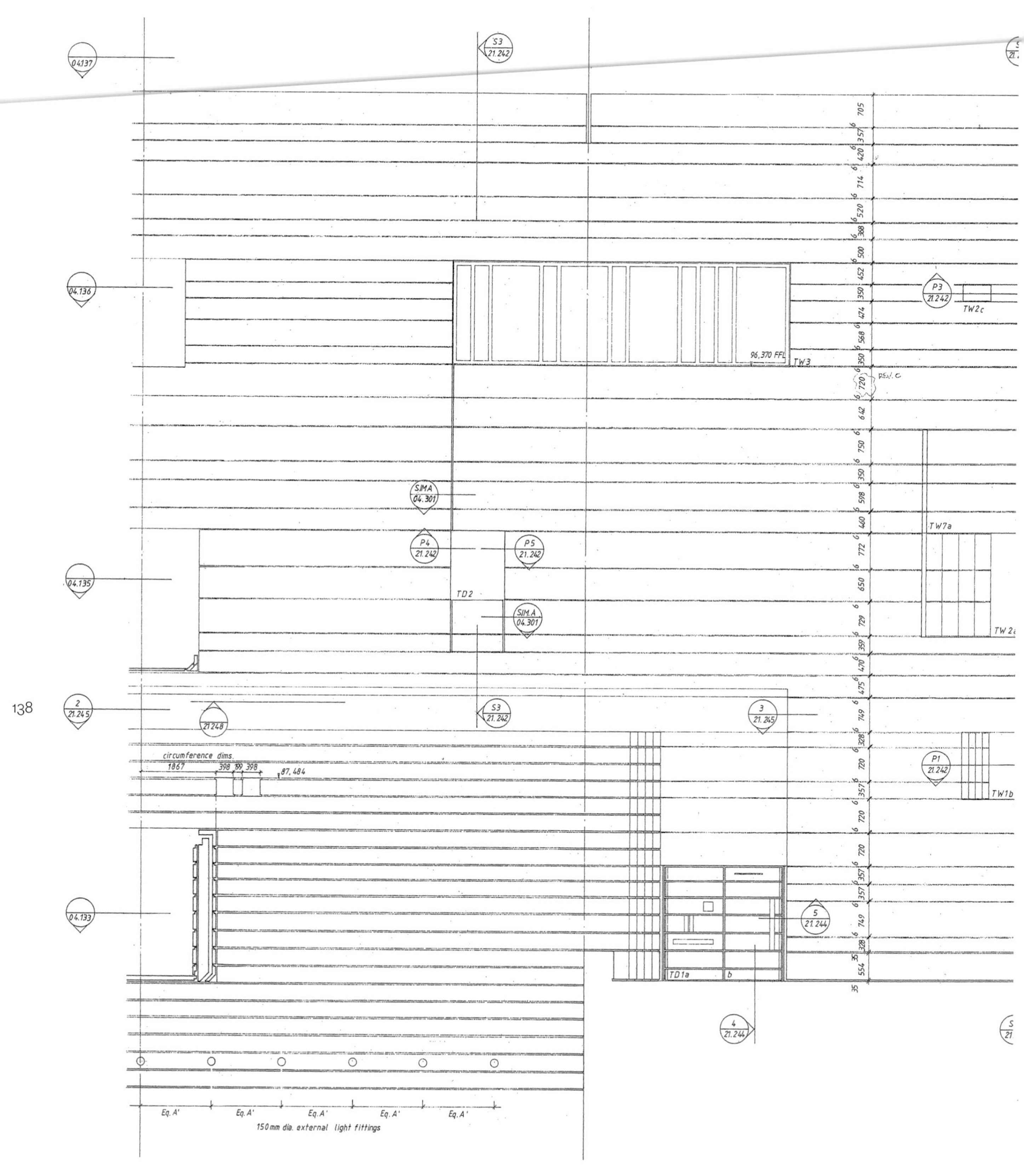
04.137
S3 21.242
04.136
P3 21.242
TW2c
96,370 FFL
TW3
REV. C
SIM.A 04.301
P4 21.242
P5 21.242
TD2
04.135
TW7a
2 21.245
21.248
3 21.245
circumference dims.
1867
398
199
398
87,484
P1 21.242
TW1b
04.133
5 21.244
TD1a
b
4 21.244
Eq. A'
Eq. A'
Eq. A'
Eq. A'
Eq. A'
150mm dia. external light fittings
705
357
420
714
520
500
452
350
474
568
350
720
642
750
350
598
460
772
650
729
359
470
475
749
328
720
357
720
720
357
357
749
328
554
35

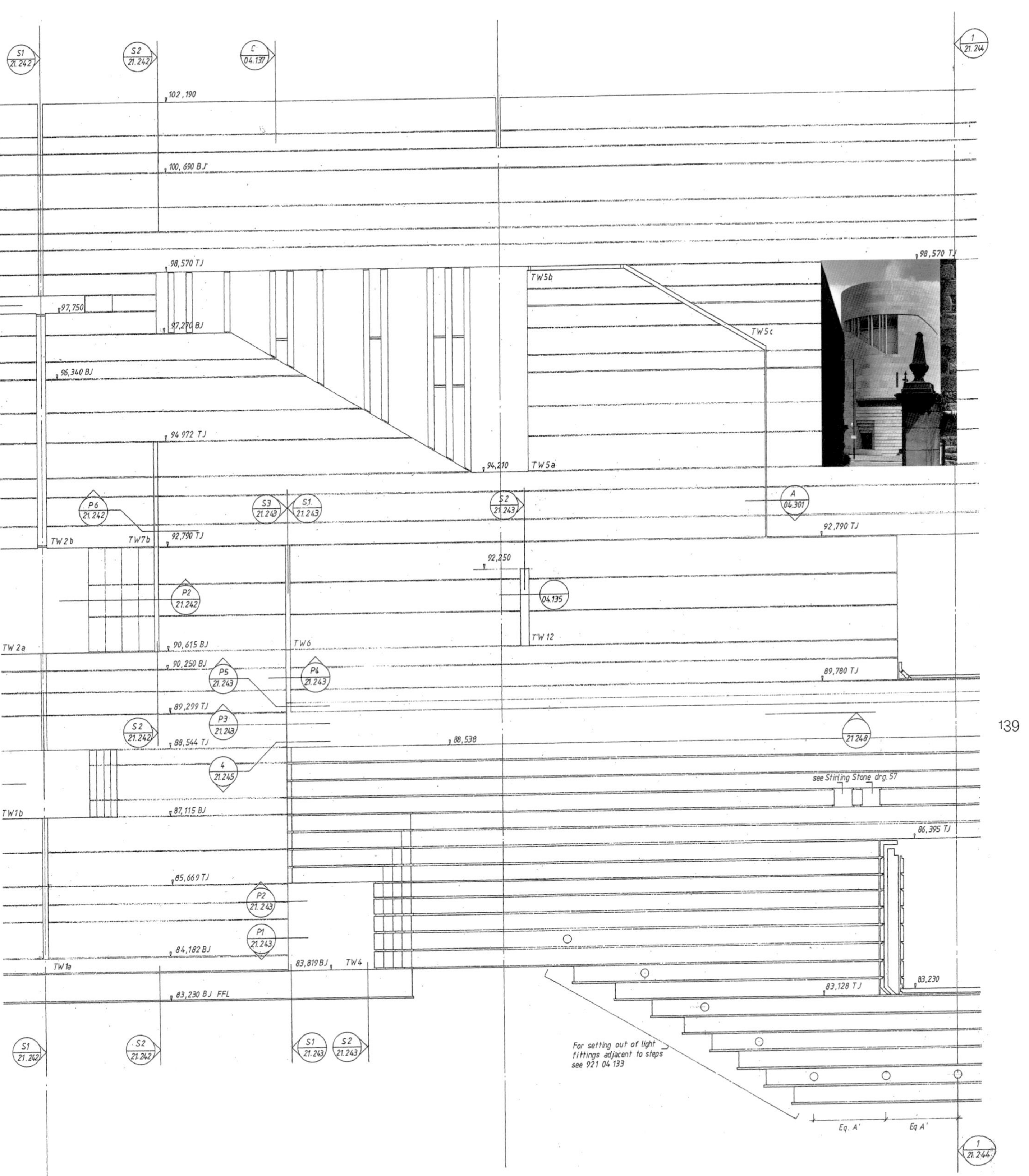

S1 21.242
S2 21.242
C 04.137
1 21.244
102,190
100,690 BJ
98,570 TJ
97,750
97,270 BJ
96,340 BJ
94 972 TJ
94,210
TW5a
TW5b
TW5c
A 04.301
P6 21.242
S3 21.243
S1 21.243
S2 21.243
TW2b
TW7b
92,790 TJ
92,250
P2 21.242
04.135
TW12
TW2a
TW6
90,615 BJ
90,250 BJ
P5 21.243
P4 21.243
89,780 TJ
89,299 TJ
P3 21.243
88,544 TJ
88,538
21.248
4 21.245
see Stirling Stone drg. 57
TW1b
87,115 BJ
86,395 TJ
85,669 TJ
P2 21.243
P1 21.243
84,182 BJ
TW1a
83,819 BJ
TW4
83,230 BJ FFL
83,128 TJ
83,230
For setting out of light fittings adjacent to steps see 921 04 133
Eq. A'
Eq A'

Built work	Museum of Scotland Opened to the Public	30 November 1998
	Gallery 22 MOS Administration Building	1997
	The Jyohanna Museum, Japan	1994
	The Divided House, Oshima, Japan	1994
	Pavilion, Glasgow Garden Festival	1989
	Boarbank Oratory	1985
	Boarbank Hall Physiotherapy Room	1986
	Marico Furniture Workshop and Residence	1979
	Maiden Lane Stage 1	1976
	Lamble Street Housing	1975
	Mansfield Road Housing	1975
	Branch Hill Housing	1974
Work in progress	National Gallery of Ireland Millennium Wing	Due to be completed Sept 2000
Competitions	National Assembly for Wales	Competition finalist 1998
	Scottish Parliament Competition	Shortlisted entry 1998
	Scottish Parliament Feasibility Study	1998
	National Gallery of Ireland	Winner 1996
	Victoria & Albert Museum	Competition finalist 1996
	Cowgatehead Library, Edinburgh	First prize 1995
	New Museum of Scotland International Competition	Winner 1991
	Strathclyde University Science Innovation Centre	Proposal 1989
	Petershill St. Paul's M.E.P.C.	Limited competition 1989
	New Theatre in Cumbria	First prize 1989
	Glasgow Auditorium	First prize 1989
	Glasgow Eurodrome	First prize 1988
	Isle of Dogs Mixed Development, London	Proposal 1985
	ICI Building	Selected entry
	Kew Gardens Building	Selected entry
	Northallerton Civic Centre	Commendation
	New Parliamentary Building	Commendation
	ABS Home	2nd premium
	Hebden Bridge Civic Centre	2nd premium
Awards	The Royal Fine Art Commission Trust and British Sky Broadcasting Building of the Year Award 1999 Museum of Scotland	June 1999
	The Scottish Design Awards (Museum of Scotland): Best New Building Scottish; Architect of the Year; Scottish Design Team of the Year; Chairman's Award; Public Space; Environmental Design; Scottish Design Awards Industry Choice; Office Interior	May 1999
	American Institute of Architecture Excellence in Design Awards Museum of Scotland	Winner January 1999
	Royal Incorporation of Architects in Scotland/Edinburgh Architectural Association Annual Awards Museum of Scotland	Winner February 1999
	British Design and Art Direction – Temple of Time, Oshima International Silver Award	Winner 1996
	BBC Design Award – Boarbank Oratory	Winner 1987
	AR International Interior Design Award	Winner 1982
Teaching	Design Tutors at the Architectural Association Dip.	1977–1986
	Gordon Benson held the Chair of Architecture at the University of Strathclyde	1986–1990
	Gordon Benson Simpson's Professor, Edinburgh University	1991-1996

Publications	*Museum of Scotland* – National Press coverage	November 1998 – May 1999
	Drum Magazine Museum of Scotland	June 1999
	MacMag Museum of Scotland	June 1999
	The Architectural Review Museum of Scotland	April 1999
	Building Review Museum of Scotland	April 1999
	Royal Society of Arts Journal Museum of Scotland	April 1999
	The Architects' Journal Museum of Scotland Focus	February 1999
	Prospect – Architecture in Scotland Museum of Scotland	December 1998
	RIBA Journal Museum of Scotland – Building of the Month	December 1998
	Architect's Journal Museum of Scotland	26 November 1998
	Building Design Museum of Scotland	27 November 1998
	Building Magazine Museum of Scotland	October 1998
	Architects Journal Museum of Scotland Profiled	April 1998
	RIBA Journal Museum of Scotland Profiled	November 1997
	Building Design Cowgatehead Library	17 March 1995
	Architectural Review Jyohanna	April 1994
	G.A. Japan Environmental Design 02	Winter 1993
	G.A. Japan Environmental Design 05	Autumn 1993
	L'Arca 58 Cumbria Theatre	March 1992
	Kenchiku Bunka Vol 47Japanese Projects	April 1992
	Building Design Japanese Projects Practice Profile	21 February 1992
	S.D. 'London Avant-Garde'	February 1992
	Macmag Museum of Scotland	June 1992
	Building Design Cumbria Theatre	18 January 1991
	L'ARCA 43 Eurodrome/Auditorium	November 1990
	L'ARCA 43 College Street	July/August 1990
	Building Design Auditorium 'Bonny + Clyde'	27 July 1990
	Architecture Today No. 2 Cumbria Theatre	November 1989
	Petershill - Selecting An Approach M.E.P.C. / D.E.G.W.	June 1989
	Building Design College Street Integration of Town and Gown	3 February 1989
	Structural News Eurodrome 'Cultural Landmark'	25 November 1988
	Building Design Eurodrome 'Cultural Landmark'	25 November 1988
	Domus Oratory	May 1988
	Church Building Oratory	Spring 1988
	Architects Journal Oratory	29 July 1897
	Bauwelt Physio Room/Oratory	February 1987
	Blueprint	1986
	Quaderns Physio Room	July 1986
	A.A.Files Marico/I.C.I. Comp./Physio Room	January 1986
	Architectural Review International Interior Design Awards	November 1984
	R.I.BA. Guide to British Architecture	1945–1984
	U.I.A. International Architect No.5	1984
	Architecture d'Aujourd'hui	June 1984
	L'Industria Delle Construzioni 153/4	July 1984
	L'Industria Delle Construzioni 150	April 1984
	A.3 Times	March 1984
	Architectural Review	April 1983
	Design Magazine 'Building the New Jerusalem' Deyan Sudjic	August 1981
	Technique et Architecture	May 1981
	8101 Toshi - Jutaku	January 1981
	8010 Toshi - Jutaku	October 1980

Museum of Scotland
Architects: Benson + Forsyth

ISBN: 1 902854 07 1

Published by August Media in association with Benson + Forsyth

Designed and edited by Benson + Forsyth in association with August Media
116–120 Golden Lane, London EC1Y OTL
T: +44 171 689 4400
F: +44 171 689 4401
E: dept8@augustmedia.co.uk

This publication is supported by the Scottish Executive as part of its promotion of Scottish architecture.

Production coordination: Uwe Kraus GmbH
Printed in Italy

Photography

Richard Bryant
Photo essay (cover, pages 7, 8, 12, 17, 20, 22, 24, 25, 32, 34, 35, 37, 38, 40, 42, 44, 45–48, 58, 59, 61, 65, 67, 68, 77, 79, 80, 82, 84, 87, 89, 121, 131, 132, 136, 138)

Hélène Binet
Photo essay (pages 10, 11, 13–16, 18, 19, 26–29, 31, 41, 50–52, 54–57, 60, 62–64, 70, 72–74, 78, 81, 88–101, 139)
Construction photographs by Niall Hendrie (pages 102–109)
Additional photographs by Keith Hunter (pages 21, 43) and Niall McClean (pages 25/1, 76)
Photograph of the Monymusk Reliquary (page 144) by James and Saul Gardiner

Contributors

Sir Colin St John Wilson RA is the architect of the British Library. He was formerly Head of Department of Architecture at Cambridge University, and is the author of *Architectural Reflections*, *The Other Tradition of Modern Architecture* and *The Artist at Work*

Professor Duncan MacMillan is Professor of Scottish Art, Edinburgh University, curator of the Talbot Rice gallery and art critic of *The Scotsman*

John Allan is a practising architect and director of Avanti Architects in London. He is the author of *Berthold Lubetkin – Architecture and the tradition of progress*, RIBA Publications, 1992

Benson + Forsyth
Gordon Benson, Alan Forsyth
Kevin Adams, John Cannon, Iain Carson, Paul Clarke, Eleanor de Zoysa, Andrew Fortune, Mary Ann Gallagher, Mark Hawker, Annabelle Henderson, Catriona Hill, Jim Hutcheson, Debby Kuypers, Gregorious Patsalosavis, Reza Schuster, Fred Smith, Andrew Stephenson, Peter Wilson, Emma Winkley, Cally Winter.

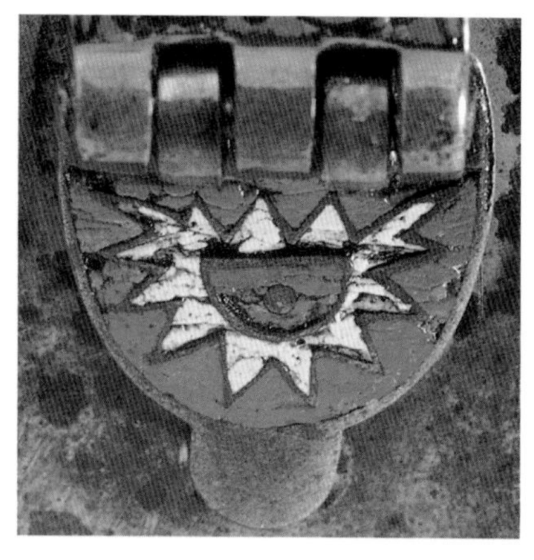